CW00566269

A SHOT AT H

Bandeep Singh

Abhinav Bindra is India's first and only individual Olympic gold medallist and also the first Indian to win a World Championship gold. Born in Dehradun, the thirty-four-year-old shooter has won over hundred international medals in the last twenty years. His last Olympics was in Rio in 2016, where he finished fourth.

Courtesy: The Straits Times

Rohit Brijnath has written on sport for thirty years for such publications as *Sportsworld*, *India Today*, *The Hindu*, *The Mint*, BBC-South Asia website and *The Age*. He is currently an Assistant Sports Editor with *The Straits Times* in Singapore. This is his first book.

Praise for the Book

'... one of the finest books on sport published in India... Read it if you love sport. Read it even if you don't.'
—*Tehelka*

'...the most outstanding book on an Indian sportsperson that I have ever read.'
—Tom Alter, *Outlook*

'(Rohit Brijnath) writes beautifully on the subtleties of the mind of a sportsman.... His ability to delve into the life of the reclusive Bindra is an achievement, and the book a great contribution to shooting.'
—Rajyavardhan Singh Rathore, *Indian Express*

'... a vivid and compelling peep into the mind of an obsessive perfectionist...'
—*The Asian Age*

'A must-read for every Indian sports fan and official alike....'
—*Deccan Herald*

'There is a lot for the younger generation to learn from the book.'
—*The Hindu*

'There is a refreshing honesty.... Without the usual gloating surrounding achievements or inconvenient subjects being brushed under the carpet.'
—*The Tribune*

'...beautifully written...'
—*Financial Express*

'...a myth buster in every sense...'
—*Pioneer*

'...honest, reflective and stimulating....'
—*Business World*

Fellow Shooters on Abhinav Bindra

'Ever since I met him in 2002 at the world championships I knew he was a great shooter. I happened to train next to him and watched what he did, how he moved, how he fired his shots. I was trying to learn his technique by watching him because everything he did made lots of sense to me...

'Abhi is the man I have to thank for my Olympic title because he was the one who taught me the most important lesson which helped me win gold in London: "It is not over until the referee says so." He taught me that lesson in the 2008 Olympic final in Beijing where he won gold, right in front of me, after shooting a beautiful final and winning on the last shot. He believed in himself until the end. I have great respect for Abhinav and all his achievements and I am proud to call him my friend.'

—ALIN MOLDOVEANU, Olympic champion in London 2012

'If anyone could win from India it was only him. The way he functions, my God, it's 100 per cent shooting. I have never met anyone who thinks so much about shooting... I was once satisfied with a 99/100 and he said, no, why not 100/100... It's when I thought, OK, this is what you need to be a champion.'

—SUMA SHIRUR, Olympic finalist 2004, Commonwealth Games champion and world record holder (air rifle)

'I haven't seen such a composed, mature and thoughtful athlete. He has a natural knack for shooting and practised like a madman when we trained together before the Sydney Olympics. He is a very enigmatic person: at times talkative and at times very quiet. I was sure he wouldn't miss the gold medal in Beijing once he reached the finals...'

—ANJALI BHAGWAT, Olympic finalist and winner of four rifle golds at the 2002 Manchester Commonwealth Games

'He's easy to get along with, he has no airs. His level of discipline and his commitment is exceptional… In twenty-seven years, he's the hardest working shooter I have seen. He puts in so much effort the whole year that I worry. But sometimes, thankfully, we used to go and chill out with some vodka shots.'

—MANSHER SINGH, Olympic trap shooter and gold medallist at the 1994 Commonwealth Games

A SHOT AT HISTORY

My Obsessive Journey
to Olympic Gold and Beyond

ABHINAV BINDRA

WITH

ROHIT BRIJNATH

Harper
Sport

An Imprint of HarperCollins *Publishers*

First published in India in 2011 by Harper Sport
An imprint of HarperCollins *Publishers* India
Building No. 10, Tower A, 4th Floor, DLF Cyber City,
Phase II, Gurugram – 122002
www.harpercollins.co.in

8 10 9 7

P-ISBN: 978-93-5264-575-6
E-ISBN: 978-93-5029-296-9

Typeset in 11/15 Berling
Jojy Philip New Delhi 110 015

Printed and bound at
Thomson Press (India) Ltd.

MIX
Paper
FSC FSC® C010615

To my parents
and
to all the Indian athletes in Olympic sports who
dare to dream

CONTENTS

PREFACE

by
Rohit Brijnath

To understand Abhinav Bindra's uniqueness, to weigh what he achieved, to acknowledge where he went, requires a quick glance at history. For over a century, India has chased Olympic gold. Games after Games. Rowers and swimmers. Archers and runners. Boxers and wrestlers. All that dreaming, desire, talent, so much of it beautiful, always coming up short. Gold just refusing to come in an individual sport till it had the smell of a curse about it. Every successive Olympics, the pressure builds, the questions come, the absurdity of it all grows. Burundi had one, as did Luxembourg, the UAE, Hong Kong. Not India.

Eventually, the gold medal sits there like a tease. It becomes an insinuation of mediocrity, it corrodes ambitions, it settles like a psychological weight in the athletic mind. Those Kenyans rising at dawn to eat up mountain trails with their casual strides; the hefty German rowers with oars tucked under muscled arms in their silken kits; the sleek Americans, all talent and science and technique in sleek bodies. Could they be beaten? By us? Did we have the nerve? Do we know how to do it?

The questions are suffocating, they tamper with the mind, they make the heart race, they don't help at the Olympics, where victory—in a theatre of ceremony and brilliance and harsh scrutiny—is so difficult anyway. It is this environment, this history, this burden, this negativity which used to coat India before an Olympics, that Abhinav Bindra, and his peers, had to contend with. They were lugging along this baggage while trying to beat a world of Olympic shooters so gifted they could trim your moustache with a pellet from thirty paces. And the exquisite appeal of the Olympics, its challenge and cruelty, is that this chance to beat the world only arrives every four years and is often over in 10 minutes, 30 minutes, an hour. You have to find your best, right then, at this appointed time. And he did.

It could only be done by an unusual man and Abhinav fits that definition. He is not an easy man to know, imprisoned in his own shooting planet and insulated by shyness. But he vibrates with intensity, a sort of silent, restrained fury to be flawless, interrupting it only with an occasional flash of dry humour. We do not spend our lives adhered to athletes; we cannot say for certain that one man's work ethic exceeds another's. But Abhinav, clearly, has an almost masochistic quality: he pushes, then he pushes harder, then he pushes even more. I spent days with him where he'd shoot, run, do sit-ups, lift weights, shoot, run more, walk a tightrope, hour after hour after hour, chasing excellence with a purity that was dazzling, and rubbishing any idea I might have had of shooters as just some species of paunchy geeks.

I admire this. I respect the intelligence with which he dissects his craft and the wonder with which he discusses it.

There is an artist within this shooting engineer. I was taken aback by how far he will go to get better, this extremity not merely of pain but of perseverance that he was willing to travel to. Small things. The meticulous way he examines his pellets, the dissastifaction even with a perfect score, the altering of the soles of his shoes by 1 millimetre, the willingness to try commando training. Anything, everything, that could help him win, and in this case confirming the idea—which makes him grin—that shooters are, well, a little odd.

Yet when he did win gold at the Beijing Olympics in 2008, his reaction was instructive. Relief and joy, the obvious responses to a grand victory, were followed later by a mild depression. The gold medal in his pocket, he was enveloped in an emptiness possibly unique to sport. He'd spent a life focused on a single moment and at twenty-five, when our lives are only commencing, his moment was done. It was an education for him, and later, for me.

Shooting, like chess, is an internal sport, the movements minor, yet it is a sport of fine nuance, of subtlety, requiring a certain imagining to appreciate it. These men rage, too, they just cannot show it. Unlike many sports, here perfection is not elusive, it is, in fact, a requirement. Fifty men, even more, stand in a line, confronted by a bullseye that's a blurred dot from 10 metres, a dot just bigger than a pinhead whose centre they are trying to hit. Fifty shooters, each one capable of being flawless on any given day. Fifty shooters whose aim you can't affect with a sledge, a glare or with your own skill.

It makes it uncommonly hard to win a major event, to be more perfect than perfect men on the perfect day.

So tough that no man, till Abhinav did so, had won the World Championship and Olympics in the same cycle.

So difficult that no man has ever won Olympic gold in the

air rifle twice and only three men have won two Olympic medals in the event. Abhinav was almost the fourth man but, as he would say, 'almost' wins you nothing. In London 2012, he came sixteenth but at the 2016 Rio Games, his last, Abhinav would come excruciatingly close to a medal, losing a shoot-off when four men were left in the final.

He lost, he will tell you, because other men shot better and he did not. He lost, he will clarify, because he was less perfect and they more. Yet he was grateful for even the chance to win or lose because three years earlier, in 2014, he had suffered the first of his epileptic seizures.

As much as it was disorienting and dizzying and exhausting, it was scary. But Abhinav did what he always does: he struggled, he found a way. By Rio his condition had stabilized, but a private man decided to write publicly about his disease for a reason: to show that a meaningful life is possible in spite of it.

Now he has retired, clumsy shooting jacket exchanged for sleek business attire, a man who changed his sport and was changed by it. He is more open, relaxed and certain. He is not fun in the conventional sense of the word, and I'd tease him about his personal life, simply because for a long while he had none. He has the occasional girlfriend, makes motivational speeches and reluctantly sits on various committees only because they might help improve life for athletes.

He doesn't wear a tattoo or buy Ferraris, and chill is not a word he is familiar with. His life was simple, it was a dedication to his craft, to the fulfilment of a dream. This was the only way he knew how to attain it. It is quite beautiful, it is also the only way he knew how to tell his story, honestly, starkly, intensely. It is a champion's journey, it is the story of a man who fought valiantly to make his own history. And with it, finally, his nation's.

ACKNOWLEDGEMENTS

ABHINAV BINDRA

After an interesting two years writing this book during which I had more fun than I had imagined, I have many people to thank. Starting with my exceptional and persevering co-writer Rohit Brijnath, with whom I shared many laughs, coffees and intense conversations on sport. Amit Agarwal, managing editor at HarperCollins India, was enthusiastic and meticulous. Kamesh Srinivasan, the fine writer at *The Hindu*, transcribed the first draft of my story and kindly checked all the facts.

A multitude of people, in varying ways, contributed to the project. Photos arrived from Germany, Kavita Muthanna designed early covers for me and Bandeep Singh interrupted a busy schedule to shoot a predictably beautiful cover.

I have fenced for years with the National Rifle Association of India and have not always been impressed with the sports ministry, but there are people in both organizations who have lent me a hand.

Through my career, innumerable people have contributed to my growth. Colonel Jagir Singh Dhillon first taught me under a mango tree, Amit Bhattacharjee tutored me on academics and life, and Maik Eckhardt stepped in to assist me at key times. My friend Ambika Jain provided valuable support; Manisha Malhotra, who heads the Mittal Champions Trust, always believed in me, and Suma Shirur was a kind and patient shooting partner over the years.

Psychologist Tim Harkness peered creatively into my mind while consultant coach Uwe Riesterer toughened me, educated me and wrote me wonderful letters that lifted my spirit. Gaby Buehlmann and Heinz Reinkemeier, who still coach me, kept me in their home and pushed me every day to make me a better shooter.

Without all of them, I would have no story to tell.

But most of all I thank my parents, Apjit and Babli, my sister, Divya, and my brother-in-law, Angad, for never losing faith in me, for putting up with my tantrums and for always loving me.

ROHIT BRIJNATH

I'd like to thank Abhinav for trusting me to tell his story and for speaking with honesty about the journey he's finished and the one that continues. Thanks are also due to his parents, Babli and Apjit Bindra, for opening up their beautiful home in Chandigarh to me and putting up with my endless interrogations. Abhinav's coaches in Germany, Gaby Buehlmann and Heinz Reinkemeier, and his consultant, Uwe Riesterer, endured long conversations on the phone and spoke with passion and precision on their art. Colonel J.S. Dhillon brought his scrapbooks and valuable memories to the table as did an early mentor, Amit Bhattacharjee. Shooters Suma Shirur, Anjali Bhagwat and Mansher Singh spoke with great affection about their peer and my old journalist friend, Kamesh Srinivasan, studiously checked the books for errors.

My gratitude is also owed to my editors Patrick Daniel, Han Fook Kwang and Mathew Pereira at *The Straits Times* at Singapore, photographer Bandeep Singh, lawyer Akhil Sibal and the tireless Amit Agarwal at HarperCollins. Sharda Ugra offered me early feedback and Namita Bhandare read the manuscript and offered suggestions. My gang in Delhi—Samar Halarnkar, Priya Ramani, Vijay Jung Thapa, Rohini Prakash, Javed Ansari, Kavita Muthanna and Harinder Baweja—fed me, drove me around, plied me with fine malts and put up with my endless chatter about shooting. My parents, Roma and Rajen, know that I give thanks to them every day for introducing me to the written word. Finally, this book would not have happened without the encouragement, laughter and love of my wife. Sarah, thanks, always.

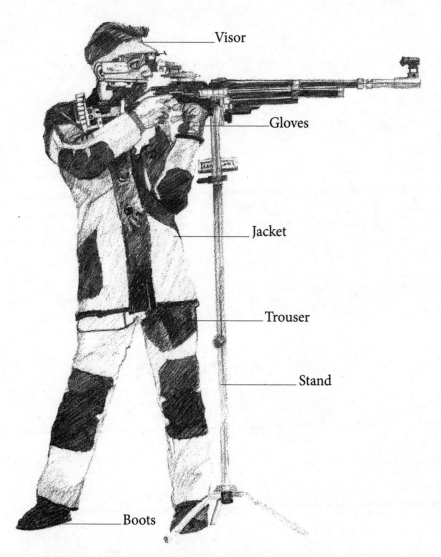

Visor

Gloves

Jacket

Trouser

Stand

Boots

Illustration by Dibakar Das

Visor: To block light, especially from above, to ensure clear picture of target.
Gloves: Made of material that grips; worn on left hand to support rifle.
Jacket/Trouser: Heavy, stiff canvas/leather garments which bring stability.
Stand: To rest rifle between shots. Also holds ammunition.
Boots: Flat-bottomed, often using custom-made insoles, which assist in ankle stability.

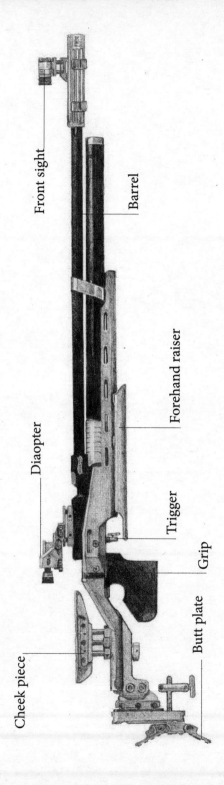

Front sight

Barrel

Diaopter

Forehand raiser

Trigger

Grip

Cheek piece

Butt plate

Illustration by Dibakar Das

Barrel: at least ten are tested for accuracy before one is chosen.
Forehand raiser: where the gun sits on the left fist.
Butt plate: can be custom-fitted to shoulder.
Cheek piece: where the heads rests, can be adjusted to millimetres.

Diaopter: the sight is fine-tuned by a series of 'clicks'.
Trigger: its sensitive weight depends on shooter's preference.
Front sight: can be adjusted to suit light conditions.
Grip: Aligned to ensure trigger finger is in precise position.

PROLOGUE
THE QUEST

It's 5 am. Winter. Chandigarh, 2005. It's cold, it's dark, I don't want to get up. I am a shooter, I stand still for a living, why do I need to run? I rise, I fall back on my pillow. I hate running, especially on a treadmill. It's as monotonous as shooting. No, it's worse.

But I need it, being fit gives me confidence, it builds my self-esteem. I am wary of complacence, I am scared of regret. I want to believe I persisted. I need to know I did everything to be the best, whether it concerns my gun, my nutrition, my technique, my brain, my body. So I must push myself to the extremities of my being. Every single day. I have to make my life difficult, break it down into minute detail and master each part.

I do all this because of that Olympic medal out there, that elusive, circular piece of metal at the end of a ribbon which means the world to me. I don't know that one day in the future in Beijing I will win this medal. All I know is that I want it like an ache. So I rise, pull on my shorts, lace my shoes, go out into the dark and the cold. And I wear out my treadmill.

1

DEFEAT AND DESPAIR
IN ATHENS

I don't dream any more of Athens. Never. I am thankful for
it. It took a long time. It took me eventually to therapy to
Germany. All defeat haunts, but this one, in the final of the
10-metre air-rifle event at the 2004 Olympics, cut deeper. It
seemed to infect my nervous system, worming into my brain
and flooding it with worthlessness. It devastated me and stirred
me to anger.

One picture tells the tale.

The walls of my shooting range in Chandigarh are like a
cluttered history of my sporting life. Photographs, certificates,
badges, scoresheets. All framed behind glass. Except one. It
is my Olympic certificate from Athens. It states that I came
seventh in the 10-metre air-rifle event. I don't look at it, but
it stares at me accusingly, an unmoving reminder of my worst
failure. It's why one day, frustrated in training, I grabbed it
from the wall and hurled it to the ground.

The certificate, glassless, is still there. The dreams of the
final have gone away, but not what Athens did to me. This is

where my life turned. There is where we should begin. With a defeat in a Greek city where the Olympics began.

All I knew in life till 2004 was shooting, my vocabulary distilled to *gun, sight, aim, breathe, target, fire*, all these words strung together and running through my head like a sporting prayer. All I was in life till then was a talented boy with a gun, defined by my ability to hit a .5-millimetre bullseye from 10 metres with an air-filled rifle made by Walther, a gun-maker that was James Bonds's preference.

All my life didn't matter anymore, because now, on this Athens afternoon, I was nothing, a sporting irrelevance. Only sport can do this to you, strip you naked in an instant in public, step on your dreams, make four years of practice incidental. In this, sport can seem absent of grey: you triumph, you fail. Black or white. Shooting is worse, you can't even blame anyone, cannot excuse failure as a rival's inspired day, a referee's error, a lucky bounce. Only one person is responsible for defeat. You.

History. It's what I came to make in Athens. *First Indian to win an individual Olympic gold.* History is not why I shot, but history was also partially my fuel. I never felt the burden of a nation waiting, but I appreciated how long it had been waiting. Olympic Games after Olympic Games, watching athletes from countries like Suriname win gold, from Mozambique, listening to outsiders sneer, 'one billion people, not one individual gold'. I guess I had the power to alter that, I presume people believed I had the power to change that. Now I'd failed.

If you had asked me, any other day, who I was, I would have instinctively answered: *A desperately lucky man.* I had wonderful parents, a loving sister, supportive coaches, never had to worry about money, yet now I felt so desperately alone, so utterly useless. It was a twenty-year-old life at its lowest point.

I had been one of the strong favourites in the 10-metre air-rifle final at Athens. I had been in splendid form in practice. *Forty-seven* players competed for a place in the eight-man final, and after the qualifying I was sitting in third place. In touching distance of a gold medal, even closer to bronze. Then I fell to seventh out of eight shooters in the final. I had lost.

But it was more than that, for losing I had known, losing I didn't like, but losing I wasn't scared of. This had a different taste, this was a collapse of talent precisely when it was supposed to bloom. I didn't want to speak to anyone, see anyone, say anything. I was mystified by my own incompetence.

Air-rifle shooters fire sixty shots in qualifying competition from a distance of 10 metres, and each shot can be worth 10 points at best for a total of 600. In the final, the top eight shooters fire ten more shots, but the scoring goes into decimal places to separate the best. It means, when it comes to the bullseye, you can score from 10.0 points to a highest of 10.9. In our world, even hitting the bullseye isn't enough. We have to hit a particular part of the bullseye, we have to exist on the very edge of perfection.

Great shooters aren't supposed to shoot 8s in an Olympic final. They rarely shoot 9s in an Olympic final. Nines are nice, they're accurate, they're impressive. But they are not perfect. Not even close to perfect. Too many millimetres away from perfect in a sport where the bullseye is 0.5 millimetre. Let's just say this: William Tell with his crossbow had to hit the apple, I have to hit the seed inside the core of that apple. All the time, every shot, that's my job.

This is where great shooters live. This is where I thought I now lived. In an international air weapons competition in Munich in Germany earlier that year I had shot 10.4, 10.1, 10.4, 10.9, 10.5, 10.6, 10.2, 10.3, 10.3, 10.3 in the final. Every

shot above 10. One a perfect 10.9. But now I was looking
at my scores in the Athens Olympics final and they were
inexplicable. Like an elite sprinter timing 11 seconds in an
Olympic 100-metre final.

9.4, 10.0, 10.0, 10.3, 9.8, 9.9, 8.8, 9.7, 9.6, 10.1.

One score in the 8s.

Five scores in the 9s.

Nothing higher than 10.3.

Damn.

I knew my craft. My gun was like an extra limb. I had
studied balance, posture, technique. I could strip down every
performance and tell you almost precisely why I failed or
triumphed. Down to the last irregular breath. I knew myself,
I knew shooting. But this didn't make sense.

My mood had been buoyant. A day or two before my event,
Indian trap shooter Mansher Singh and I had chauvinistically
kidded about what we'd need to do to win Olympic gold.

'Maybe I should enter the women's double trap,' I laughed,
simply because it only had ten serious competitors in it. *We
had nearly fifty.*

'Yeah,' he smiled, 'but you'd need more than a gun change
for that.'

My form was flying, too. My German-Swiss coach, Gaby
Buehlmann, later insisted that technically and mentally, I was
a superior shooter in Athens to the one I was four years later
in Beijing, when I won Olympic gold. India's Suma Shirur,
both superb shooter and friend, told a reporter years later
that 'Abhinav was in excellent form in Athens. I don't think
at the 2006 world championships, where he won, he was even
close to it.'

Ironically, inexplicably, I even *felt* I had shot great in the
final, that I had done everything right. *Yet this was the lowest*

total I had shot anywhere in the world at any level. It was a total I couldn't shoot even if I was trying.

Questions coursed through me.

Had I overestimated myself, so driven by ambition?

No.

Had I miscalculated the difficulty of being an Olympic champion, the incredible amalgam of training and luck and performance on the day?

No.

Had I underestimated the value of just getting to an Olympic final, being one of the world's eight best shooters, in just my second Games?

No. A final was good but it wasn't enough. For me, seventh was as good as seventeenth.

Had I overlooked the intensity of my first Olympic final?

No.

Of course, an Olympic final was new for me, unknown territory, the pressure foreign. This was the place where you wonder, am I just a training world champion—great only in practice—or a real one? I could wake up at 3 am in my underwear and shoot a perfect 10 on command. But this was the Olympics, the unpredictable universe, people watching, cameras recording, the world's finest collection of talent nudging you from every side. Where a tiny mental error, or an infinitesimal misalingment on my hips, could mean victory denied. Nevertheless, I believed I was ready.

Had I been undone, slightly, irreparably that day, by my own expectation, by that of my family?

No.

Uwe Riesterer, a German who was my performance consultant, believes Indians handle expectation differently. His generalization goes like this: Constantly tell an American he's the best, and he will saunter into the arena and say 'Let's kick ass and beat the hell out of everyone.' Tell an Indian he's the best and he tends to be defensive: 'I am the best, I better not make a mistake.' It's a reasonable theory, especially for me and Indian shooters of my generation—the new breed is different, bolder, more certain, like India itself—but that day it didn't apply to me.

I had been led to believe, from boyhood, that I *could* be the best. It was a belief broadcast to me more often than a propaganda message on China Radio. But this message was vital for me, for I was naturally negative, driven to almost a mild depression when results were erratic. My family was like a pack of boxing seconds, lifting me when I tired. So many times I wanted to quit, fall into some hole of self-pity, but my family never gave up on me. They kept me going, they reminded me of my talent. Never a burden, always a support.

So many theories abounded of why I failed, so many explanations, so many assumptions. Later, I'd weigh them, but right then, that night in the Olympic Village, I was unable to sleep, I kept thinking, something was wrong. The jury is going to discover there was a mistake with the target, the competition has to be redone, because these were scores I couldn't explain. But morning brought no solace.

You have to understand my reaction. Shooting, like all sport, is about incremental improvements. I started by wanting to be a district shooter, now I was at my second Olympics. Piece by piece, like a gun being assembled, I was being put together, and now I felt like the final polished product. I was no longer content getting to finals, I was winning finals.

I had started 2004 in Colorado Springs at the Rocky Mountain Championships—a series of three events in three days—with a 597/600 and a total of 103.5 in the final (103.5

was an average of 10.3 every shot for ten shots, and any score in that region is considered a good final performance). In the second event, I shot a perfect 600/600 and a 103.6 in the final, for an impressive total of 703.6, much better than the world record then. This didn't count as one because it wasn't an official event sanctioned by the International Shooting Sport Federation (ISSF). It didn't matter. World record scores are infrequent; 600/600 is infrequent—in ISSF competitions it has happened only three times.

So powerful was the confidence accelerating through me that I felt, put me in a final and I will win it. In Europe, before the Athens Olympics, I won gold again in Germany, against a field comprising Dick Boschman of the Netherlands, Wolfram Waibel of Austria, Torsten Krebs of Germany, Peter Sidi of Hungary, Artem Khadjibekov of Russia, Rajmond Debevec of Slovenia, Konstantin Prikhodtchenko of Russia. Nobodies to you, but for us, at that time, these were the heroes of the bullet business. I felt I was as good as them; in finals, ironically, I felt I was better than them.

So I came to Athens expecting gold, yet I left wanting to vomit. Not only because I failed, and *how* I failed, but also because of *when* I failed. Any time is fine, except now, except Olympic time. These Games are impossible to overstate for the runner, the shooter, the archer, the wrestler, the boxer.

Athletics aside, there are no hefty prize money cheques on offer for us. Week in and week out, it's all paper certificates and tin medals. It's a planet of few headlines. Negligible sponsors. Not many agents. Small fan bases. In a way, without diminishing other sports, our pursuit is pure. Pure gold. The Olympics is the single moment that beckons us, defines us, and it is a moment that arrives infrequently.

The cricketer has Test matches through the year, the tennis

player has four grand slam events in twelve months, the golfer
the same number of majors annually. Constantly, there is an
opportunity for redemption, a chance to stake a claim for
greatness. Not for me. My only chance comes every four years.
My only chance is seventy shots in 125 minutes every four
years (the first sixty shots are to be fired in 105 minutes, each
of the final ten shots within 75 seconds).

We have to be a little insane to do this, a trifle obsessive,
almost as single-minded as shaven monks who sit for years
meditating under trees in search of distant nirvana. No joke. I
once got yak milk from China because I was told it enhances
concentration. (It didn't.) I attached electrodes to my head
to view the activity in my brain when I shot well. I lasered
off my love handles. Let's be clear: we're not you. We're not
better than you, or other athletes, just caught in lives mostly
weirder than most. Shooters can't suddenly shout 'fuccckkk'
as football strikers do after a missed opportunity to score, we
can't throw guns as one might a tennis racket, we have to
absorb everything, swallow conflict, keep it tightly leashed
within, not let it out, give up our humanness to become a
machine. It's probably what makes us neurotic.

Athletes in general tend to talk a lot about processes and
journeys and the need to savour them, because if we thought of
our reality—investing our entire beings, our savings, our sweat
into a single Olympic day—we'd go crazier. We're looking to
become highly tuned instruments almost agitating to perform.
It is a high, a unique feeling only athletes and musicians and
actors might have. An Australian Rules football player once
said that at season's beginning he was so sharp, every muscle in
his body so alive, that it was hard for him just to walk. Every
time he did, he wanted to break into a run.

The pressure of the Olympics is that right then, at that

precise two-hour period every four years, I have to be perfect. Or just more perfect than everyone else in the world. And the world of shooting is reasonably large. Germany itself has 1.5 million shooters; across the world, in an inexact estimate, there are close to 70 million. It's why we're nervous, why athletes throw up before competing, why we chant, sit quietly in corners, put on particular socks in a particular order, hold on to superstitions, look to God. It's why gold is so meaningful.

This is what the Olympics' appeal is, for it is the ultimate proof of readiness. Earlier in 2004, I had casually mentioned that the Olympics was just another competition. I was lying. Deliberately. I was trying to detach myself, trying to remain relaxed, trying to stave off pressure. But the truth is that the Olympics *is* everything, it is the mission.

There is no higher achievement in my sport, no finer examination of sporting worth, no more excruciating confirmation of skill produced under the suffocation of tension. In India, we all grow up to the yell of a distant 'Howzzat' from an adjoining field, but for some of us, our temples go beyond a pitch. They become instead a ring, a court, a track, a pool, a range. Instinctively, as a boy, the moment you actively pursue a sport, in your childish dreams—which never quite die—you look to its ultimate expression. The crown that represents excellence is the crown you wear in your sleep. For tennis players perhaps it is Wimbledon, for badminton players the All-England Championships, for golfers the Masters.

For me, it was this ancient Games to which an Indian first travelled in 1900. Our bond to the Olympics came through a team wielding hockey sticks as if they were wooden wands and a wrestler named Khashaba Dadasaheb Jadhav, who won independent India's first individual medal, a wrestling bronze, in 1952. No shooter had won here. No grand record of individual excellence at the Olympics existed. The gold medal was remote. Never seen by most, never touched. This very foreignness of it made the journey more mysterious and arduous. Yet it was also an inspiration. Everyone, after all, wants to be the first on any moon. So the Olympics is 99.9 per cent of the reason why I shoot; it is also the best place for me to judge how well I shoot.

Yet here in Athens, after four years of changing coaches, weighing hundreds of bullets, detailing guns, sitting with psychologists, firing in darkened rooms, taking a screwdriver to every tiny damn detail, you want to have something to show. I had done everything. Yet I had nothing except seventh position in the final.

It is deflating, it is humbling. No one understands. No one except other athletes. That day, Russian Olympic shooting medallists Lioubov Galkina and Tatiana Goldobina came up to me in the dining hall and had tears in their eyes. We're not close friends, it's just a bond athletes share, an appreciation of pain. At one point, I just kept laughing and can only explain it as being in some sort of shock. When someone asked me if I wanted to eat, I answered with feeble amusement: 'No, thanks, I'm still digesting my 9s.'

But right then, wrapped so tightly in defeat, winning anything, like a world championship two years later, or an Olympic gold four years later, seemed unreal. I told one of my mentors, Amit Bhattacharjee, 'What have I done? I am a waste of space.' I mentioned to the American coach Dave Johnson that at least the last shot of my shooting career had been a 10. At that point, another four years to the Beijing Olympics seemed pointless, seemed too tiring, seemed simply not worth the investment if this was going to happen.

It was all over. As a shooter, I was finished. At twenty, I was ready to retire.

2

THE PARENT FACTOR

All my life, shooting has been a struggle. A contest with the self. Every 10 has been a battle, every performance has demanded that I look within for an answer. Just below my apparent calm there is tremendous conflict. To win you need an internal rage, a desperation, a hardness, and eventually I became a shooter who relished a fight.

If my stability was imperfect on a given day, perhaps because my stance was awry, or my body not relaxed, then I'd fight it. Ten times I'd raise my gun to fire, ten times I would put it down, fighting to find the tranquil balance that shooters crave. I didn't quit and I need to thank somebody for that.

My parents.

Are champions born? I don't think so. It is a bunch of extraordinary people who make champions out of ordinary kids. Would Tiger Woods have been who he is without his father, Earl? I'm not sure. Great, yes, unique, who knows? Unquestionably, champions are born with something, like a sprinter's fast-twitch fibre, or champion swimmer Michael Phelps's long torso-short legs physique that seems fashioned by God for the purpose of cutting through water.

But that is not enough.

Dreams require a team. And my Olympic and world championship golds arrived because my parents and a clutch of experts groomed a young boy to strive for excellence.

I believe destiny makes the world spin the way it does. But I also believe that positive energy drives champions. Great athletes don't just exhale this positivity, they surround themselves with similar people. Not yes-men, but believers. When people buy into your cause, cheer your dream, it's like an armour-plating of sorts: you're not alone. When this cheering is fake, and I've smelled that, too, it stinks. In India we tend to limp along because our sports are shrouded in negativity.

Every successive Olympics was presented as proof that something was wrong with us Indians—we were unable to win gold, we lacked the right strain to produce athletic heroes. We were seen as not strong enough, tough enough, disciplined enough. For athletes this can be disheartening, for winning is hard enough without the constant suspicion—from officials, forget the public—that eventually we will be proved incapable. Growing up, I faced this negativity. As the 1996 Olympics approached and I first understood, at age thirteen and from a distance, what an Olympic gold was, I found it was also portrayed as an unachievable dream. Eventually it took the collective intensity of my family and coaches to successfully unravel a puzzle that had perplexed Indian sports for over a hundred years: you have to stretch yourself to the limit and leave very little to chance. Only then does reward arrive.

The foundation of my confidence came from my parents. I believed because they believed in me. After the Athens final, with my world collapsing, my mother, Babli, came to me and said: 'The best you could have done anyway was silver, but that's not your goal. Your destiny is to win a gold.' My mother never quit on me. Never. She was my reassurance, my faith. She spent cold days of my youth in Germany, just getting me ready for the range, just waiting for me to come home, never wavering in her belief. How do you forget that?

My mother, daughter of a man fond of shikar, was a fifth-generation descendant of the legendary general Hari Singh Nalwa, the commander-in-chief of Maharaja Ranjit Singh's army. He once fought a lion armed with only a shield and a sword. My mother, single-handedly, took on slightly lesser foes—Indian sports officials—with as much bravery.

My mother is a woman of many fine parts—she has a Master's degree in psychology and is an athlete of some merit. She played softball, table tennis, hockey, basketball and was a part of the Panjab University's first women's cricket team. Dedication, determination, discipline—which Anil Kumble used to preach to schoolkids as the three Ds—were attributes she was familiar with. It's why the German coach Heinz Reinkemeier (Gaby's husband—they coach me as a duet) says, 'She is a very special mama. She is tough.'

My mother's fuelling of my dream, to let me chase sport and not a law degree, is perhaps rooted in her past. Having lost her mother at thirteen, she was desperate to be a doctor, but in more conservative times her father prevailed upon her to get married. She would not do that to me, she would let me go, not interrupt my dream but assist me in its pursuit.

If she gives me emotional sustenance, my father, Apjit, gives me spirit. He is my hero, my role model. He has backed my dream unflinchingly with every fibre, every resource, every encouragement he possesses. He'd be knee-deep in business deals, confronted by problems, but shooting was never dismissed. I was travelling the world, and he was the man left with a list of things to do: coaches to speak to, equipment to be bought, formalities to be completed about travelling with guns. He'd get his secretary to pester journalists with my results, he'd fax them news, results, quotes. He didn't just get it done, he did it with an enthusiasm that was inspiring.

It may be tempting to believe that my father was living his dream through me. For many parents, children are the vehicles to sustain their unfinished dreams, as if there is some unfulfilled athlete, some disaffected dreamer, within them. It was not that simple in my case. My dad gave me the freedom to make the choice. Once he was convinced of my conviction, he backed me. In short, my dream became his dream.

My father, a Sikh, was born on 4 June 1949 in Lucknow. My grandfather, Bir Singh, was an army officer and retired as a colonel. He had played hockey for the Services along with the legendary Dhyan Chand. My grandmother, Kartar Kaur, specialized in Punjabi spiritualism and eventually could recite the entire holy book, the Guru Granth Sahib.

My father went to Yadavindra Public School in Patiala and attended the Punjab Agricultural University in Ludhiana and Panjab University in Chandigarh. His life altered with a scholarship to Denmark. He did his doctorate in animal sciences, became fluent in Danish, practised as a veterinarian and led a comfortable life. Then fate, not for the first time, interceded.

In 1971, the then prime minister, Indira Gandhi, visited Denmark and my father was attached to her as an interpreter. Conscious of the brain drain from India, she told him that India needed young men like him. The work he did was work India needed. My father loved life there, but a more persuasive argument would arrive in the form of my grandmother. Loathe to travel anywhere, she bravely hopped on a Lufthansa flight and arrived only to find my father with cut hair disguised in a badly-wrapped turban. She came to convince him it was time to come home. It was a mother's plea he could not refuse.

Life was kind yet testing for my father, it knocked him down yet he always got back on his feet. His plan for a breeding programme in Dehra Dun using Danish cows ran into a sea of red tape and only a visit to Mrs Gandhi, and a phone call from her, could cut through it. Business boomed, only for foot and mouth disease to kill his entire herd. He bought and sold animals, diversified into food processing, and gradually found success again. But life never promised to be smooth.

Mrs Gandhi was assassinated in 1984 and madness prevailed. Our home was attacked in Dehra Dun and a 300-strong mob tried to burn the house. On a terrifying day, where I was a two-year-old in a farmhouse under seige, my father and grandfather had to fire in the air to disperse the crowd. Finally it moved away, but not before burning down our limestone factory.

Eventually the family shifted to Punjab and my father became an industrialist. When problems arose, and they did, he was aggressive in finding solutions. If his lawyers said there was a 99 per cent chance of an idea failing, he would ask them to explore the remaining 1 per cent and find a way. Struggle was his style and eventually it became mine.

Perhaps, in all this, there was a subliminal contest going on within me. A son's need to prove himself worthy of his father. Intriguing theory, but not convincing to me. But coach Heinz Reinkemeier was sure that this was one of my motors. He saw a distinct connection between my father's success and my need to emulate it. Except in a totally different field. As if I had no choice. As if I was prisoner to the pull of my DNA.

3

THE SMELL OF GUN OIL

I was a fat boy, a normal gregarious kid, who wasn't keen on reading, hated physical activity and was ambivalent about playing sport. Physical training classes were akin to hard labour and I would find the flimsiest excuse to bunk them. The Doon School was my home briefly as a kid for a few years, but it didn't fit my personality. Let's just say I was a homesick mama's boy. Even though sport is one of the joyful escapes of boarding school, I wasn't intrigued. Watching, yes; playing, yes, but without any evident passion. I'd attended a cricket Test at Lord's in 1996 as a boy, watching Javagal Srinath send back Michael Atherton in the first over, but this sport did not call me as a participant. For a while I played golf with my father and hoofed around a football, but I gave up easily. Call it a lack of talent.

My father, bless him, tried. Every day when I was in Doon School, he wrote me a letter. Every day, how's that for love? But his letters had one common theme: try sport, son. He had played sport as a boy, he'd seen the passion with which it was followed when living in Denmark, and he believed sport allowed a person to develop himself and stand out. Studies were fine, but sport was a vehicle for recognition far beyond mere money. It offered, he believed, the highest glory.

Dad tried. He pushed. It didn't work.

And then I found something else.

Guns.

Like boys and fighter planes, these shining, smooth weapons had some mysterious, almost mystical, hold over me. Even now, like some familiar scent, I can remember the smell of gun oil from my childhood. My father had three weapons, a W.W. Greener shotgun, a .22 Czech Bruno rifle, and a Webley and Scott revolver. Once a month, I would sit, fascinated, as he dismantled them, sliding cleaning rods into the barrel and coating them with oil. When he went to the local gun shop in Dehra Dun to get one repaired, I went with him, and was astonished by the array of rifles before me.

I was about ten when my father first allowed me to shoot. He held the shotgun, I pulled the trigger. Quick to sense my fascination, he gifted me air guns on my birthdays, like those old Daisy's which I could barely bend and collapse to feed pellets into. They're still stored in a lost corner of my house. My mother was nervous about a kid with an air gun popping away at cans and bottles, but I surrendered to this addiction. It calmed me, it reassured me, it was mine. Entire afternoons would drift by with me loading, aiming, firing, reloading, as if this was some routine that perfectly fitted my personality. The individuality and solitude of shooting, the reality that any success or failure rested entirely with me, was intriguing. I began to get a strange sensation, as though this was something I was meant to do.

Like many kids, I was capable of acts of irresponsibility. In my case, it was persuading my maid and her daughter, Tulsi, to rest balloons and bottles on their head, while I shot at them.

The maids were brave, I was foolish. Fortunately, I was also a good shot. When my mother found out about my sniper impersonations, there was hell to pay. Human targets were understandably banned, but shooting wasn't discouraged. Not even when her lawn became a carpet of broken bottles. The size of the bottles determined my progress: I started with beer bottles, advanced to cough-mixture bottles and peaked at ampoules, which my father religiously collected for me from a friend who was a doctor.

How does anything start, a career build? Passion first, chance next? Rana Gurmit Sodhi, who later became Punjab's sports minister and was a strong supporter of athletes, was a family friend and a fine shooter. He saw me breaking those bottles one day and there it began.

He sensed I had potential and suggested to my father that professional training could help me. So much of India is about knowing the right people, everyone has a friend of a friend who can help. My father needed a coach. Sodhi's friend, Lieutenant Colonel Jagir Singh Dhillon, was one.

The colonel had been around guns all his life. He'd shot in the first national shooting championships in 1952 and had stopped only in 2004. He had shot at the Asian Games twice, in 1970 and 1978, and been a coach in 1982. And he had done one more thing. He'd shared a room with Milkha Singh. The colonel was then an aspiring shot-putter, his roommate a great runner under construction.

Both men joined the army at the same time and the colonel eventually told me compelling stories of Milkha's devotion to his dream, stories that told me that even the runner's contemporaries were astonished by him. Milkha would parade up and down a hill in Secunderabad, where a masjid stood on top, with a backpack filled with 20 kilograms of sand to strengthen his legs and lungs. Sometimes he trained under the moonlight, certain that it made more sense to prepare in cooler conditions. He had no real coach then, no lessons in technique, said the colonel, but he had a capacity for pain. The fact that I remember these stories even today is evidence of the influence they had on me. Greatness, I understood early, was a long, sweaty road.

The problem was getting Dhillon to agree to coach me. Sodhi kept promising to set up a meeting but he was a busy man. But stubbornness was part of what defined me. So I took the initiative, sat at the computer and typed out this letter to the colonel. I was thirteen years old.

> *Sir,*
> *By now Mr Rana Sodhi must have got in touch with you regarding coaching me for shooting. Sir, I am very interested in shooting but don't know how to go about it. I humbly request you to kindly coach me. I am prepared to work as hard as I can & make you feel proud of me one day.*
> *Please let me know the timings, fee, as soon as possible. I am ready to start working hard from tomorrow itself.*
> *Looking forward of being your student.*
> *With respectful regards,*
> *Abhinav Bindra*

Sodhi had, in fact, already spoken to Dhillon. But the colonel was unsure about me. 'Who is this boy,' he would say, 'who is promising me already that one day I will be proud of him.' Was I too soft, would I buy the right equipment, could an Olympian be forged out of this thirteen-year-old? He thought, I waited. But the letter startled him. The clarity of what I wanted had an impact. I was ready, now so was Dhillon, and he sent word:

Come.

I remember the day Sodhi took me there. I remember returning from school, skipping lunch, and going for the meeting, so full of apprehension and elation, like a boy before his first exam. I was immediately impressed with the colonel because he talked details. He asked me to come the next morning at 8 am. I was there at 7.45. It surprised him.

He was an old school gent who thought the rich preferred not to sweat and those who sweated couldn't afford to shoot. My attitude altered his view. I love shooting and sweat, the challenge of hovering flies, the burn of the sun, the need to blank out one universe and get lost in another one. Cool rooms and carrom weren't my thing. Still aren't.

We started with an Indian rifle with an open sight. It was a basic gun, with an 'I' in the front and the 'U' at the back for aiming. Then we went shopping for a better one, even if just a poor quality carbon-dioxide powered weapon. The rifle is everything, it has to fit the shooter, like a tennis racket or a golf club; it is about feel, balance, weight, comfort. The sportsman doesn't want to think about his equipment, he has to just believe in it, trust it, and so quality matters.

I needed an air rifle, a junior model, and after perusing shooting magazines, the colonel recommended a gun manufactured by Beeman Precision. My mother's sister, Tina Chopra, who lived in Sussex, New Jersey, in America, bought it and handed it over to my father, who was travelling there. In those days bringing a rifle into India was cause for nervousness, but my father paid the requisite duty and ten days after ordering my gun, there it was. I still have a photo of me with it. Some days I look at it and smile.

I trained every day with the colonel. No exceptions. He had a range built in his backyard, and under the shade of a friendly mango tree I chased greatness. We shot at old-fashioned paper targets that had to be reeled in on a pulley system after every shot, the paper changed, and reeled back in place. A shooting jacket was ordered from Germany, a heavy, swollen tunic that helps stabilize the shooter, and in the 40-degree summer heat I wore it and shot. Bullet after bullet. Hour after hour. A table fan arrived one day and sat there like a sentinel, capable only of squeaking out hot air. I didn't care, I never complained, I only wanted to shoot.

A transformation of a life was under way, an adventure commencing. The gun and I became everything, the rest of my existence stood still. Nothing mattered, not hanging out with buddies, not even cricket watching for a while, for which I had such affection. Shooting plays hell with friendship, it's too internal and obscure. If you're chasing a tennis career, pals might saunter across to watch you practice, rubbish your backhand, and discuss Serena's forehand. If you're an aspiring cricketer, buddies will accost you with their views on Sehwag's footwork and Dhoni's haircut.

But who watches, and talks, bullets? Who's interested in our dressing-room talk and whether the posture is correct and if there is chatter in the brain? Loneliness became a price I had to pay, for shooting had become like an infection of the brain. Now I care. Nowadays this isolated, cocooned world of the shooter affects me. Now I search for company. Now I think my way was almost unreasonable and believe you shouldn't start shooting with such religiosity till your mid-teens. But for years I was too bloody-minded to care. Blind to everything but my dream.

This sport now consumed me to the point where some people in school thought I was weird. Maybe I was, but maybe to win gold you need to be a little twisted. When the colonel said pick up the gun, I did. If he said, hold it for five minutes, I did. If sweat trickled down my face, I didn't move.

My schedule was immoveable. I returned from school at 2 pm, had lunch and was in the colonel's house, 10 minutes away, by 2.40 pm. Training continued till 5.30 pm, whereupon I returned home for schoolwork. On weekends I trained twice a day. And I was never late for practice. Never. The colonel estimated later that that I spent roughly 2000 hours under the mango tree. It is no longer there.

I usually trained with the colonel, but occasionally in Chandigarh they had Sunday shooting at a poorly-maintained facility in Sector 25. It was next to a cremation ground, which is kind of appropriate, for on lonely days it had a deathly feel. But it was the first time, and first place, that I entered anything resembling a competition and just handing in that initial entry form was stirring. I saw my name printed in the newspapers and felt that frisson of excitement that comes with a first achievement, however minor. A. Bindra. It had begun.

4

NIRVANA IN THE SHADE

A boy needs teachers, an athlete needs early mentors, and I had two fine ones. One corrected my aim under a tree, the other checked my mathematical accuracy in the house. Colonel Dhillon could dismantle a shotgun blindfolded and tell you its make from sheer feel; Amit Bhattacharjee, if blindfolded, couldn't initially tell if he was holding a shotgun or my grandfather's walking stick. Either way, both offered me more than knowledge, they gave me a hand of confidence.

To call Amit simply a 'teacher' would be an incomplete explanation. Eventually he became elder brother, ally, guide, sounding board, punching bag. He came to my house as a tutor and gradually became a believer in my mission. If I was feeling dejected, I went to Amit. He offered me positivity and a smile, immeasurable gifts for an athlete.

Amit, then a part-time teacher who was preparing for his civil services examination, was the very answer to my mother's prayer. She pushed sport but she wouldn't let go of academics. Balance, she insisted, and Amit provided it. He was amusing but strict. Homework had to be done, but he listened as well, intrigued by my enthusiasm, taken by my wilfulness when I said I would win national gold.

My mother, an organized woman, had my day planned to the minute. No messing about. In a way, it was like living in a cage, no room for a boy to be silly and defiant. But Amit won my friendship by allowing me to express myself. At home, tuition was usually for an hour. For kids it's a lifetime. My response was to order a pizza, hoping it would cut into our study time. Amit was clever. He smiled, ate the pizza, and doubled my tuition time to two hours.

One day, I wanted to drive his car, one of those alloy-wheeled modified Maruti 800s. My parents were away, the guards at the gate were convinced by a story of books to buy, and finally, I was in teenage heaven: behind the wheel of a Maruti 800. What I learnt that day wasn't driving, but that I had a friend willing to stretch himself for me. So he became my confidant and my first secret to him was a familiar athletic complaint: studies and sport were becoming impossible to balance.

Amit responded. He spoke to my teachers at St Stephens School, helped get exams postponed, told them I had potential and that they would be proud of me one day. My principal, Harold Carver, a decent man whose steadfast support I can never forget, responded; my vice-principal, victim of crank calls from me saying, in a growly voice, 'Don't disturb sportspeople,' did not. To him, it seemed, Indians in the sporting arena were a travesty, a waste of time. Again, Amit was my buffer. He helped me with homework and even faxed it to me during competitions. Every such act was quiet confirmation from him that what I dreamed could be done.

As time went on, I was changing, and so was Amit. I dived into academia, he learnt guns and sport. Seriously. He watched coaches, he inhaled their training methods. He ended up studying alternate medicine, sports psychology and sports management. He learnt meditation, different techniques of yoga and flexibility training. In short, he became a pillar of strength in my drive to achieve an Olympic medal.

On my later travels, I sent him cards. One week we debated an Indian cricketing performance in Zimbabwe, the next I teased him about how *he* was preparing for my forthcoming exams. He took me sightseeing, trying to make me grow as a person, but he would not indulge every silliness. When I picked up a cigarette in the mid-2000s, he was appalled, but I was merely following the instructions of a fellow and fun-loving shooter, whose advice pre-competitions was pithy: walk, massage, smoke. It just didn't work for me.

Amit, my parents, my sister, friends, Colonel Dhillon, were my support troupe, a comfort to me when I competed through the years in foreign lands. Back home, believers matter. The athlete has down days—form flies, media bruises, equipment malfunctions, rivals improve. Sitting spent in yet another hotel room, the curtains dull, living on room service, the world can look bleak. But it's then that you can hear the cheering from a distance in your head and you remember you are not alone. You never forget. Like the day Amit handed me a note in 2006. On it he wrote: 'You will win gold in Beijing.'

But in 1996, at thirteen, when I started with Colonel Dhillon, the Olympics was too big, too far, too out of reach. As a boy it was like a separate universe of the splendid, a distant planet of athletic perfection. I remember watching on TV the gifted Jaspal Rana at the 1996 Olympics in Atlanta, and the sad shabbiness of the ill-fitting Indian uniforms. My sister, Divya, swears I told her then, 'One day I will win a medal.' A boyhood boast, probably, for as I watched, the

Olympics unnerved me. Gold was then an absurdity. Just wearing an India blazer one day seemed fantastic enough. For now my dreams were small. Just being district champion meant the world.

I had won the Ropar district event in February 1996, at thirteen. There were few shooters in the fray but no boy cares about such trivial numbers except the one that says 1st place. My father, who was at the event and was asked to give away the prize, was thrilled. The colonel was satisfied. He was a committed teacher whose finest lesson to me was work ethic. If I loved practice, if I believed sweat was the finest polish in sport, he was the reason. It all began here, at this Ropar range, and never left me. Later in life I'd go the other way, I'd overtrain, become restless after dinner, and go back to the range. This perfectionism hurt me because I was always unsatisfied, yet it also helped me.

Shooting had my attention, it triggered my intensity. Part of it was accidental. I wanted to prove to the colonel that being a rich kid didn't equate with sloth. Part of it was simple brilliance by the colonel. He tempted me with fame. Come first, he said, and I would earn a headline. Make a record and I'd get a picture in the paper. For a kid, this was an irresistible seduction. I was fascinated, hooked. My parents had given me everything. But fame I had to earn for myself.

It worked for me then, but not later. Later, I understood that my journey was more complicated and that fame was shallow. Fame doesn't last, it cannot stand in comparison to the pursuit of excellence. I also wanted self-respect, and other people's respect and pride in what I had done (even if I hadn't won). After the Beijing gold, I was invited everywhere, to dance shows, to cooking shows, reality shows. Maybe I could have even lobbied for a bit-part in a Bollywood film. Bit-part,

Ok? But I shied away from it all. However, that was still to come. For now, at thirteen, at fourteen, fame was the incentive. Now getting an honorary badge for shooting a certain score in competition was a rush. Once, when the badge didn't come, I cried for a week and did what Indians do at least once in their lifetime: cursed the postal department.

I was not by any stretch a natural shooter; I'm not that good, not such an innate artist. But I was not without some natural advantage. Admittedly, if you examined my genetic blueprint, one thing you wouldn't find is any athletic DNA. Coordinated movement wasn't my thing. My German coach, Heinz Reinkemeier's favourite story is of me and Valentina Turisini, the Italian Olympic silver medallist, playing badminton in his garden in a university town in Germany.

A neighbour strolled by and inquisitively asked: 'Who are they?'

Replied Heinz: 'They're Olympic champions.'

The neighbour was stunned: 'I cannot believe it; I have never seen two such untalented movers.'

Heinz, always up for a laugh, agreed, and threw in a line about us playing badminton like old-timers with hip disease. Very funny, Heinz.

But if I don't have V.V.S. Laxman's hand-eye magic, or Leander Paes's instinctive athleticism, I do have one thing: fine motor control. You know those movies where the hero gently draws the detonator out of the bomb with 0.4 seconds left on the timer. I'd be good at that.

Let me explain. My trigger is sensitive, it takes just 30 grams of pressure to set it off. Almost to the point where, if a platoon of arguing bees sat on it, it will fire. But I have enough control in my finger to pull it back 20 grams and then hold it, hold it, hold it, and then exert a little more to fire, as gently as a butterfly's breath. It's cool.

I have other things. Small things. I have concentration, and Colonel Dhillon loves to regale visitors about the time I shot under his mango tree, unafraid, or simply unaware, of a low-slung hive and inquisitive bees, so impenetrable my world could become. I enjoy stillness and even while watching a movie I hardly move. I have a sense of aim which led my coach, Gaby Buehlmann, to once say: 'He could put his legs up on a table and still shoot a 10.'

But primarily, I am a persistent student, the shooter as swotter. This is my personality. My dad and I would huddle around Meccano sets and buy aircraft and car models and painstakingly construct them. One tiny part after another, threading it together, never skipping a detail. This became a function of my schoolwork as well. I'd stick to a maths problem, persevere, grind teeth but never go forward till I had finished the previous one. In shooting, this is essential, a gradual, systematic accumulation of knowledge.

My life, meanwhile, was beginning to revolve around the 10. The bullseye. Nothing else would do. If I scored a 9, I would scream, throw my glove, my rifle, even a box containing 500 pellets, all of them skittering across the grass (and later hunted for on bended knee). A bad shot was intolerable, my tantrums were legendary. The colonel still has tattered, small notebooks, filled with detail on every shot I took from thirteen to fifteen, interspersed with notes that are a trifle embarassing now:

'It is a useless sport, I will leave shooting soon.'

'I shall quit (after a few 9s).'

Imperfection wasn't in my dictionary. I wanted answers. Solutions. Quickly. Later, I'd understand that introspection would bring them, not a loss of temper. Still, it spoke of my rage to be better and partially accounts for the fact that I was greying by the time I was twenty-one.

But the colonel was clever and calm. He never shouted. Instead, he laughed. He saw that I was just releasing my frustration. And he was more interested in my ability to shoot the 10s.

He told me that irrespective of the score I had to analyse and tune myself for the next shot. Even if I shot a 10, I had to shoot a better 10. If the shot was edging towards the right of the bullseye, I had to pull it back to the left. Millimetres, understand. What he believed was written on a sign that was pinned to his notice board:

'Whatever your mind can conceive, your heart can believe, you can achieve.'

He taught me well. He taught me to think big.

Once I asked for a glass of water on a hot day. He went in and got it. I did not take a sip from it. He was amused and surprised, but said nothing because the session was still on. Later, he asked me why I had asked for the water if I wasn't thirsty. I answered with a rueful smile and by bending down and pulling out a target from under the rubber mat on the table.

I had shot an 8 and did not want him to see it. When he went to get the water, I slipped it under the mat.

I wanted only 10s and so did he.

5

THE AGE OF UNREASON

Doubt shadows the sportsman. Stalks him. Affects him. Doubt goes with me everywhere—to the arena, to the practice range, it's there when I awake and when I sleep. Doubt is my enemy because it unnerves me, makes me overthink, but it's also, in some weird way, my friend because it helps me become a sharper shooter. Everyone is trying to get to a place of reassuring calm, of certainty, where instructions and decisions flow between brain and hand and body without impediment. It's a fantasy, at least for me. It's a place I want to get to, but never quite reach. One day I doubt if I can trigger smoothly. I fix it. Next day, I doubt if I'm as stable as I should be. This is the pleasure and pain of what I do.

Doubt comes in two parts. I doubt myself. People doubt me. That's life. But I learnt early that in India the doubters are many. Especially in the place where you don't expect to find them. Your own field. People who should push you, doubt you. It's frustrating but eventually there is only one way to use it. As fuel. That's what happened to me.

Shooting fitted me, it's like my cheek was waiting for a barrel, my finger for a trigger, my eye for a sight. So, very quickly my scores were high. In a Sunday competition for juniors at the Chandigarh state shooting championship at the Patiala Rao shooting range, I shot 200 out of 200. Nice. But no big deal. The following Friday, 30 August 1996, was a big deal. I shot 600 out of 600. Perfect. The world record stood at 597/600, shot by Wolfram Waibel of Austria at the World Championship in Munich that year. He also held the Olympic record of 596/ 600 at the Atlanta Games.

Now the world record was mine. And I was thirteen.

Except it wasn't mine. The competition wasn't recognized by the UIT—the Union International de Tir, which was the earlier name of the world shooting body, now known as the International Shooting Sport Federation, and so the score wasn't recognized. Colonel Dhillon sent a letter to the UIT to ratify it, but they said, too bad. I shrugged; I knew what I had shot, what it felt like. There is an injustice that you feel keenly as a boy at the first taste of such unfairness. Yet, at the same time, you're young, and your best days are only ahead; you care, but not that much. The score felt cool. So did the speed with which I shot. Competitors get 105 minutes for 60 shots, I took 50 minutes. Later, I would calm down, then I was a cowboy with a gun.

My parents were thrilled. In old-fashioned style, a letter was sent to the colonel. It simply said: *thank you*. It also spoke about the winning of a gold medal in Sydney 2000. I had been shooting for only a year but my parents were ambitious. They were my believers, the anti-doubters. Every letter henceforth to the colonel would have the same two words: Sydney and gold. You can't say they weren't consistent. So was I.

The better I shot, the more people disbelieved my ability. That kid, those scores, not possible.

The cruellest cut came at the All India G.V. Mavlankar shooting championship in Ahmedabad in November 1996. It

was the qualifying event for the national championships and
I recorded 400 out of 400. Officials were stunned and refused
to accept it. In front of my name stood no result.

Had I done something wrong?

No.

But the score was considered impossible.

An Indian kid? No way.

The colonel argued my case. He said, 'Don't say it's
not possible, it just happened!' Even after he asked for an
observer—an official who stands quietly behind shooters to
ensure they do not break the rules. Normally observers are at
hand, but that day they were absent. So the colonel requested
one. He told them also of my perfect 600 in Chandigarh. He
said I had scored 399 out of 400 in October in Delhi in the
presence of officials such as Colonel Jaswant Singh and Rajiv
Bhatia of the National Rifle Association of India.

But reason failed to puncture suspicion. Their minds could
not comprehend what their eyes had seen. Something was
wrong, they said, we're just not sure what. They refused to
ratify the result, gave the gold to the second-placed shooter
and ordered a re-shoot for me (to qualify for the nationals)
in Delhi. I felt sick. These men were supposed to breathe life
into excellence, not reject it. I was only fourteen.

They insisted that my pellets, which had a round nose, not
the usual flat one, were not legal. It was a cheap tactic. My
mother faxed letters to Eley, the company that manufactured
the pellets, and to the UIT.

Horst G. Schreiber, the UIT secretary general, said round-
nosed pellets were allowed to be used and made smaller holes
on the target. The technical department at Eley wrote to say
that round-nosed pellets would not make a clearly defined cut

through the paper target like the flat-nosed pellets. But there was no illegality on my part.

Still, officials were unconvinced. I asked if any official had seen me do anything unfair. They were mute. My mother argued that they could find fault with my shooting but not with my integrity. But sports officials in India don't need evidence, don't need to build a case, they just do their thing and strip athletes of confidence. The rebel in me made a brief, terse statement to the media. I said: 'I am not bothered. I am not out to please anyone. Let the critics say anything. I know what I have achieved.' Most people want acceptance, but I wasn't looking for it.

I was alone at the trials in Delhi, trying to qualify for the nationals. I arrived at 8 am and waited for the foreign coach, Dr Laszlo Hammerl. He arrived in the afternoon. Tension sat at the range. One shooter, fifty people watching. As if to see if I was a fluke, a fake. It was demeaning, but I managed to qualify. Then I practised, for the range is like a refuge for me; it is also the place to build back confidence. I shot two matches every day, creating artificial pressure to find that precious match temperament that competitions require. When I got to the nationals in Asansol, I shot a 548 and won a bronze (in the open section).

I was a boy, but I had my first scar. The first pockmark of doubt on my brain. It was a blessing. It reminded me that at every step I had to prove I was good enough. It taught me that doubt didn't rattle me as much it inspired me. In his Hall of Fame speech, Michael Jordan remembered coaches and officials and players who had slighted him, who had underestimated him. I never forgot either. In my heart rested not hate but defiance: I'll show them. My time would come

There was a terrific irony to all this. Eley, the pellet manufacturers in Birmingham, England, who had heard about my 400/400 performance in Ahmedabad, were impressed. They congratulated me on my 'fantastic success' and encouraged me by saying greater things surely were to come. They also confirmed that Eley would send me 50,000 Wasp No.1 pellets every year, along with Eley promotional items for me to carry on with my shooting.

Thousands of kilometres away, people who didn't know me, who had never seen me, were already believing in me. From them, came no doubt.

6

LEAVING MY COMFORT ZONE

The young athlete knows nothing, and has no idea what he doesn't know. He has an unformed beauty, an unpolished talent. His ambition is raw, his dreams are huge, but he cannot get to greatness without information. On technique, routine, competition tricks, guns, training—he knows nothing about the nuances and subtleties of his craft. Not that the height of the heel of a shoe can matter. Not that different brands of pellets shoot differently. He doesn't even know about the rules. For years I shot without knowing them. Neither did many officials.

It's why the shooter needs to beg, borrow, plead for a plane ticket and go out into the world. He needs to listen, watch, hear, learn by osmosis. He needs to get an education. Especially if he's from India. Because here expertise is hard to find and legends don't sit in local locker rooms. At least not in my time.

I was lucky, no argument. Money helps, of course, but money doesn't make you a champion; something inside and indefinable does. I know that because I have seen so many Indian athletes held hostage to their circumstances. And therefore prisoners to officialdom. If you have an athlete's career in your hands, it is an intoxicating power.

Going abroad initially was the equivalent of attending a first-year course at a shooting college. It helped that Colonel Dhillon accepted that I needed extra expertise. It was another sign of his wisdom. Coaches otherwise tend to clutch on. It's hard to admit you have nothing more to teach or that someone else knows more.

So I wrote to the UIT and they recommended a German shooting school in Wiesbaden.

It's intimidating leaving your comfort zone, but I had my eagerness, and I had my mother, who was worried that I'd go astray. Maybe she'd seen too many bidi-smoking shooters at national camps. I was a slightly built fifteen-year-old, barely able to carry my own rifle case. It unnerved the security at Frankfurt airport, which first saw a spectacled kid and then realized he was carrying a gun.

We—my mother and I—lived in Hotel Olympia right above the shooting range in a small room. Think of it as a hostel with a restaurant. But we had our own phone. Well, sort of. On the ground floor landing was one of those black metal phones. Put in coins, dial, yell. No one ever got a call on that phone except us. If it rang, with a ring sharp enough to pierce the building, everyone knew: it was my dad.

Some days were difficult, the food, the loneliness, but my desire kept me going. When I left for training, my mother washed clothes and looked out of the window into a lonely cold and waited for me. Sometimes she'd go for a walk, sometimes she'd watch me shoot. This is what they call unconditional love. Often, and sadly, we go blind to this in sport. We see the competitors, but not who they lean on. We miss the parents putting child before job and ferrying kids to obscure destinations for tennis events across India; we miss the mothers sitting patiently beside pools as a daughter cuts quietly through the water for hours; we miss the fathers religiously dropping off sons for cricket nets before work and after on their Bajaj scooters. They wait for, and on, us.

It's hard to go anywhere for a length of time without meeting a character. In Wiesbaden it was Mr Schreiber, whose first name I forget, who ran the hotel. I didn't like the food, all cheese and meat, but he would insist I finish it. Thank God for napkins, which is where a lot of it surreptitiously disappeared. The only television in the hotel was in a common room, where I became an inadvertent expert on Bundesliga football. Schreiber, one might say, cared deeply for his team, Bayern Munich: one day when they lost, furniture flew. But he was a fine man whose family I became fond of.

Everyone at the range in Wiesbaden helped me. They liked my interest and I became an object of their interest. An intense kid from India, shooting rifles, was not part of the usual Wiesbaden day. It wasn't that India didn't have worthy shooters, for the excellent Jaspal Rana had won a world junior gold in Milan in 1994. But in Germany, to be fair, he was still to become a familiar name.

In this atmosphere of excellence, I thrived. Watching top shooters produce phenomenal scores next to me produced an immediate impact. It's the way it is in sport. Play with someone better and it inspires you to match them. Ego comes into play. You look, you learn, you find a way to become better, so much better that you can beat this better person. In those days, there was no consistency to my shooting. I was young, erratic, capable of spurts of excellence, but unable to sustain it. In a manner of speaking, my regular score was 560. When I returned from Wiesbaden after one month, I was shooting 570.

Ten-point improvement. Just like that. It was fast, it was huge. It was also possible to make such a leap at that level. But the further you went from 570, from 580, from 590, the harder every incremental improvement became.

Shooting 570-580, as we did in India, wasn't enough. Because I had now seen what the world was shooting. They were rattling off 590s, some days 595s. It was scary yet stimulating; it told me how far I had to go to catch the world.

Shooting in Wiesbaden was also a privilege because there were no power cuts. The machines never broke down. The range was never unclean. Environment is important for a shooter, for any sportsperson. You feel good about your craft, you feel energized. You are also never distracted from your mission. When ranges fall into disrepair, it's like no one cares, it is like a disrespect to the art form you are trying to pursue. In the range in Tughlakabad in Delhi, prior to the 2010 Commonwealth Games renovation, electricity would cease, air conditioners stop, targets break down. You'd stand there sweating in your shooting jacket or trying to shoot with water dropping onto your head through a leaky roof. When I was a kid I loved shooting under the colonel's mango tree, but Germany was a new, fascinating world.

Wiesbaden was where I took the first steps of my independence movement. Was I pampered? Protected? Was there a feeling that 'This is a nice boy from India, let's give him a good time and he'll come back. It's good for business?'

Probably.

So I had to learn shooting was me, gun, target. No mother could count on the range. No coach standing behind me. I liked it.

I started going regularly to Wiesbaden, often twice a year from age fifteen to about seventeen, for a few weeks at a time, and was under the supervision of its coaches, Astrid Harbeck and Bernd Schaufelle. Sometimes I shot with the Luxembourg national team. Sometimes I sat and watched Germany's junior shooter Rebecca Frank, who once shot five sets of 399/400. By 1998, I had started to touch the mid-580s occasionally, which was a decent level. Certainly enough for the coaches from the German federation to suggest I should attend the 1998 world junior championships. Their advice was uncomplicated and sensible: exposure and competition was the only way. Not everyone agreed. Our national association was slow to respond. So was coach Sunny Thomas. Eventually, the trip was cleared but the cost was mine. I could afford it, but what if I couldn't?

The 1998 World Championships, in Barcelona, was my first international competition. I was nervous, apprehensive, eager. I shot a 574, finished forty-fourth in the junior section and was pretty happy. It was enough to earn me selection for the Commonwealth Games in Kuala Lumpur in September. There, on the cusp of sixteen years old, I shot 571 and finished sixteenth. This time the score left me unhappy.

Yet there was good news. No longer was I the kid shooter who knew nothing. Now I knew something. I knew I was still only learning how to compete. I also knew that my 574 in Barcelona was insufficient. I had to muster 20 points more. Somehow.

7

THE SHOOTING DAY: TOILETS AND TREMORS

My range, at home in Chandigarh, is my chapel, workshop, refuge. Accompanied by the muted hum of air conditioners, the sound of my prayer is the bark of a rifle. I have an indoor 10-metre range linked to a larger 50-metre range that extends outdoors. They are cluttered with the tools and detritus of my craft. Gun cases lie stacked and 50,000 rounds of ammunition in tin cans await firing. Shooting jackets lie draped everywhere as if at a haberdashery store and at the side an enormous mirror stands at reflective attention where I pose to correct the alignment of my hips. From a window, sunlight sneaks in to warm me when my form is cold.

In a corner lies a framed, crank-action Winchester with a picture of Annie Oakley, the American markswoman who, so goes the legend, could knock the lingering ash off a cigarette from a decent distance. It's too good a story to even want to refute. The walls are pockmarked with pictures and scoresheets and certificates. A shooting table stands before me, cupboards

As a baby (*right*) and at my house in Dehra Dun with my sister Divya after taking part in a school play (*below*).

I fell in love with guns at an early age. Here I am practising under a mango tree at Lt Col J.S. Dhillon's shooting range in Chandigarh at age 13, with my first rifle (*above*); and firing a toy pistol on a family holiday at age eight (*right*).

The first flush of excitement. With coach Col Dhillon and hockey legend Pargat Singh at my first national games in Bangalore in 1997.

Walking out after a crushing defeat at the Athens Olympics in 2004, with shooter Manavjeet Singh Sandhu on my left and Rana Gurmeet Sodhi, the man who got me into shooting, on my right.

Left: With long-time coaches Heinz Reinkemeier and Gaby Buehlmann, who have been very influential figures in my life and with whom I share a special bond, and their son, Joe, at the Taj Mahal.

Below: With my ally, guide and sounding board Amit Bhattacharjee, who has been with me through thick and thin.

Below: In Rajasthan with Gaby (fourth from left), Heinz (second from left), shooter Suma Shirur (third from left), her husband Siddhartha (extreme left) and Joe (extreme right).

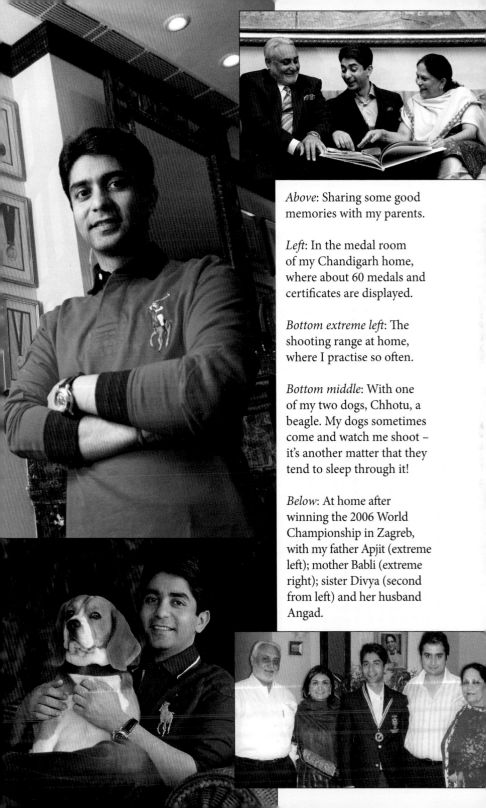

Above: Sharing some good memories with my parents.

Left: In the medal room of my Chandigarh home, where about 60 medals and certificates are displayed.

Bottom extreme left: The shooting range at home, where I practise so often.

Bottom middle: With one of my two dogs, Chhotu, a beagle. My dogs sometimes come and watch me shoot – it's another matter that they tend to sleep through it!

Below: At home after winning the 2006 World Championship in Zagreb, with my father Apjit (extreme left); mother Babli (extreme right); sister Divya (second from left) and her husband Angad.

Left and below: Before the Beijing Olympics in 2008, I wanted to leave nothing to chance. Here I am getting neuro-feedback – to see how my brain and body respond to the highs and lows in my shooting – from South African psychologist Tim Harkness.

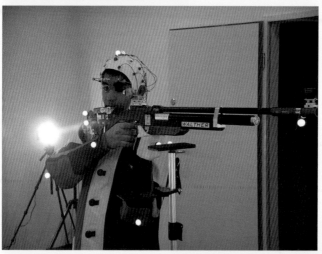

After the Beijing win, when I didn't know what to do with myself, I even consulted, as a fun thing, a palmist about my future.

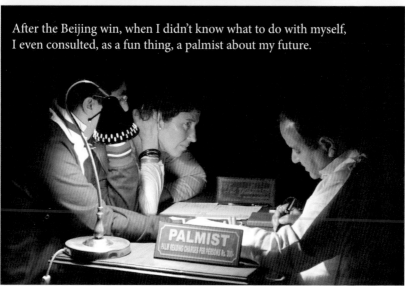

Good luck and all the Best to you
for the Olympics 08!!!
Only you set the limits!
Uwe + troops

As my German consultant Uwe
Riesterer (*left*) eggs me on, I somehow
conquer my fear and manage to climb
a 40-feet-high 'pizza pole' in Germany.
The feat gave me extra confidence
going into Beijing 2008 – if I could do
this, the medal could not be all that
difficult.

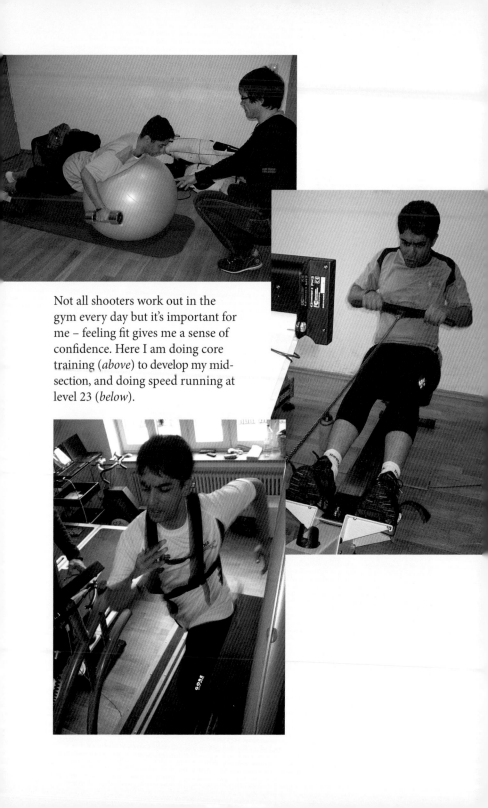

Not all shooters work out in the gym every day but it's important for me – feeling fit gives me a sense of confidence. Here I am doing core training (*above*) to develop my mid-section, and doing speed running at level 23 (*below*).

Being close to nature and testing my endurance helps me clear my mind and focus better. Here I am going rowing in Lake Chimsee in Germany (*left*) and snow-walking in the Bavarian Alps (*below*) – it's not as easy as it looks!

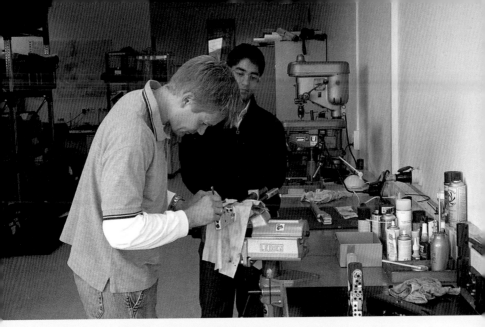

Getting my gun fine-tuned at the Walther factory in Ulm, Germany.
Guns need servicing at least three to four times a year.

A pipe dream: Working with a water pipe in place of a gun to improve
my balance and stability during training at my range at home.

A sweet victory for me at the Commonweath Games in 2014, as it came at a time when I was battling epileptic seizures.

A special moment with my father after winning the gold at the Asian AirGun Championship at the Dr Karni Singh shooting range in Delhi in September 2015.

The final trip: Cutting a cake on the last day of the training session at home, before leaving for a 62-day trip in preparation for Rio 2016. In the picture are my father Apjit and mother Babli, sister Divya, niece Naintara and nephew Agastya.

It's all about balance: My Pilates teacher in Germany, Tina Hense, reshapes and fine-tunes my body as I prepare for Rio 2016 (*left and below*).

An ideal distraction: Building a Mandala at the Berlin studio of artist Ernst Handl, brother-in-law of my Pilates teacher Tina Hense. Each circle and colour in the Mandala reflected my mindset before Rio 2016.

I'm flexible: Yoga became an important aspect of my fitness routine before Rio 2016.

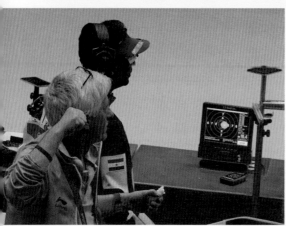

A close-knit team. I shared a special bond with my physio Dr Digpal Singh Ranawat (*above left*) and coach Heinz (*above right and below left*), and the positive and happy atmosphere helped in dealing with the stress of competition.

The final goodbye: My last morning at the Rio Village, with Gaby and Heinz.

Leading the Indian contingent at Rio 2016, and in the process fulfilling my dad's dream to be a flag-bearer at the Olympics. *Right:* With my physio Digpal Ranawat after the march past at Rio. Ranawat was a pillar of strength for me during all my struggles in the last few years.

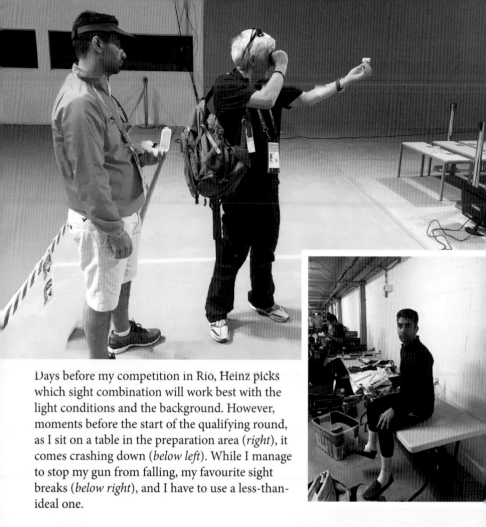

Days before my competition in Rio, Heinz picks which sight combination will work best with the light conditions and the background. However, moments before the start of the qualifying round, as I sit on a table in the preparation area (*right*), it comes crashing down (*below left*). While I manage to stop my gun from falling, my favourite sight breaks (*below right*), and I have to use a less-than-ideal one.

are scattered in an ante-room, all littered with rods, cables, screws, air tanks, butt plates, spanners, triggers.

On a shelf rests a projector and occasionally, I will project a film onto the target and moving figures will dance all over it. I am testing my focus, challenging my concentration, ensuring my eyes are locked to the bullseye, nothing else. My gun sits, it waits for me. It is all angular steel, all screwed-on tubes and parts, like some modern version of what I am told Edward Fox used in *The Day of the Jackal*. Two monitors blink at me, one offers up my score, the other is part of my laser-operated SCATT Training System.

When I lift my gun and bring it to bear on the target, a squiggly green line traces this 20-second movement on the SCATT monitor. Is my line smooth? Is it clean? Am I shifting? Colours become my education. A yellow line shows the moment 2/10th of a second before my shot, a white line indicates my triggering. They tell me: Did I take too long? Did I jerk? Where was I aiming? Finally, a red line on the monitor denotes my follow-through. In a precise sport this is precious information. On certain days, after every shot I will study my movement on the monitor. Then I start again. You can't smell sweat in this clinical room, but I promise it is there.

Someone once asked me if I was a nervous shooter. Wrong question. Everyone is a nervous shooter. It's why we need more toilets at ranges. One hour before an event and each one is full.

Think of it like this. Take a panic attack and multiply it. A thousand times. And then you get me. On competition day, I fidget and fuss. I am assailed by anxiety, I can feel adrenaline injecting into my system. Footballers relish it, but not shooters. We don't know what to do with adrenaline. We want a monk's calm, or a state of arousal only to a particular, precise point. Instead it's like our insides are in some washing machine switched onto high. You never get used to this.

Never.

Fear and nerves I carry everywhere. Except to the practice range. I like shooting for nothing, no medal, no match, because there is control, a distinct connection with your inner being. It is talent being expressed with pleasure. But shoot for even five rupees and it's different. Like a Taser to the nervous system. The body becomes more aware and fearful, reactions slow down. It's like a beautifully polished, tuned machine refusing to work. In training, skill just happens. In competition, I feel I have to make it happen. Yet I know, to shoot well, I can't force it. You have to allow it to happen. This is my struggle.

In my early days, traumatized, I decided to shoot fast. Get it over with, be normal again. It was reckless, it didn't work. Then I started talking to myself, one small sane part of me trying to cajole the shaking competitor within me:

You can do it.

Trust yourself.

You've done the training.

Nice. It didn't work either.

Other times I would scotch-tape a piece of paper to the table in front of me. As if to read my own instructions would focus me, distract me from the bile rising up my throat. I'd write on the paper, 'Follow through.' Which means 'when the shot is over don't jerk your neck to look at the score on the monitor.' Or 'Breathe.' Or 'Concentrate on triggering.'

Finding solutions to anxiety was almost like a hobby. You try everything, almost nothing works. Eventually you learn to live with it, you hate the fear but you accept it. You train your mind to work through it. Before the Beijing Olympics, I had arrived at a place where my worst state was still a manageable state.

Shooting is embedded in my brain, frivolity isn't. At twenty-nine now, I am beginning to learn that smiling isn't a sin. Am I fun? Not on the surface. For too long my interests were too few, my life condensed to my sport. No girlfriends. No parties. No hobbies. No distractions. I watch movies, carrying ten to twelve around on long trips, but they are only my escape. Next morning, ask me the story and I couldn't tell you. Food is not a fascination, though the older I get the harder I search for Indian restaurants abroad. Familiarity becomes comfort.

Of course, when I first lived with Gaby and Heinz and she said, 'Make your breakfast,' I replied 'How?'

Boil an egg? This technique I did not know.

I approach shooting like a scholar, as I do life. I'm a learner, a career student, if you like. Knowledge fascinates me and on television I am addicted to the news: What is happening? What should I know? I approach all sport with delight but also in a similarly analytical manner. I enjoy performance, but it is not entertainment in the conventional sense only that I seek, but also something else. My pleasures are almost academic, as if the action that has just unspooled on the field has to be not just watched, and enjoyed, but investigated.

So much thrill lies in prediction: who will win and why? When an athlete is performing with authority, the instinctive reaction often is to think: this is it, here is the winner. But the critical moment in sport is often when realization slithers into that athlete's brain: 'Damn, I can win this. I should win this.' That emotion, which he has not been aware of, must now be managed. Occasionally, an athlete will start thinking of a press conference. What he will say. What the headlines will say. In that instant, he has moved away from the present and into distraction.

My passion beyond shooting is an Indian one. Cricket. It seems some trick of DNA, but in truth it is simply environment. Look out of an Indian house, a train, a car, and there is always a boy with a bat. Cricket allows for no escape, so it might as well be embraced. Tendulkar can be watched forever, he has this quality of genius that is undecipherable. He is distinctive for reasons not always evident. When a player hits a boundary we appreciate it, but when Sachin hits one the pleasure is purer. It is not a case just of shared passport, he just has the ease and command we all crave. I find a similarity with Roger Federer, a fluency that obscures the sweat these men put in. But the later Federer, 2009 onwards, appeals to me more because if once he was too effortless, now he appears human and fallible. Perhaps mechanical men like me are just jealous of artistry.

I admire Rahul Dravid for separate reasons. He is more soldier than artist, he bats unhurriedly but with the stubbornness of a priest whose faith is being challenged. He is a self-confessed cricketer of certain limitations, but his overcoming of them, his compensations for them, these victorious battles he has with himself, are astonishing. The signature of his greatness is commitment and a parallel is to be found an ocean away in Australia. Steve Waugh was as clever, he knew how to summon the best in himself.

These men were creatures of routine. So am I. 'Soldiering on' is our phrase. On any competition day, qualifying is at 9 am but I awake at 5 am. Always. The range is usually some distance away, often on the city outskirts, where there is enough space for pellets and bullets and shells to whine safely into the distance. Breakfast is mandatory but it is difficult. Food doesn't make it easily down a throat constricted with fear. At the range I am irritated for there is a long line at the armoury. In all sport, you have to learn to wait when all you want to do is compete.

My equipment is packed. Haphazardly. A shooting jacket, trousers, shoes, gloves, a compression suit worn below the jacket, glasses, ammunition. All stuffed in. I am ready. The jacket is a second skin, a heavy one, it weighs 5-6 kilograms and offers stability, the shoulders softer where the butt fits, the back like a panel of hard cardboard. At competition, a machine checks its stiffness and thickness: a little extra helps, but a little extra is illegal. The shoes are hard. I don't like that and I once soled mine with rubber that is used for Ferrari tyres.

I altered the thickness of my soles because the floors at ranges can be different. One day wooden, next day cement, third day carpet. Each one perhaps a millimetre or more different in height. Why do I do these things, this fiddling with soles? Because I can, because it makes shooting fun, because change has an effect that's not real but psychological. Like taking a placebo. It reassures me.

I am at the range an hour ahead. My stand, where I place my rifle after every shot, is close to me. In front of me is the monitor that blinks my score and the odd screwdriver, and perhaps an Allen key. Nothing else. Just me and the bullseye looking at each other. I spend time trying to align my hip to the target, looking for a visual clue, a line on the floor, a pipe on the roof, to give me a straight line. Sometimes I use a laser. These days Gaby does it for me, marks the table with a pen where precisely my line is to the target.

At the range, I wait, I study opponents. In Beijing 2008, during the qualifying, the Chinese shooter Zhu Qinan, standing next to me, looked closed to the world, uptight. I thought, this is going to be a hard day for him. Before the final, he was laughing, talking, it was unusual, it told me he was not himself that day. Maybe people watch me. Who knows what they say?

Rugby players tape fingers and stretch. Tennis players fiddle with rackets in the dressing room. Batsmen swipe the air with their bats. Not me. I can't hold my rifle till 10 minutes before the event. Man and gun just sit side by side. My rifle is ready. It works on compressed air and there's a cylinder in the dressing room to fill it.

When I first lift my gun, I lift it high, at 12 o'clock position and about 5 millimetres above the target. Don't ask how I know it's 5 millimetres. I just do. Shooters are like that. We live our life by slide rules. I bring my gun down, slowly, methodically, it takes fine motor control to do this, very fine. Staying motionless, a statue that breathes, is hard enough. But when you bring a 5.5-kilogram object—the rifle—into play, and put it to your shoulder, and ensure it doesn't affect your balance as new muscles start working, that is an art. It's why I need the control. As I align the rifle to the bullseye, I can't relax too much; if I do I will move. So it's a like a controlled collapse, a gradual sinking into the shoes. That's why I hated the hard shoes. It made it harder to sink.

I don't like Chinese shooters. Only kidding. But they're lucky, it seems their bodies are perfect for shooting. Pliant. Flexible. My body is disobedient. I can't naturally put my left elbow on top of my hip joint and into my ribs. It just won't go there. So I compensate. I lean a little forward, the right hip up, but that stretches and hurts my back. So much for the presumed flexibility I was supposed to have as an Indian. Some days I wish I was Gagan Narang, big and massive, whose elbow just plants itself solidly in his hip.

In the movies, Clint Eastwood lifts his rifle, points it,

squints, a sort of narrowing of already narrow eyes, and knocks a gunman off his horse from 400 yards. I'm not that cool. For me the act of aiming, and what I do with my eyes, is not simple. Post-Beijing I had Lasik surgery, but before that my eyesight was -2.75. Even worse, my peripheral vision was dismal. Sometimes, it was like looking through a piece of paper with two pin-holes in it. Your vision is tunnelled. You don't see much else except a blur. Part of it is by design, you get so focused on looking ahead, you miss the world. To some degree, it's also why people considered me arrogant. Really. When they passed me, even two metres away, I couldn't see them and so I often didn't acknowledge them. It's why Gaby thought I was always alone.

On the range, my eyes make life even more complicated. With the assistance of my German coaches, I build a bizarre contraption. Over my left eye is a blinder, which semi-covers a lens. My eye is open behind the blinder. It has to be. It plays a role in balance; furthermore, the television monitor that tells me my score after every shot is on the left.

On the right side, I wear one lens, like a monocle, in front of my eye. Another lens hangs at a 45-degree angle. When I am searching for calm, for balance, I don't look at the target, I look to my right, into space. If there was no glass there, I'd see a blur. A blur is bad. Because when I am ready to shoot and look straight again, I am going from a blur to a sharp image and have to refocus. It throws me off. Weird, I know.

First, I dry fire, which is shooting with no pellets. I am trying to position myself, find the right muscle tension, locate a balance. I am also like a two-year-old inside. A baby. A kid. I don't know what's happening. Fear is back, or did it never leave?

We're standing in a line, shooter after shooter, two metres

from each other yet utterly oblivious of each other. In Munich, there are a hundred shooting points, at the 2010 Delhi Commonwealth Games there were 80. Like a congregation of snipers.

Then I'm shooting. Tink, tink, tink, the range sounds like it's in the middle of a hailstorm. I hear nothing. My window of opportunity to pull the trigger is small. Tiny. A tenth of a second possibly. It's that moment when the sights are aligned, when your inner and external beings are in sync, and an instinct tells you: Now. And you pull. It has to just happen. If you're too aware of your surroundings, you might over-think. Should I shoot now, wait, what? If you're too blank, you can miss this moment.

It is a state of consciousness I am constantly trying to find, and hold onto, for the separation between victory and heartbreak is nothing, it is cruel.

While unsuccessfully defending my title at the 2010 world championship in Munich, fifty-three of my sixty shots in the qualifying were 10s. Not great, not bad. But the flimsiest, tiniest errors felled me. Four of my other shots were worth 9.9 in real terms, but counted only as 9s since there are no decimals in qualification. The 9.9s were, thus, almost perfect in a perfect sport. I was only .1 away from a 10, the breadth of a drawing pin, but each time I only got a 9.

It is annoying, it is a huge penalty, it points to the unforgiving nature of shooting. Cricketers can edge the ball yet stay alive, footballers can mis-kick before goal and get another chance, tennis players can miss lines entirely and try again the next point. There is a relief in that. But my cost is different, it is harsher. The scoring structure of shooting means I can't afford any mistake and it makes me defensive.

Too many things can go wrong, too many things to keep

me at 9 and away from a 10. It could be a fluctuation in muscular tension in my body causing a jerk in triggering. I don't even know which part of the body it has come from. It could be movement, for I may appear still, but I am often shifting, imperceptibly, a few millimetres back, a few forward. It could be my aim: it may have shifted gently left or right, or up or down. In that case I need to give my sight a 'click' which readjusts it by 0.1 millimetre, either vertically or horizontally, or left or right. It could be my shooting jacket that doesn't sit well or my pellets that are less accurate than another make. Some days the backdrop irritates and the lights distract. Some days a heavy shooter fills your peripheral vision and you feel the vibration of his movement. Other days an apprentice shooter makes large movements, too many of them; he slams his rifle back in its cradle and distracts.

I know all this and I have to forget all this.

If I shoot a 9, I don't react visibly. I can't. Even though it's a crap shot. Even though if I have a couple of 9s, it's over. This is a perfectionist's sport and mistakes hurt. But occasionally—only occasionally—a 9 is good. The tension leaks away. Now I'm shooting for pride and I shoot well. But mostly I look ahead, I forget about the 9s. The last shot must become irrelevant, if it nags away in the head it distracts with its negativity. Even a good shot, even a 10, has to be cast from the mind. A passing moment of triumph registers, confidence swirls. But the next shot is a separate masterpiece, it must be approached without any hindrance—either despair or overexcitement—from the immediate past.

I can abort a shot seven times. Eight times. Ten times. Aim, not fire, put down the gun, breathe. As many times as I like within the prescribed time. I am not that talented, not a natural shooter, remember? I have to work, I have to fight, to find that moment, a precise equilibrium of body and brain. I think I am smart and that's a problem. I am self-critical to the point of eccentricity. I once shot six straight perfect 100s and left the range unhappy. Being less intense can be good, it keeps you from overdoing your analysis.

All that control, aiming, feeling, concentrating, it's unbelievably exhausting. I have a saying: if I want to win I have to get to the minus part of the Duracell battery. Close to empty. I did this in Beijing, but you can't always do this, can't always dig so deep. I have to work so hard to win, I can't do it all the time. So sometimes I address a specific issue, or work on different strategies. Most people think I am an over-thinker, and they are right. I don't recommend my method.

Except that I won gold using it.

8

GUNNING FOR SYDNEY

a) Ready...

It is uncomplicated. You take your practice form. Fly to Europe. Stand next to a German or Norwegian or Dutchman, with a CV as long as your elbow, ten years and two Olympics older than you. Then see if you can shoot well. Can you replicate practice form in competition without shaking? It is the ultimate sporting examination.

In India, we have a famous word for trips abroad: EXPOSURE. Everyone needs it. Even if your ranges are littered with talent at home, as India's are now, you need to taste different environments, light conditions, range backgrounds. Just waking up in a place of foreign voices and strange breakfasts can be unsettling. Your mind takes journeys it shouldn't. The more you travel, the less surprised you are.

But in India this was a struggle.

Travel!

Exposure!

Eyebrows rose as if you were asking for a free ticket to go shopping on Oxford Street. In 1998, when I was just sixteen, competition in India was limited. Just one national championship where 250-odd showed up (now roughly 3500 do) and weeks of trials and camps. Same place, same people, same shooting. A new environment was vital but the National Rifle Association of India (NRAI) was unconvinced. However, this is the beauty of sport. Timing.

In one of the 1998 trials, just when it mattered, I shot a 579, defeating senior, experienced riflemen like T.C. Palangappa and A. P. Subbaiah. Very nice people, for whom getting beaten by a kid was not very nice.

This was always an issue. Age. In effect, I was a prodigy, a boy in what was a man's sport and it can be strange. At the Commonwealth Games the same year I roomed with the veteran shooter Ashok Pandit: he was in his forties, I was fifteen. Like father and son.

Shooting is democratic. Ostensibly anyone can win a medal. A teenager in his first Games. A forty-eight-year-old in his seventh Olympics. The issue isn't age, it's readiness, it's where your form is at a particular moment. Age can hurt. Age can steal part of your flexibility. It can dull your triggering reflex. It can affect your neuro-muscular control. But all this can be overcome.

No finer story exists than the one about the Hungarian Karoly Takacs, recounted by David Wallechinsky in his Olympic compendium, *The Complete Book of the Summer Olympics*. A world-class shooter in the mid-1930s, Takacs injured his right hand in a grenade accident. So he switched to his left hand, practised, and won gold at the 1948 London Olympics. He was thirty-eight. In 1952, at forty-two, he won a second gold.

Time is not the enemy. Form is. In shooting, it comes in abrupt phases. It's a sport of constant hiccups. You can embrace perfection, win, stumble for five years, then win again. Even for shooters it can be incomprehensible. If there's a peak age, we're still looking for it.

Shooting in India is now turning younger and the reason is opportunity. Pigtailed girls with pistols walk ranges. Boys with rifles are no longer uncommon. But back in the late 1990s, Indian shooting was the preserve mainly of mid-thirties Army shooters. Only Jaspal Rana, brilliant and controversial, who seemed like he had emerged from some Louis L'Amour western, was young, and even he was eight years older than me.

At fifteen, I was unusually young. And young people in sport are always expected to know their place. Back of the line, kid. Grow steadily like everyone else. Jump the queue, while wearing steel braces wrapped around your teeth, and people get antsy. No one wants to get beat up by a fellow who comes to the range with his mom. I understand this, but it is uncomfortable.

These days the shotgun guys are my pals. They're different from rifle shooters. We're quiet, they are wild extroverts. Maybe it's all in the sound. Exploding targets as they do is more aggressive than puncturing them like I do. I like them, they're not me. But way back then, I was a social misfit. No one to talk to, nothing in common, no sense of comfort. Predictably, there's always talk about the young kid with the new guns, not from everyone but from enough people for one to sense it.

Oh, he has the latest equipment.

Hey, he's spoilt.

How hard I practised was secondary. Now it's easy to shrug off, then it got under my teenage hide, sitting there like an irritation.

I tried to be unobtrusive. I would arrive at the range 30

minutes earlier. Or get dropped off a couple of hundred yards before the gate, because I didn't want to show I came in a nice car. I ate with everyone at Nehru Stadium. Was careful not to splurge when travelling abroad. Didn't want to stick out. It was useless, it's hard to disguise you're a kid or well-off or own a nice gun. And some things I couldn't control either, like my mother insisting I stay in a hotel during camps and be comfortable during training. It was thoughtful, but didn't help.

Eventually my attempts to fit in were becoming a distraction, a waste of energy. I stopped caring about anything but performance. I became businesslike: loading, firing, leaving. Even in competitions, even later in my shooting life, this became my style. Whether I lost, or won, I'd leave. After winning World Championship gold in 2006, I left five minutes after formalities ended. The range wasn't a place to make friends, it was the site of my mission. From the outside, I might have looked standoffish, but this was a mechanism to cope with the pressure. Just get the job done and leave. So I didn't chirp, didn't cut corners, I just focused.

But beating the older shooters, like that day in Delhi, was vital. I had won by 10 points, a fair margin. Indian coach Sunny Thomas had called me in to talk about international exposure. The system of communicating results was slow and he hadn't seen the results yet. 'You're not ready to go abroad,' he said. First prove yourself in India, he argued correctly, first beat the best here. Just then, in a piece of immaculate timing, a peon brought him the results. He glanced at them and was taken aback. Scores are the finest allies for they are almost impossible to argue with. Now Thomas, a genial man who has held the shooting team together for decades, altered his tone, his manner changed, respect arrived. Going abroad wasn't as hard anymore.

b) Set....

Sporting lives need a focus; they need immediate destinations and also distant ones. An athlete goes to the nationals, but dreams of the Olympics. He is chasing many things at once, perfection and victory: the first is not always possible, but you can never get close to the second without chasing the first. I was tip-toeing into the shooting world, starting the run through club competitions in unknown German halls and getting a first taste of World Cups. But always one word danced in my head. Sydney. The 2000 Olympics. I was, young, gifted, inconsistent and I wanted the world.

Shooting, like all sports, has an established hierarchy. The Olympics, held every four years, is the Holy Grail. Close behind in worthiness is the World Championships, which is also held every four years. In eminence, the Olympics dwarfs it; in competitiveness, the World Championships can be stiffer, for each nation is allowed three entries per event, not two like the Olympics. Ranked next in prestige are the World Cups, which are held four times a year across Europe, Australia, Asia, America.

The quota system has altered over time but now it is as follows. To get to the Olympics, you must finish, in the two years preceding the Games...

... between first and fifth at a World Championship,

... first, second, third at any World Cup,

... first or second at the Asian Championships.

It may seem like a lot of chances, a lot of quota places. Till you remember that only seventy-odd make the Olympics in all three men's rifle events. Till you see the thousands of shooters worldwide trying to qualify. At just one World Cup, in Munich in 2011, there were roughly a thousand shooters just in the rifle and pistol sections.

If you want to qualify for the Olympics, this is your hunting ground. This is where you earn a quota place. This is where you are reminded the Olympics are not a gift.

So, in the spring of 1999, closing in on seventeen, I began my chase for the Sydney Olympics in Europe. These were small events, adequate for finding form and arranging technique, and my beginnings were correspondingly small: a silver at the Luxembourg national championships. A few years later, I'd shoot higher than the existing world record at that range, and they gave me life membership of their club. Thank you, gents.

The World Cups which followed in 1999 were my first real smell of world-class competition. Leif Steinar Rolland of Norway, fifth at the Atlanta Olympics, in one lane; Marco De Nicolo of Italy, Havana World Cup champion from 1997, in another lane; next lane, boy from India who hadn't got his first Gillette yet.

At the 1999 Munich World Cup, I finished eighty-ninth; in Milan next, I slipped to ninety-fourth place; in Atlanta, I was sixty-ninth. I was disheartened but educated. This was like being a young player on the PGA Tour. One good round is possible, four is hard. Anyway, at a World Cup there are thirty people who can shoot 595/600. No one wins every day, no one can. This is a sport without a dominant Tiger Woods.

Rapidly a tutorial was being administered. This wasn't my home range, it didn't feel like my home range. The world was watching and invisible to them was the sweat forming on my skin. When I went home, I was another shooter. Calmer. More confident. Abroad I couldn't break 580/600. After the World Cups, I shot a 594 in Bangalore. One point better than the world junior record held by Rasmus Lund of Denmark at 593. It also qualified me for the South Asian Games in Kathmandu, where I won a silver.

I was shooting well and not just for someone who was seventeen. I just wasn't shooting well enough for the Sydney Olympics. I won bronze (team pairs) at the third Commonwealth Shooting Championship in Auckland in 1999, and won the national junior and senior titles in Phillaur. My score was 593. No one, ever, in forty-three nationals, had shot so high. But I still didn't have a quota place.

The Asian Championships in Langkawi, Malaysia, in January 2000, offered an opportunity and we were ready. Our rifle coach, Laszlo Szucsak, had a neat theory: to polish diamonds you need diamond dust. The more we shot abroad, the clearer we saw that the best shooters were within our reach. Psychologically, this was a boon. If greatness looks intimidating close-up, paradoxically it also looks more human. From 10 feet, no one looks like a superman. Anjali Bhagwat was proof of such Indian capability, her scores were world class, even in practice, where she whipped me by 5-6 points. Getting beaten by girls is not always fun, but by this brilliant woman it was just fine.

But Langkawi was a letdown. I needed at least silver but won bronze. Yet there was hope. The international shooting federation has Olympic wildcards, or what they intriguingly call 'hardship quotas', for deserving shooters. But they needed to be impressed and the last chance was the World Cup cycle in 2000.

It's a strange life, of travel, shoot, lose, learn. Man battling himself. Improvement lies in the scores, but also in technique. Great shooters in my event might win only ten major medals (World Cup, World Championship, Olympics) in ten years, if they're lucky, and definitely not all of them gold, so the shooter must understand defeat, not befriend it but learn to walk with it.

It's easier to play against someone, an active rival who can affect your skill, who has a shining day which allows you to sigh, 'He was too good.' But for shooters, defeat is often a pure failure of the self. To stay sane, defeat requires bizarre justification. Like 'Oh, I really didn't want to win that competition,' or 'This event isn't really important to my build-up.' But it hurts, deep within, like an open wound in the mind that is beyond suture.

On I went, chasing the Sydney Olympics. In that city itself, in the 2000 World Cup, I was twenty-fourth. In Milan, which was next, I was joint fifteenth, but in Munich, whose range inevitably inspires me, I shot 596 out of 600 to equal the junior world record. It was the first time the Germans saw me shoot at such a level and they were astonished. Watching opponents watch you, mark you down for the future, this is fun. It was one of my points of arrival as a competitor.

So there I was. In my first World Cup final. At seventeen. Very cool. But my final was scrappy and I missed the bronze by 0.1 points to eventual Sydney Olympic champion Cai Yalin of China. My scores were a telling study, a superb 10.7 to start with, a dismal 8.8 as my fourth shot, a 10.0 as my final shot, which was average. Here was another lesson: in the finals, shooting becomes another sport.

It starts with pace. Qualifying shooting is absent of urgency, it allows the shooter to follow his personal clock. He has to fire sixty shots in 105 minutes. He can put down the gun, he can reassess, he is *in* command. In the final, you shoot *on* command. In 75 seconds, the trigger has to be pulled and this clock has a weight, it is a pressure in itself. There is *time*, but subconsciously you know you are *being timed*.

In the final—which always has eight shooters—an alertness sits in the brain. The heart rate rises like a man late for a flight.

It is only 10 shots, not 60, so each minor mistake, just the .2 between a 10.6 and a 10.4, becomes enormous. As it is only 10 shots, there is less room to claw your way back. Tension increases the minor tremors. The shooter knows a 'deep 10', a 10.5, for instance, is within his grasp, he has trained to the point that he believes he can do it *any* time... but can he do it at *this* time?

Right now.

This shot.

In qualification, victory is almost abstract, it is not the purpose. In the final, victory is precariously close, it looms, the shooter must grab it, and this massive realization, this smell of gold, makes him lose his motor control.

Really, finals are a beautiful pain.

But despite my defeat in the Munich World Cup final, I found some solace in my improvement. I had been, for a short while in Munich, one of the top shooters in the world, and it was a thrill. But Sydney still taunted me. The 'hardship quotas' had been asked for and we hung around like young men after a job interview, unable to proceed with our lives. It meant our Olympic preparations were irregular. It's strange committing yourself in training for an event you may not be in, but only we were to blame. If we were good enough, we would have qualified.

c) Gone....

Athletes wait, we're like the people in railways stations in India, slumped on suitcases and wearing a shrug. We're constantly stuck in a sort of limbo, and if patience isn't written into our personalities, then we have to learn. The act of sport is itself quite short. Ninety minutes in football. Roughly two hours plus in tennis. Under two hours in shooting. The rest of our

lives is spent waiting. Waiting at airport lounges, waiting in
hotels for the team bus to take us to training, waiting to fire,
waiting to go out to bat in cricket, waiting by the phone for
a selector to call.

But this time I was lucky. The first to get the 'hardship
quota' was me; the first to feel uncomfortable about it was
also me. Shooting is not subjective, the holes in the target and
the scores on the computer are an unarguable reality. Anjali
Bhagwat, who'd made the finals of World Cups, was shooting
better than me, better than anyone, she deserved it more than
me or anyone else. But I was young and the world loves the
prodigy, so maybe that is why I got it. Sport isn't fair, I know
that, but for all our competitiveness, which is as sharp and
cutting as a razor, athletes know injustice.

So I did the only decent thing possible: I wrote to Anjali
and said it's yours. I was ready to transfer my quota to her. My
parents might have been stunned, but I was sure in my mind.
Anjali was surprised and later told a reporter, 'He felt very sad
and thought I deserved it. I felt so good.' I think she still has
the letter somewhere.

Then fate intervened and a few days later, she got her
quota, too.

The team practised in Bangalore at a camp, I worked at
home. Coach Laszlo Szucsak from Hungary, a decent man, felt
I needed the quiet and calm of my own range. Embarrassingly,
it was superior to Bangalore's. I had less power cuts. Fewer
distractions. Less instances of equipment breaking down.
We're talking about the range to prepare Olympic shooters.
It's beyond sad, it's pathetic.

At the Sydney Olympics, my father ordered me an
electronic target system. It is basic equipment in shooting. It
means instead of a pulley winding back a paper target every

single shot, the score of every shot appears on a monitor next to you. Changing the paper target every shot is more movement, and more movement hurts technique. When the score appears electronically, you know it immediately, you adjust immediately. Almost every shooting club in every range in every European town has at least a few shooting lanes with electronic targets. For years India's best ranges didn't. Now, thankfully, we have eighty electronic shooting points in Delhi and Pune. It's great, but it's not enough.

Briefly, I flirted with the idea of travelling to the US for a week before the camp to undergo Lanny Bassham's mental management programme. Bassham lost an Olympic shooting gold in 1972 but won in 1976 and used his experience to forge a system that helps athletes manage pressure. As he once explained: 'Pressure is like air. Too much and you have a hurricane. Too little and you suffocate. But in the correct amount it is the breath of life.'

But Laszlo Szucsak wasn't keen on the idea, he thought his system—physical training and shooting long stretches—was just fine. I respect Szucsak, but like many coaches he was possessive. Not everyone is. One of Gaby's most significant virtues was her openness in letting me work with other coaches.

So I started an expensive process. Consulting Bassham on mental tactics and strategies on the phone. Even in Sydney, during the Olympics, when I was struggling and he provided me with positivity, we communicated, but this time over email. Phone bills were getting too high. Back home, I had joined the camp for a series of trials, but there was good news—Jaspal Rana was around. A former roomie, a buddy, a shooter who helped me appreciate that after a day's practice you need to peel off the competitive mindset and get away, Rana was special. He was an independent athlete in a time when most spirits were muffled. Now athletes speak up, they have found their voice, but then circumstances didn't allow it easily. Fear of official sanction was strong. But Jaspal never bowed down, never did anything unless he was convinced. He taught us: forget controversy, stand up for yourself.

Then we were in Sydney, blue skies, chirruping volunteers, polished stadiums. I went to the opening ceremony, my only one in the Olympics so far. In Athens and Beijing, I was a contender, concentrated on my moment, unready for distraction. Here, I had the lightness of a debutant, feeling both humbled yet unique, for I was a member of this exclusive fraternity of the chosen. The Olympics till then for me were words on the pages of a history book. Distant images of excellence on a television screen. But to be there, in it, part of it, to taste the environment, to be not a watcher but part of the watched, was overwhelming. So much of it dazzles, from the scale to the history, from the ceremony to the spectacle. It lifts the spirit, yet intimidates. It infects the athlete, or most of them, with purpose. To spot Marion Jones, to see the Williams sisters, may bring awe to a shooter from a corner of India. Yet we, in a way, are the same—in our sense of mission, in our stoked egos, in the tension that invades us. Still, as a kid, only seventeen, I was not just competitor but spectator, sauntering off to the hockey, gymnastics, swimming, taking a first-hand look at greatness.

I would sit in the dining hall in Sydney and study people. Athlete as voyeur. Some meals stretched to two hours for this was a favoured entertainment. I was bewildered by the appetite of swimmers, fascinated by the camaraderie of teams, debated the language of faces, walks, bodies.

Athletes can have a particular strut, a bouncy, rolling,

indolent walk that is some parts energy, some parts watch-me. Their physiques are immediate clues to their craft: the weightlifter's thighs, like bonsai tree trunks, give him away; the elongated torso suggests a swimmer; oversized shoulders that don't match a slim waist is the gymnast's giveaway.

The exceptional athlete sometimes projects, he wears confidence, like the unreal calm of a surgeon about to journey through a stranger's brain. But often this is just deceit for athletes are also actors, they learn to disguise emotion and send contrary signals. Under the apparent cool might nestle deep insecurity. Faces tell these stories and Cathy Freeman's spoke of stress. Australia's lithe 400-metre runner, a powerful Aboriginal figure, was under pressure to win and her struggle was evident. Sometimes the athletes themselves are not sure how they look from the outside, which is why Heinz told me in 2010 to carry a mirror with me. Facial tension, he said, can change how your body feels. So you look in the mirror, you adjust, you fake confidence. But still, sometimes, nervousness just can't be hidden, you can see it on other faces and in some warped way this makes you feel better. Their misery gives you security: you are not alone in fearing.

At the Games, national flags were unfurled outside the village windows, a sort of staking out of territory. It was also a geography lesson, a reminder that to win you must beat the world. Tuned athletes walked the pathways and in this vast collision of dreams you could forget what you were there for. A gold in a first Olympics is remarkable, it shows uncannily quick and intelligent adjustment. Often, gold requires a patient internship, and I was accumulating lessons for my future.

I had arrived twenty days before the Games. First mistake. Twenty days becomes boring, in Athens it would be three. I also arrived at 3 am. Second mistake. Accreditation takes time, it is exhausting. In fact, accreditation can be done in advance, I discovered. It was akin to a student taking detailed notes for a future exam:

> *Go to cafeteria, take jacket, it gets cold.*
> *Get ready to eat McDonalds, Olympic food gets tedious.*
> *Check transport timings, go to the range not feeling rushed.*

Only two Indians of a substantial contingent stood out. Karnam Malleswari for her bronze in women's weightlifting, which sparked a wonderful celebration in the Village late at night after her event ended and she returned. A bunch of us had gathered earlier in the Indian team office at the Athletes Village, and to watch her performance together, to see one of us shine, was to feel a powerful sense of team. One billion, damn, at least one medal. The other standout was Anjali Bhagwat, who became the second Indian to make any final since P.T. Usha's 400-metre hurdle heroics in Los Angeles in 1984. Her finish in eighth position was due only to inexperience at such level, but it was a brilliant effort.

Anjali shot well in Sydney. I was shooting rubbish in practice. Struggling with my rifle, struggling with steadiness. But at least I was ready to struggle, I felt the need to push. My Olympic score was 590, my arm shaking because I was delaying my shots. Tension, explained coach Szucsak. Tension infects everyone, which is why low scores at the Games are unsurprising. Just one point better than me, 591, made the final, but instead of despair I wore a quiet pride. This was the best day of shooting of my twenty days in Sydney; the best day of shooting when it mattered most.

I was a good shooter, but not yet a shooter in command. I was a talent—I had turned eighteen on 28 September, during the Olympics, and was the youngest shooter there—but without the requisite control. Sydney was a valuable classroom. It told me the Chinese were an emerging threat and I asked Amit Bhattacharjee to research them and film them. It also told me that at this elite level I was not a stranger. It is wonderfully liberating for an athlete to know, YES, I BELONG HERE. And five minutes after my last shot, a single defining thought went through my head. I can win in Athens. No 'hardship quotas' required.

9

THE GRAMMAR OF GUNFIRE

The shooter in front of his target is akin to an artist contemplating his canvas. At a stretch, on my good days, my work, a series of perfectly placed holes, forms a neat picture. Pointillists, especially, might approve. Shooting, for many folks, scarcely appears a colourful, imaginative pursuit. Guns, by colour usually, and by what they represent, own a grimness, a planet of black and white. But there is a similar sense of communion between the worlds of guns and art. Quietness is a virtue, stillness a quality, form is everything. Lost in contemplation before our different-sized pieces of paper, the world drifts into irrelevance. It is the most perfect of private spaces.

Introduced to this artistic world by my parents, I am now, at twenty-nine, drawn to canvases, as both painter and watcher. On tours to Europe, I break the monotony of my technical world by drifting off to auctions of antiques and traipsing through museums and galleries. Some of it might come from my consultant coach Uwe Riesterer, who viewed my constant habitation of the range as akin to that of a caged tiger whose pacing eventually leads to paranoia. 'Have intellectual challenges,' he used to rail. 'Read, go to museums, listen to music.'

I am not fussy about cars, used to collect watches, like to dress neatly. But art intrigues me, I am fond of a variety of painters, from Husain to Raza to Subodh Gupta to local unknown artists. Art calms me, it allows my mind to unlock itself from shooting and travel to a different place. Else, my life is restricted to airport, hotel, range. I enjoy the detail in paintings, I am awed by imagination, and sometimes I try it myself, standing in front of my easel and brushing oil onto canvas. Of course, embarrassed by my ineptitude, I trash my art work. Only one remains, a Buddha head which an excessively kind friend wanted to keep.

Many athletes consider themselves as artists. Shooters, too. Even as we puncture paper, we think of ourselves as creative. Every 10.9 in shooting is an original, expressive piece of work. At least for me. It takes feel, delicacy, touch, it requires the senses to be sharp. But that said, I am essentially a shooting techie, a range engineer. Like a car fanatic who likes to dismantle his machine and admire every part, I like to disassemble my sport and comprehend every piece. I am a fiddler, a slave to technique. And I found in Gaby and Heinz, in late 2001, kindred spirits in this adventure.

He was a former rifle shooter, later an assistant coach with the German shooting team, a friendly, funny man. Occasionally a human being gives off a vibration, has a certain style, that instinctively appeals to you, and Heinz, writer of books on shooting, was that man. In difficult situations, he opts for laughter. Gaby, in sharp contrast, exhales intensity, she promotes suffering, she wears a look that requires little interpretation: it says, let's-get-the-job-done. One meeting, and you think, she must have been a competitor. And of course she was, a five-time Olympian, the first woman to shoot 400/400 in competition, so technically sound in her movements, a brilliant machine on auto-pilot, that a coach told me to go and watch her. I did. But I was in such awe that courage failed me and I couldn't get myself to talk to her. Big mistake. It took three years, after an introduction through Jaspal Rana, before I joined her and Heinz. And have never left.

It was not a perfect relationship. Later, years later, Heinz finally confessed. He did not initially believe in me. Not in 2001, when we first met—I was eighteen then. Talent I had, but something else was bothering him. An Indian kid could ride an elephant, was his quaint summation, but success in a highly technical and technological sport like shooting? No way.

Europe was the heart of shooting, with a few Americans 'disturbing us', as Heinz liked to say. In Austria and Switzerland, talent littered the country. Germany itself had 12,000 ranges. For a population of 80 million. Go to a village, you'd find a range. Shooting was not alien to India, and Maharaja Karni Singh even won a silver medal at the World Championships in Cairo in 1962. But our history was littered more with shikaris standing victorious next to slain tigers than track-suited fellows with medals. My family had no competitive shooting background and India—in the 1990s and early 2000s especially, but even now—has few ranges. Fewer coaches. No sports shops selling world-class guns. No ammunition easily available. No culture of shooting competitions in small clubs on weekends.

Heinz looked at me and saw all this. He considered my short-sightedness and thought, 'I never saw a shooter with such bad eyes.' To maintain balance in a room you need 3-D perception, which I didn't have. It's why I moved more than others. Heinz shook his head. 'It's impossible to overcome these obstacles.' It couldn't be done, it was a dream too far.

But Heinz is also an exceptional, brilliant man. He and Gaby are also both sports psychologists, who relished the idea of challenge. So they decided: 'Why not?' As Heinz put it, I had 'a certain heart', a 'meditative presence, with skills in concentration and awareness'. Almost, he grinned, 'like an autistic boy living in his own universe'. Perhaps that was the attraction, for he admitted that they liked to work with people who were 'not normal, but interesting'. They also saw my family, the conviction, and they understood this wasn't some idle pursuit. They were serious people. So were we.

Heinz told me all this when our friendship was cemented. I grinned. I eventually changed his mistaken impression of Indians and elephants. That took a while. Much quicker, I made another impression on him. A good one. On day one, I refused to leave his range. 10 am till 10 pm. Everyone had packed up, waved farewell and gone. I kept shooting. Morning to evening. Caught in that idyllic feeling that comes with single-minded devotion, trying to build a fort of a million perfect 10s around me. Gaby was taken aback. Later, she told a friend: 'You have to be crazy to be a shooter. But this crazy we've never seen. He could keep shooting all day, and I recognized something special in him. His motivation was fantastic. That was one thing with Abi, we never had to motivate him.' Then, they shook their heads, they dragged me home.

Rumour insisted that if a Chinese shooter failed to score a 596 in training he had to miss his next meal. Not here. They tried to relax me, got me to laugh at my mistakes, turned the volume down on seriousness. 'Too intense, Abhinav,' was a frequent refrain. In their group, as is the way in Europe and Australia, a convivial atmosphere prevailed. Jokes and teasing, especially of the fresher, are part of sporting routine. But jokes and teasing are not always an Indian staple in the sporting workplace. Me, I had no sense of humour. But eventually, slowly, agonizingly, I learnt to give back.

I was shy, too, Eastern boy stuck in a Western world. In Gaby's house, if you wanted food, you grabbed it from the fridge. You washed your glass. You made yourself at home. This was foreign to me, as if it was almost rude to rummage through someone's kitchen even though I lived with them. For Gaby it was painful. Always they had to ask: don't you want to eat something? Only then I did.

But their relationship with me rapidly altered: from coaches they grew to be my friends and finally became my family. We discovered a strong human connection, and over the years I would live with them endlessly, in a house of books, of hearty conversation, of Heinz teasing Gaby about her cooking. Here, physically, for I slept the sleep of someone who belonged in their house, and mentally, for I trusted them, I was home.

But first they had to alter me.

One day my father called, and Gaby told him: 'He is very nice, but competition is not nice.' I was a fairly typical Indian boy, polite and respectful (or at least that's how we see ourselves). Heinz and Gaby grimaced. Competition is stressful, it is fearful, and Gaby, once, trying to ignite my aggression and locate my toughness, tersely told me: 'There is no mama here you can go to, so don't be a spoilt mama's boy and go and do your job.' In competition they wanted a harder, meaner shooter. Maybe they taught me too well because I became one.

Eventually I learnt to dislike my competitors. Not in the literal sense. It was not an active hostility towards my fellow shooters, or a disdain for them as people or as competitors. No, it was the creation of an occasional and artificial dislike for an opponent, to propel myself. It's not an original philosophy, for athletes often create scenarios in their heads to discover motivation and fuel themselves. Steve Waugh, it is said, manufactured a sense of being under siege to play better. Mats Wilander went further. In an interview, he once said: 'I've played a lot of matches where I don't care if he's a great player, I just don't like you. I don't dislike (you), but I can find something in you that I don't like to fuel me.' It made sense to me. If I felt these men around me, these brilliant fellow shooters, were trying to take my medal from me, it simply made me work harder.

That was later. But then, in 2001, I had a thousand questions, Heinz and Gaby had a million answers. They were shooting academics of a sort and we talked constantly, discussing the grammar of gunfire. One night—and this was on the phone—Gaby and I spoke for two intense hours, just on tension in my neck to tension in my little finger. Heinz, amused, exasperated, as he listened in, thought we'd gone insane. Even our meals weren't quiet, an idea emerging, a chair pushed back, a chicken left uneaten, as we leapt into shooting positions and examined them.

I was trying to create a robust technique, a confluence of standing, thinking, breathing, holding, sighting, firing that wouldn't break down. I was making minute changes in equipment, all based on feel. It was an environment I craved, what Heinz called 'zero tolerance'. They were teaching me what I would somewhat master eight years later: learning to be perfect on an imperfect day.

So it began. My technique was analysed, stripped down and rebuilt. It had to be. Because when strengthened it becomes the athlete's most reliable friend. An athlete may stand in a hostile arena, late on a day, his shoulders tired and feet heavy. Victory may be flirting with him, tension might be nibbling at his brain. But amidst the stress on his best days, his technique does not collapse. His head does not wobble, the alignment of feet, hip, arm stays true. He has found a correct, efficient method of functioning, he has polished and waxed his mechanics so well, that even in strife he can rely on it to work. This is what I needed.

The shooter can produce a fine score with improper technique. If his head isn't rested properly on the butt of his rifle, but is being held up by neck muscles which will eventually tire, he can manage. If his hips aren't pushed forward to the specific degree, he can manage. If his left leg isn't carrying the required weight and the muscles are working overtime to create small equalizing impulses, he can still manage. But for a while only. In the arena, as pressure freezes the joints and disturbs his equilibrium, he will start to fall apart, bit by bit, shake by shake, his mistakes adding up. The body shifts as it is rattled by a series of tremors, and poor technique cannot sustain him. It is akin to a building with an inadequate foundation caught in a minor earthquake.

My technique was passable, it had taken me to a world record score. So shooters, both local and international, wondered:

Change?

Now?

What for?

But risk is part of the oxygen of my existence. Some days I think there's a Wild West poker player in me wanting to get out. Risk is also invigorating, trying something new helps stimulate the mind in a shooting environment that is based on repetition and flirts with staleness. Risk is also a route to greatness, whether it is going for the lines when breakpoint down in a tennis match or overhauling a golf swing. I didn't want to shoot a world record one day and fade away the next. I required consistency. I figured that to arrive at the next level, to become a shooter in complete command of my world, I had to change.

I was only following a well-worn tradition. When Tiger Woods took a spanner to a swing that had brought him numerous majors it was nothing but the exceptional athlete's appreciation of long-term goals. He wanted a swing that would last. People were surprised, but shouldn't have been. Not changing a winning game, or altering a winning team, is a flawed theory for it suggests a game, or team, cannot get better. It is untrue. Everyone can get better and they have to because everyone else is getting better. Great athletes interrogate themselves, review their games, it is precisely how they avoid stagnancy.

So Gaby and I started our technical tango. Small things, vital things, things that would take years to harden into instinct. I was attempting to build a biomechanically perfect, stable position. I was ensuring my gun was close to me so my neck did not dip and turn too much, for every slight movement affects everything. The human head weighs five kilograms. It gets tiring. I was ensuring that my right shoulder, which felt like cement, released some of its tension. The body is being taught, but it remembers slowly.

Gaby hovered over me, like a mechanic with a wrench, trying to tune a machine. My hips were at 11 am in relation to the target and Gaby shifted it to 12. At 12, you're in a straight line, weight being distributed correctly.

Try it.

Pick a photo frame to shoot at. Put your hips at 11 am. Raise an imaginary rifle. Then do it at 12. Feel the difference.

At 11, your hips move slightly more, you use more effort to pick up your rifle from the stand and align it. At 12, you only move the upper body, you isolate it. It is minuscule, but in shooting it is massive. It is not easy and, frustrated, Gaby would remind me to stabilize my body. Use your deep core muscles, she'd shout; utilize the muscles that you use for doing you-know-what, she'd hiss. Of course, she said it in slightly more colourful and descriptive language.

Nothing happens in isolation when fiddling with the human body. This is a complicated machine. Move the hips, other parts move, too. It is why change warrants patience. Just a few inches altered in a stance took me three years to incorporate. It required special conditioning with a physio because I lacked the flexibility in my lower back to maintain that position.

This is a game within a sport. The athlete is desperate to see if his changes work, but aware he must give it time to work. Time for the mind to wholly embrace change even as uncertainty lingers: Will it work? Is this right? Time also for the body to adapt. The muscles, so attuned to a particular movement, must be stripped of that memory and must respond to new instructions.

The shooter's structure, his shell, how he stands, arranges his bones, is his outer position. His inner position is his arrangement of the muscular tension within. Tension is tricky, you need just enough muscles working and you need the right muscles working. Activating the gross muscles, the biceps, the shoulders, is easy. But they don't stabilize you.

Stability muscles are tinier, harder to activate. It's like having an ear to your own body, a sort of stethoscope for your muscles, so you are attuned to every fibre, every ligament, every lever working within. In the neck, no tension is allowed; in the shoulder, none is invited. The leg muscles are working, quietly, constantly, allowing for balance, just tense enough to lock the knee. In the feet, nothing, no tension, just as relaxed as they might be in a spa. The hands are, meanwhile, doing an exquisite muscular dance. Only the trigger finger on the right hand is loose, the rest must own enough tension to keep the gun steady. The left arm is absent of tension, but the wrist has sufficient cement in it to ensure it does not bend. The better connection the left arm has with the hip—even to the point of using a belt into which the elbow snugly fits—the more relaxed the arm is.

Wait, hold on, we're not done. Welcome to Zero Point. When you pick up a rifle and aim at an object, Zero Point is where every shooter naturally points to in relation to the target. Either too high or too low. So out come the screwdrivers. Adjustment commences. Shorten the rifle by reducing the stock and Zero Point goes down. Lengthen the stock and Zero Point goes up. Widen your stance and Zero Point goes up. This matters. The target is exactly at 140 centimetres; if, because of how tall you are, or because of your natural stance, you find yourself naturally aiming at that height, it's an advantage.

Gaby, Heinz and I are looking at everything, going through the entire manual of rifle craft. Their discipline, their perseverance, moved me then as it does now. Heinz has spent hours fine-tuning my ammunition and rifle; he'd walk me through an ancient schloss to clear my head in the open air where suggestions are often absorbed more easily than in the intensity of a range; he'd sit me down in coffee shops if even just to people-watch and discuss some latest political upheaval. Gaby had her own way. Once she frog-marched me to their village gym just for acrobic classes. This gyrating of hips, she'd do it with me, but on one condition. She wouldn't watch me: for when she did, she collapsed in laughter.

Nothing is inconsequential, untouched, ignored by us. From mounting a rifle to setting the sights. My sight is high. If it's too low, it's hard on the neck because you must bend forward to it. My body feels odd, the new movements foreign. In competition, this translation of a coach's orders into practice, is hard. One part of the brain wants to return to an old comfort, another demands you keep pushing for change. In the midst of competition, a battle with the self is occurring and scores will be low. Results have to be foregone, so easy in theory but hard on the ego in reality. Outsiders can speak a lazy language; the moment you stutter, irrespective of reason, there is talk of 'collapse' and 'slide'. But a critic's slump is often the athlete's learning curve. He believes; he has to. His best friend at this time is faith.

Heinz and Gaby came to specific competitions to observe me. I liked that. Shooting is a reclusive pursuit. You can't walk anywhere in the range, you can't shout, you're not demonstrative, you can't take your frustration out on an opponent. You're just locked in, every desire let go only in a gentle tug of a trigger. So it's nice to have support, and I felt a deep kinship with the couple. Even now, the relationship gone ten years, I return to them like a boy with enthusiasm. For always they have a new idea, a new philosophy, a new method. Always they listen to me, the shooter, not dismissing my concern over a minor detail as coaches might, but tuned to my feelings. Then, when we started, I thought, damn, they're interested in making me better. They care. I hardly have faith in myself, so it's difficult to have faith in others. But with them, yes.

I remember a fretful day at the Munich World Cup years later, as I attempted to qualify for the 2012 Olympics. I can't eat, I muttered. Without a word, like a mother feeding a distraught child, Gaby put a chocolate in my mouth. How will I go through this, I whined. Metaphorically she held my hand and said: You will go in, you will sight, you will focus on balance. Quietly she took me through my routine. The suggestions were basic, but they brought calm. In such moments, you just have to believe. There is no time to question. If there's no trust, you think, what does she know? But she always knew. She, and Heinz, I always trusted.

10

BREAKTHROUGH AND BATTLES

Golf stars, some of them, have private jets. Nice. We shooters learn to meditate at airports. We're the guys with the pale faces from not enough sunlight accompanied by long, guitar-like cases. Alas, Antonio Banderas in *Desperado* we're not. We're also the guys always there at the airport nearly four hours before a flight. Show the gun to the airline, to security, to customs. Show papers, fill forms. Sigh a lot. Once, in the old days, my gun went through the X-Ray machine in Delhi without anyone realizing those bits of broken-up steel were a dismantled weapon. It did not fill my heart with confidence over security.

The wiser you get as a shooter the less you want to travel with a team. It's painful. One gun to be examined at Chinese customs is painfully acceptable. But twenty! You sit in dank airport halls, exhausted, as serial numbers are matched to every gun for security reasons. In 2008 I had to spend nine hours at a police station in Nanjing airport before I was cleared. It doesn't end there either. After the airport comes only the promise of a long car ride ahead. Shooters never go to hotels.

They drive straight to the range to deposit their guns. It is always a long day.

But in late 2000, at eighteen, my journey resumed alone, in small towns in Europe, me and my gun traversing the continent. In winter, Europe freezes and people turn away from the cold and often to indoor rifle ranges. Over the years clubs have sprouted and competitions born, till shooting has found both a history and a season. At these small events, almost like a European circuit, talent gathers: it could be shooters tuning themselves for the European Championships, or experimenting with technique and finding form. But it is a nice standard.

I was alone, challenged by the cold, waking up in small Danish villages where the sun disappeared after a two-hour flirtation, but helped by strangers in forgotten airports as I struggled with my unwieldy gun cases. Only once was I duped in Europe, by a self-proclaimed mystic, who conjured my grandfather's name out of thin air, proceeded to tell me my future as he saw it and left me $100 dollars shorter. He was an Indian. I was confused by language and confronted by surly waiters in tiny cafes with no menus. Once, after a small conference in sign language, I was presented with a steaming dish laced with blue cheese. Somehow I hadn't managed to convey that I ate anything *but* cheese.

The days were long and lonely. The Europeans travelled almost as teams, the Poles in one corner, the Italians chattering in a restaurant, the Germans practising together. I sat in my room, my companion a flickering television, and it was the start of my addiction to the news. The carpeted corridors of basic hotels were quiet, undisturbed. Years later I would grow accustomed to the audible footsteps of Korean ladies in Changwon hotels, who would slip their calling cards under my door. But here, nothing; here only the cold silence of winter. On days I shot poorly, the room felt smaller and it seemed the world and the walls were collapsing on me. I felt bereft some days, furious on others, once wrenching the curtains from their hooks in rage. Uwe Riesterer, who had booked the room for me and was apprised of the damage by hotel staff, sent pictures to my parents of my petulance. Fortunately, I was the courier of these photos, happened to peek inside the envelope and proceeded to destroy all evidence. But even through the most desolate and tedious days, I pushed on. I never quit mentally for I was desperate, I was hungry. I knew no other way.

Sport never halts after an Olympics, only a fresh cycle begins, a year torn from the four-year Olympic calendar. When the 2000 Sydney closing ceremony concluded, effectively Athens 2004 commenced. Sport is sustaining in this way, it is replete with new beginnings. In four years, for the defeated, is another Games. Another chance. It is this hope we cling to, this hope we need.

But the years can add on and it becomes a marathon run with only a few lingering water stops. In fourteen to fifteen years, I took a long breath only when I injured my back in 2006, and for five days for my sister's wedding in the same year (which was fun, but led me to tell my parents: twenty-five people at my wedding, no more). No holiday, no switching off. Later, I would identify precise goals and competitions to peak in, but now I was young, energetic, greedy. Every year, twenty-five events, sometimes thirty. If there was a match anywhere in the world, I was there.

Back home—by now 2001 had dawned—my grandmother had succumbed to cancer, but no one told me. It is how families protect athletes. She had given me two lucky coins that always stayed with me, and used to call me, as grandmas will, 'her shining star'. For a while I was, winning five consecutive gold medals in lesser European events at one point, a winning that stoked the ego and released infinite joy. But it is remarkable, maybe even strange and beautiful, how the meaning of victory changes, how the mind digests success over time, how a trophy comes to represent so many things in a single career.

Back then, as a young boy just starting, victory was pure, like the innocence of a first kiss. My God, you think, I am something. Later, victory becomes relief, for you expect yourself to win, you demand it of yourself. But knowing you are good enough to win engulfs you with a different pressure. Finally, victory becomes not irrelevant, not secondary, but just not the greatest pleasure: it is staying faithful through time and tribulation to a process, it is the travel to greatness which is most rewarding.

My scores in 2001 were low but not for long. World Cup to World Cup—Atlanta, Seoul, Milan, Munich—I could feel comfort and improvement. In Atlanta, I had a 590 and finished joint seventeenth. In Seoul, I scored a 591, finishing joint fourteenth. In Milan, I had a 594 that placed me sixth. And then on 10 June, I won my first World Cup medal in Munich with a 597 followed by 103.5 in the final. It was a bronze, a point behind gold in a field of 105 shooters; it was a new world junior record; and it was early proof that Gaby/Heinz/I were an intelligent fit.

It was also, like so many performances are, a subtle message. The Germans, who knew me well from my visits, had seen me shooting 570s, even 580s. But this bewildered them: a 597, at eighteen, was too quick! There was appreciation yet also disbelief. A German junior coach, a rough fellow, actually stood right behind me and trained his telescope on the target to be sure everything was working correctly.

I shot with instructions from Gaby. In Milan and Munich, she was clear: be aggressive, put a score on the board. By the rules I had 105 minutes to fire; in Milan I took 33 minutes, in Munich I took 44. Aggression doesn't necessarily translate into speed, it means you are focused, it shows intent, it means being brave with your trigger. The moment your sight is aligned, you squeeze, you pull, you react. No waiting for surety, no waiting for a clearer picture, no giving in to hesitancy, just believing it is the right time. But a shooter's aggressiveness cannot be a conscious act. If he is thinking about it—'be aggressive, be aggressive'—he might trigger too early, an overreaction born of the voice in his head. Instead this aggression should be instinctive.

A last challenge remained in 2001. The Commonwealth Championship in Bisley, London in late August. My focus was two words: medals, India. Forget all the patriotic chest-beating; shooting for your country, as a team, is fun. On opening day at the Commonwealth Championships, Charan Singh and I won gold in the air-rifle pairs. In the individual event, I won by 11.9 points with an all-10 series in the final that left me grinning: 10.2, 10.4, 10.1, 10.2, 10.1, 10.7, 10.2, 10.6, 10.0, 10.3.

One bittersweet postscript remained to a long season. I learned that I would be receiving the Arjuna Award. Instituted in 1961 to recognize outstanding achievement in sport by Indians, this was an honour. But I was particularly moved by the knowledge that when my Arjuna Award was handed to me in Rashtrapati Bhavan, a man in Delhi whom I loved was watching on television. My grandfather was ailing and did not want to come to the ceremony in a wheelchair. But he watched his grandson stand before the president and be honoured. It made him smile. I treasure that. Because the next day he was no more.

Experiment was now the first word of my shooting hymn. Always I looked for advantage. In end-December 2001, I commissioned a new trigger system. It was an electronic trigger. As opposed to simple mechanics, it ran on battery. The electronic trigger was more constant, but eventually I let it go. It couldn't be tuned to deliver the sensitivity that a mechanical trigger offered; it felt dull and heavy.

Feel was another word in my hymn, a harmonious sense of being in control. And I was feeling reasonably good. The plan for 2002 was straightforward. No junior shooting. Build for the World Cups, peak at the World Championship in Lahti, Finland, shine at the Commonwealth Games in Manchester, and the Asian Games, in Busan, Korea. When you write it down, it looks simpler.

I was in Europe before the rest of the Indians. They were shooting the nationals. I didn't see the value of the nationals. The world with its varied distractions and multiple talents was our challenge, not other Indians who we shot against routinely. I shot twelve matches in Europe, tearing paper with pellets from Luxembourg to Grafling to Aarhus. I won golds, silvers, bronzes, my trigger felt comfortable under the finger, my progress was smooth.

Suddenly, in 2002, the World Cups were there again, me and the best, back to jousting for gold, now searching for an Olympic quota place, and checking whether technique had settled. Shooting is not badminton or tennis or baseball, where a fraternity of players, families, coaches, technicians, move every week to a city. Only now are two World Cups held back-to-back, else you shoot, retreat like a priest into solitude, chant in an empty room from a holy book on technique, then return to competition.

The Olympic quota place was within smelling distance, one good day in 2002 and I was in Athens. But it didn't come in the World Cup in Milan. I shot a 590 to be joint thirtieth and my head reeled. Something had gone wrong. Errors creep in without conscious recognition of them. Feel disappears. Concentration lapses. All in such tiny measures you don't even notice them till you introspect or a coach points them out. Perhaps it was as simple as my new jacket, a change necessitated by the airline's masterful loss of my luggage and equipment. Did it feel odd, sit awkwardly, affect my elbow jamming into my hip? I had almost no time to fix it.

Lahti, site of the 2002 World Championships, was 100 kilometres from the Finnish capital of Helsinki. This was a nation of picturesque landscapes and a fine history in shooting. The temporary range was built in front of a ski jump. It was beautiful, a word shooters don't usually use for their place of work. Not like golfers who amble along in the most finely manicured arenas. It's only the chess players, locked in smaller rooms, who make us feel better. I was nineteen, in my second World Championships so early, caught in a whirlwind. Was I good enough already to be in a final here? Good enough to strike a medal? Good enough to win one of the six quota places for Athens?

The mind craves quiet, but questions careen loudly through the insides of the skull. This was my chance, India's chance. Quota places belong in fact to nations, one shooter can win them, another shooter can be sent. But effectively, if you are good enough to secure them, you are good enough to go. India's emerging status as a shooting nation—through pistol shooters such as Samaresh Jung and the air-rifle women's squad of Anjali Bhagwat, Suma Shirur and Deepali Deshpande—was becoming a story. Enough for me to convince an Indian reporter, Kamesh Srinivasan, to attend the event.

He wanted to understand shooting and his paper was in love with sport. *The Hindu* was the single newspaper that was democratic when it came to covering Indian sport. They sent reporters everywhere. Shooting. Chess. Athletics. Tennis. They were not single-god worshippers of cricket. It's why sportspeople read the paper. It's why Kamesh came.

He probably wished he hadn't. India wasn't ready. Gold in the senior World Championships wouldn't come. All that a talented contingent could manage was a bronze medal in the junior women's sport rifle prone event by Rajkumari Dodiya.

My trip was a nightmare. My gun did not land with me. I did not have a room. The government had cleared the team too late. Somewhere a babu with a file and a slow walk in Delhi didn't give a damn about hotel room bookings in some Finnish town. So we struggled. Every other team stayed in one hotel. We were scattered. It was irritating. The shooter invests his whole being into his craft, the bureaucrat waffles. There is no synergy here. For the shooter, detail, as tiny as how many grams his trigger must be, is vital; for the official, a major detail like early hotel bookings is shrugged off. Just a room to yourself, no fuss, no changing, settles the mind. At this point, only elbow, gun, trigger, sight should matter. Not where the hell are we staying.

I shot lousy at the 2002 world championships in Lahti. The worst score of my season. Not because of the hotel room. Not because of anyone else. But because I was still learning about big competitions. My 589/600 comprised an unflattering series of numbers: 95, 99, 99, 98, 99 and 99.

In my first five shots I had four 9s. In my first five shots my tournament was over. Sport is that exquisitely cruel. Kamesh Srinivasan's analogy was that it was akin to Sachin Tendulkar getting out first ball in a one-dayer. I wasn't the best Indian, that was Ashok Kumar, who was a point better than me to be placed joint thirty-fourth, while Sameer Ambekar was joint seventieth with 585.

I needed a 596 or better to make the final. I took a risk. I shot fast. It didn't work. Coming fortieth at a World Championships is like a hook to the kidneys, it leaves a bruise. You learn a taste which never goes away, the taste of pride when it is being swallowed. It required introspection but not overreaction. It was defeat but also a tutorial. It was a week when I was reminded about patience. I learnt I had to work through nervousness and absorb pressure, rather than just quickly pulling the trigger. Anxiety is horrible, it corrodes the insides, it interrupts and confuses decision-making, it authors a feeling of helplessness. But you can't fight it, you say 'come, friend', you learn to let it sit inside you and shoot well in spite of it.

But I am patient. That is my skill. I argued with myself: I had chosen a plan, it hadn't worked, such is sport. I flushed down the memories of this beautiful town. I was ready for a grimmer one. Manchester. Victory at the Commonwealth Games there in July-August 2002 would be perfect. It would be compensation. The Queen opened the Games, I watched on television (we shooters weren't in Manchester, but further away and separated in Bisley, London). The weightlifting men did some decent lifting till a couple turned out to be on an illegal diet. It is dispiriting for a country and embarrassing for a contingent to have drug cheats within. But then the women's hockey team won gold and so did boxer Mohammed Ali

Qamar, who trailed on points coming into the final round yet won and captured everyone's heart. When a fellow athlete does well, it sends a ripple of inspiration through a contingent. You look at his Indianness, you see yourself, you think: so can I.

For us shooters, separation and distance brought a sweet bonus; it offered us a better sense of team. We fed off each other, watched each other, rooted for each other, absorbed anticipation and excitement from each other. It was a sweet time for shooting, caught in a temporary innocence, talent ready to flare and unencumbered by expectation. Soon pressure would arrive, tension with it, questions, too—where are the medals? why so few?—but not yet. This was the beautiful beginning.

We made a strong and long-distance contribution. Anjali Bhagwat and Suma Shirur were unbeatable in the pairs competition, while Major Rajyavardhan Singh Rathore and Moraad Ali Khan blew away a sensational field to win India's first double-trap gold medal. Australia had Sydney Olympic silver medallist Russell Mark and world champion Michael Diamond. England had Sydney gold medallist Richard Faulds. But the Indians were irresistible.

I, alas, was not. In the pairs competition I shot only a 590, but Sameer Ambekar shot a career-best 594. It was enough to give us gold by 20 points over Malaysia. In the individual event, heartbreak showed up unannounced. I lost gold to a fifteen-year-old Bangladeshi boy, Asif Hossain Khan—on the last shot of the final. Somehow that hurt more. He had a 9.9, I had a 9.1. And I had shot a 590 in the qualification while Asif only had a 587. It was an embarrassing, painful, mocking defeat. All the medals on the European circuit, all the improving scores in the World Cup, and now this?

For a while the mind is dazed, uncomprehending: a

Bangladeshi kid in his first international competition has outskilled you? But in sport, even a novice can offer a lesson and Asif did. And it was this: Finish the job. Stay focused till the last shot. It is always a crucial shot, often a deciding one. Medals tilt on this shot so it comes with a special pressure. I would learn well. Four years later, I would win the World Championship on my final shot. Six years later, I would win the Olympics on my last shot. Now I wasn't ready. But sometimes you need to lose, painfully, for a weakness to become a strength.

2002 only got worse. It's the way it is sometimes with sport. Momentum takes hold of you, good form builds or sometimes bad luck just takes firm hold. Returning from London, I lost my luggage. Two days later, Lufthansa returned my custom-made rifles. One's trigger assembly was damaged, the other's stock was broken. My Asian Games, in September-October, was threatened.

Guns are everything. It is a piece of metal to you, it is the instrument of my talent for me. Golfers think they know sensitivity till they meet a shooter. My guns, initially, were like a part of my being. I worshipped them, treated them as possessively and sensitively as one might a child. In time, a detachment grew. But forever I was careful with them. For they were like a Stradivarius, pieces of art requiring diligent tuning.

The rifle I use now weighs 5.5 kilograms (it is the maximum weight), its calibre is .177, it fires a pellet that weighs 5.3 milligrams, it travels at 175 metres per second. It is a Walther LG 300 and its serial number is my email address. First, you buy it off the shelf. Then you start work on it. It's why my range at home looks like a professor's messy laboratory of old guns—ten or twelve of them—vices, stands, screwdrivers, jackets. I am constantly in a frenzy of tinkering. Refining a grip. Shaving the stock. Redesigning the butt plate. Bjorn Borg once was able to tell that his racket was 3 grams heavier than normal. It's a fussiness I feel in my bones.

My trigger has a particular pressure. My barrel is matched with ammunition. The weight of my weapon is carefully arranged. The stock is heavier, using a 30-gram piece of weight that is used on winter car tyres. The rifle sight can be smaller. The light filter can be changed. If the range is bright, it can be made darker. The grip is altered to suit my hand.

It is a rifle built only for me.

It has a physical feel which becomes a psychological comfort. Even if I buy a similar gun it can take a manufacturer six months to tune it to my eccentricities. My gun makes me secure. Without it I am not myself.

Now the damaged gun was sent to the Walther factory. But it was closed in the autumn for a fortnight. Invective flew through my mind. The National Rifle Association of India rode to the rescue by offering two guns for sale. But it's like driving a BMW and then shifting to a Mercedes. It got worse. I didn't have time to get to Europe to work with Heinz and Gaby. I know, it sounds like excuses, but it's what happens, circumstances gang up like a pack of bullies. You shrug, you have to just ride that particular storm. In the end, no one cares, record books don't have asterisks for bad luck and lost luggage.

In the midst of confusion and depression, a little sunlight squeaked through. I had been selected for the Rajiv Gandhi Khel Ratna award for 2001, edging out tennis star Mahesh Bhupathi, Anjali Bhagwat, woman boxer M.C. Mary Kom, who had won a silver in the inaugural World Championship, and hockey player Sumrai Tete. I was misquoted as saying I didn't deserve it, but certainly at nineteen, while I was young and shooting well, I only had a World Cup bronze in my collection.

'Deserving' is a fair question, deserving should be rigorously debated. Awards are nice as long as in India we're careful not to devalue them. Arjuna Awards were occasionally dispensed like out of a vending machine and the more freely we disperse them, the less valuable they become. Pure performance, over time, should determine awards, not sad lobbying by officials in dusty association rooms.

Athletes don't measure themselves by plaques and scrolls. Honour is nice, winning something is better. But the plaques had a purpose. They often displayed a government or corporate house's interest in a sport. They kept athletes relevant in the media universe. If honestly given, they are proof of progress and confirmation of work ethic. The athlete is mostly an insecure beast, the awards tell him his path is true.

But the award does something else as valuable, it celebrates the athlete's sport; for that briefest of splendid moments his discipline is news. His sport matters. It emerges from obscurity, from beneath the weight of cricket, to breathe and strut and pose for the cameras. This time, along with my Khel Ratna, coach Sunny Thomas was deservedly given the Dronacharya award and pistol shooter Samaresh Jung was presented the Arjuna award. It was a fine moment for shooting.

But no high in sport lasts for long. Disappointment was nestling nearby. In South Korea, at the Asian Games in September-October 2002, with a borrowed weapon, I made the final but only finished seventh. It was unfulfilling, but from India's perspective it was compensated for with a silver medal from Anjali Bhagwat, Suma Shirur and Deepali Deshpande in the women's air-rifle team, and silver from Mansher Singh, Manavjit Singh Sandhu and Anwar Sultan in the trap team.

Disappointment visited, but dejection stayed away. I knew I was in the midst of improvement, I knew I had made the correct decision by deciding to refine my technique. Risk would one day find reward. I was willing to meddle, I was willing to sacrifice good form for great form down the road. Patience, patience, patience, I told myself. Only one thing mattered, one day, one year. Athens, 2004.

11

AMERICAN HERO

When I finished my fitness test, Uwe Riesterer, stocky and scowling, looked down at me. 'My grandmother,' he grunted in typical fashion, 'could have done better.'

Thank you, Uwe, was a first facetious thought.

A second thought was: I need this guy.

Sporting self-fulfilment is a lonely journey but it is not one made alone. You need nurturers, confidants, challengers. You need someone to lean on, talk to, be pushed by. You need teachers on technique and mentors to spark confidence.

You just need someone to be yourself with some days, to pull down the competitive mask, to unveil your naked, shaking, unsure self before another human who won't judge you. Champions will produce moments of such sublime skill, so utterly and seemingly oblivious to pressure, that the temptation is to invest them with an otherworldly power. My God, they must be superhuman. But only when they weep at the trophy presentation, their insides revealed, that we are reassured: they are just human beings. So are seemingly robotic shooters like us. But no one knows our humanity better than the people around us.

I picked Uwe, twelve years a member of the German team, to work with me even though he made me cry. Even though I once walked home two kilometres late one night in Germany, all hot fury in a cold rain, after a verbal altercation with him.

Uwe prodded, poked, tested, dared, he defied me to become better from the day I met him. His craving for conflict unnerved me, but it was done with a purpose. He was the anti-Gaby, the uncomplicated coach. They did not care for each other, their styles in contrast and conflict, and my picking of these two varied philosophies was telling: I wanted the best advice from all worlds. I would try anyone. I would work with American coaches in Colorado, use trainers from South Africa and physios from Australia, often simultaneously. I was seeking knowledge and no one person had it all.

Uwe's mantra was not my style, but it was simple:

Go. Shoot. Sixty shots. Win. Come home.

Rough, basic common sense, even if eventually I wanted more detailed answers and he often didn't have them. Don't overtrain, he shouted, come hiking with me in the Bavarian Alps. I hated it, but gradually I was seduced. I'd like to tell you it was the beauty and tranquillity of a spectacular landscape that bewitched me. Alas, no. Of course, the Alps and the Colorado Rockies, untouched, pure, affect you. But for me this was primarily a contest with the self. To get up there was to feel stronger. If I had a choice, I would have taken a cable car up. But it would not have helped me become a better shooter.

Uwe taught me, he gave me permission to think, he encouraged it. Such independence is not always recommended in India. Respect is overstated and argument is discouraged by coaches. Athletes are not shown answers but their place.

But with Uwe this wasn't a guru-shishya relationship in its traditional sense as much as a partnership. He challenged, I challenged back. He taught, I questioned. Terrible mistakes are made when athletes reflexively go 'yes, yes' to every command and restrain their own imagination. The athlete cannot mute his instinct because competition is a lonely business and instinct is sometimes his only reliable friend in the arena.

Like Amit, like Gaby/Heinz, Uwe was my teacher who sharpened me for life and competition. We met in 2001, I was eighteen, and he reshaped my philosophy rapidly. My impression of shooting was simplistic: nice gun, stable body, the harder you practise, the better you get. Not entirely wrong, but unidimensional.

'But this is not shooting,' Uwe would insist. Shooting was a holistic exercise that went beyond mere technique. 'If your body isn't working,' he explained, 'you cannot execute the skills. You need to be a world-class athlete. If the left leg is pinching, then you can be disturbed.'

Gun, ammunition, stance? Bullshit, he said. If you're not strong, it won't matter. So, sneering at my physique, sneering at other coaches who worried about muscles causing tremors and killing stability, he decided I required a stronger base to compete from. Even his mother, who only started shooting because his dad did, and then won thirty-five German titles, told me: 'Push. You have to push.'

Which is where the Mongolian-German came in. Munkhbayar Dorjsuren is an ace shooter, world champion and twice an Olympic bronze medallist. She was also a tough athlete. She, and a few other women shooters, would be handed 15–20 kilogram backpacks and Uwe would just say: Run.

Six kilometres, eight kilometres.

You do this, he said, you run through pain and a barrier breaks down. Next time a pressure situation emerges, you know its flavour. For me, a stand-still competitor from a shooting tribe that saw running as a plebeian pursuit, this was absurd.

Backpacker? Not me.

Himalayan trekker? Forget it.

But when women shooters shrug on backpacks and run, it also provokes the competitive ego. I had to run, I had to keep up. Fortunately, Uwe had an invisible streak of kindness. Or maybe my mother's long-distance phone calls suggesting that he not push me too much made him relent. Either way, he would occasionally make a backpack of the same volume as those for the girls but with less weight. It meant I didn't lose heart, it meant the girls didn't tease me for being a wimp. It was a constructive atmosphere and confirmed for me that sport was not a mere game but a life experience. I was being challenged, and I had to find my own way.

The mountains, where he took me, city boy on a reluctant nature walk, had a purpose. 'It opens your brain,' Uwe said. A hike, three hours, four hours, five hours, in clean air, pushes the body to its physical limit. You sit on a rock and life is simple, all you want is a drink of water. Nothing else. For him this was satisfaction of the moment, life lived in the present. It was supposed to liberate me from my world, where I was either searching the past for what went wrong, or trying to predict the future.

Around 2002, when I temporarily stopped working with Uwe, his hardness too foreign for me and upset by his refusal to let me focus on my technique, he refused to drop me. So he remained a consultant and became a good friend of my father's. Much of what Uwe told me was infuriating, yet I admired his raw honesty. In the heat of the moment, I found his comments searing, rude, brutal, but at cooler times I'd sometimes appreciate their value. Honesty matters. Honesty is having people around you willing to say what you don't want to hear and it's vital. But honesty without appropriate timing can be counter-productive.

Once, later in my career, I struggled at his range in the village of Grafing. A 9 after 9 after 9 after 9. Impossible. Uwe, I told him, your targets suck, they're malfunctioning. But he goaded me, refusing to believe his targets could be defective. It's not the machine, he said, it's you, the man. Incensed, I packed my guns, barked at him and left. Perhaps he was trying to anger me, energize me, push me. Some days it worked, that day it didn't. But for all our endless disagreements, our fencing, Uwe helped me greatly and eventually became vital to my Beijing quest, through encouraging word and positive action. He also turned me into a fitness freak.

By Beijing, I could even stand and squat on an exercise ball.

That's cool, believe me.

It is Uwe who first told me: 'Go to America.'

He was right.

I had been part of the International Olympic Committee (IOC) Solidarity Scholarship programme for a while. It offered me two choices: $500 a month, or an option to train and be educated in the US, either in California or Colorado Springs.

Uwe had coached the US team, which was based in Colorado Springs, and was unhesitant about me attending in 2001. I'd be far from home, learn to be independent, find toughness and get the polish of a world-class system. My family agreed and education was the decider: I'd study shooting and, by attending university there at the same time, bring home a Bachelor's degree in business management.

Eventually, I did both.

A variety of athletes trained at the US Olympic Training Centre—swimmers, boxers, volleyballers, weighlifters, winter athletes—and there was a wider sense of camaraderie. Different men, competing women, but on similar missions. In this city, the Olympics meant something. I could hear it in the inquisitiveness and enthusiasm of taxi drivers and strangers once they knew where I was headed: what do you play, where do you come from, what are your dreams? In this centre, the Olympics meant everything. The place smelled of fun, ambition, respect, sweat; the centre hummed with energy. It was a place where history lived, where the past was pride and where the future was built. A place where you could trace every US Olympic athlete on a computer and walk the Hall of Fame, a place of such athletic beauty that visitors arrived every day. In a single year, roughly 140,000.

Visitors do not regularly arrive at the National Institute of Sport in Patiala or the Sports Authority of India in Bangalore. There is not much to see, no Indian sporting history carefully installed within the walls. The first, while improved now, for long was just the crumbling edifice of a dazzling palace. The second is a beautiful, green expanse of land. Only the swanky new sports centre in Pune, built for the 2008 Youth Commonwealth Games, has any appeal, though the shooter who was bitten by a rat in his room there will certainly not agree.

But here is another difference between the nations. In India, athletes step forward with hope, in America, at the centre, athletes walked with a bounce. They expected to win because they were people accustomed to winning; they had been carefully polished to win. At Sydney, India won a single bronze, while the US collected ninety-seven medals, forty of them gold.

Confidence was like some birthright here and they approached the Games without the cynicism whose fumes athletes are forced to inhale every day in sporting India. The Americans truly believe they are the best, and luckiest, country. They weren't going to the Olympics carrying awe and content just to try, they were going to the Olympics to succeed, make history, be remembered. It was an adventure, a collective one, and I was awed by the importance they gave to team and the building of it.

Great athletes littered the corridors. Hey, here's Apollo Ohno, the legendary skater, there's Matthew Emmons, the to-be Olympic hero, there goes a younger, yet-to-assert-himself Michael Phelps. Their vitality stunned me and more importantly, infected me through a sort of osmotic effect. Watch, copy, learn, imbibe. If you train with them, and beat them, the discovery is beautiful and immediate: I can be great, too.

The Olympic centre was not ostentatious, but it was slick. From sports medicine to mental training, everything was catered for. This was an integrated approach to greatness. A cafeteria ran 24 hours, offering Oriental, Western, Italian cuisine, offering different food for different disciplines, catering to every weight category, from diminutive gymnast to hulking weightlifter. It was a thoughtfulness we were then yet to replicate in our camps, expecting diverse athletes to function on more or less the same diet of dal, chawal, egg, chicken.

Arre, bhai, weightlifter ko extra chapati de doh (just give the weightlifters a few more chapatis).

But greatness is not just the preciseness of hand-eye coordination, it is also the preciseness of carbohydrates that go into your system.

We ate constantly because we were burning calories.
Colorado Springs is at high altitude and it was my first
experience of breathlessness. This was America and I was
always running, climbing, getting familiar with muscles I had
been strangers with. It was my first initiation into systematic
and serious physical activity. Shooters might look like
frequenters of libraries, but we're fitter than you think.

We worked in the gym, hiked 20 miles some days, the
presence of another athlete enough to make you push yourself.
Close to the sports centre, they had chiselled steps into the side
of a mountain. A mile of stairs. The first time I did it, starting at
4 am, it took me 80 minutes. By the time Athens arrived, I was
finishing in 28 minutes. I was always the last in the beginning.
Not in the end. It was exhilarating, there is camaraderie to
three to five people testing themselves against pain together,
lifting each other as dawn breaks on a mountain.

Sport was also combined with education, a sort of
collaboration between the University of Colorado and the
US Olympic Committee. Everyone studied and the faculties
were accommodating. Classes at the university were flexible
and a liberty to train at leisure remained. Not every athlete
feels a passion for books and I hated studying, but it was an
education in many parts. First, I noticed that the sharpest
guy in class was a wrestler. So much for stereotypes. Second,
the girls appeared to admire the swimmers and volleyball
players more than us shooters. Alas, here the stereotype fit.
Third, the classes distracted us from the grind of sport, where
excellence is a child of ceaseless repetition. It is a balance the
fretting mind requires.

The classes helped the athlete think with more clarity, and
this lucidity of thought is an ally in competition. But mostly
it reflected well on a US system that did not see the athlete

as simply a victory machine; it acknowledged the reality that success has no guarantee. If anything, the reverse occurs, or, as a Tibetan monk once told *Time* magazine at the 1992 Olympics: 'More will lose than win.'

Study, in a way, was readying these athletes for the life after. It is vital, for to be in your mid-twenties, untutored in anything but back flips and shooting targets, is dangerous. In India, no one cares, no system exists. The injured athlete is cast aside, the retired athlete forgotten. In the US, some athletes get part-time jobs with sponsors. In India, life after sport is not official business.

The shooting section was run by a fistful of people, headed by a chief executive officer, followed by a director of operations. Official fervour equalled athletic ardour. Their budget was not vast, maybe even less than India's, but they were particular with it. Training was detailed. Funding studied. Numbers of medals to win discussed. Together they were tilting at excellence, aware that more money only came from more medals. There was a smell to American shooting that I liked: it was the perfume of accountability. It was also a respect for athletes and their work.

Being a detail geek, their planning left an imprint on me. Competitions were picked, but with a reason. Every individual had a plan tailored for him. There existed recognition that while we used similar guns, and peppered the same targets, we were not clones. In form, confidence, security, effect of criticism, we differed. Their system was sensitive to this. I know shooters who had misplaced their form but were supported financially and given two years and a fair chance to regain it. The athlete felt a supporting hand on his back and it was a relief.

I lived in a small room at the Olympic Centre, with a bunk bed, table, chair, no bathroom attached, in what was a former air force barracks. In the first year, I did not even have a television. It was not what I was used to, but it was also perfect, almost monkish and humble in its Spartan-ness. It was as plain and neat as my ambition: to be the best shooter alive. There was also a minor problem. This finicky shooter was a world-class mess. Clean rifle but untidy room. My mother might have called in a cleaning brigade if she ever saw it.

The US team was kind to me: I was the outsider, but never felt like one. Rifle coach David Johnson was welcoming. Psychologist Dr Sean McCann was crucial at a time when I was very emotional about my performance. I constantly watched sport because everyone there watched sport. If I wasn't training, I was spectating, going off to see ice hockey, football, basketball.

Training was also invigorating, it was absent of the monotony of rigid 8 am-6 pm camps. Innovative training, or breaking the mechanical sameness of shooting, isn't some cutting-edge idea. It just requires initiative. We shot in groups, against each other, which spurred a natural competitiveness. The coaches simulated finals, they ordered us to shoot in fewer seconds than we might usually get, they amplified the pressure by making us compete head to head, or as teams, where the better shot was worth a point and the first team to 24 points won.

It was common sense training that left me refreshed and hungry. It isn't difficult to strip training of monotony, but it requires effort, a series of interested coaches and driven, high-performance managers searching for ways to involve and engage athletes. Sometimes I'd travel to Fort Benning, where the US army had a marksmanship training unit. Training with men like Jason Parker, reigning world champion in the air rifle at the time, was a privilege.

In the mirror, I began to see myself differently. I saw a better sportsperson. A shooter with more muscular self-belief, certain I could live the professional sporting life. It was a gift I still treasure, it was like another piece of my sporting jigsaw. A piece built of so many things: the professionalism of the sports centre, the tough life, the cool air, the enduring friendships, the need to show that an Indian could flourish amidst these people. It led to some of the best shooting of my life.

Words don't matter, only actions do. This is a sporting staple, but somewhat untrue. Words do matter, words from coaches, from books, from others athletes, from the heart. And so it was in Colorado Springs, where I lived off and on for three years, from 2001 onwards. Six days a week my colleagues sweated. Often I sweated seven. Some slept on Sundays, I trained. Maybe because of words.

Maybe because I was taking literally the words that I passed every day, read every day. Words that resonated within me. Words that were printed all across the US Olympic Centre.

IT'S NOT EVERY FOUR YEARS. IT'S EVERY DAY.

12

THE CONFIDENCE GAME

Shooting is a cousin of archery, a relative of chess. We're the nerds of sports. In sports' caste system, we sit towards the unathletic bottom, in a sort of quiet exile from any celebrity. When people occasionally ask me my profession, my reply—my business is shooting—often ironically results in an instinctive connection with Bollywood. Perhaps they presume I am a light man. So now I introduce myself as a 'sports shooter'. This has its rare sublime moments. A German, based in Australia, and I started a discussion on a plane about the Delhi Commonwealth Games. He asked my opinion, so I gently volunteered I was part of it. He mentioned he had travelled to the Sydney Games and I confessed I had been there, too. Whereupon he asked, well, what level do you shoot at? To which I replied, well, actually I won the last time in Beijing. One might say he was taken aback. But mostly we don't mind this anonymity, we understand. Our skills you can't always see and thus appreciate. But let me put it this way: Lionel Messi has great balance, but he should try what we do. Not move. He'll shake. I promise.

Shooting has its own culture, its specific intensity. We don't sit in lounges and play video games and wait for rain to end or matches to arrive like in tennis. We go, shoot, train, leave. Sure, we talk guns, and training schedules, what ammunition is shooting well, what barrels are being used. But not too much more. There are no girls on the boundary line to talk about. No team dinners whose menus need discussing. Or whatever it is that cricketers do between overs and when fielding at slip. The fine details of the magic required to win is mostly kept to oneself. As a kid, I blabbered a bit, I got excited and wanted validation from another person: *Hey, you know, I am working on this strategy.* Now I sit there like a sphinx.

We're finicky people, we're more sensitive and insecure than writers with a new book on the stands. A single sentence thrown casually in our direction can rattle us. Mind games aren't unknown, but in shooting it's expectedly subtle. It's not a sport of nudges and sledges, just gentle, cutting asides like 'Oh, you could do a 600 tomorrow,' just to ratchet up the pressure. So, almost reflexively, you start thinking: *Damn, could I, am I overconfident, what am I doing well?* Already the mind, this beautiful beast, is going places it shouldn't, asking questions when none are required. On the morning of the competition, when instinct is supposed to take over, the sentence can suddenly pop into your head and you shoot a 9.

Maybe it's why everyone on the bus wears headphones. I used to wear them with no music on. Like a 'Do Not Disturb' sign. In Beijing I carried around a book whose title I still don't know. It was my protection from journalists. I just didn't want to talk. The result was I gained a reputation for being a little impenetrable, giving off an unfriendly, unconcerned air. My friend, the shooter Suma Shirur, once told me, no sarcasm intended, that my ability to cut off was my biggest advantage.

I was in a bubble of concentration and I didn't want to come out of it because that state of mind is too precious.

And the particular state of mind all athletes crave is confidence, this belief that we are in control, that form can be produced automatically, at any time. It is the knowledge that sweat has found fruition and technique has assembled correctly. It is the calm flow of a complicated craft. It is the picking up of a gun with the presumption that a great score is imminent. It is a bit like what Beethoven might have felt like on days when he pulled his stool up to a piano. With a year to go for the Athens Olympics, I had not earned this perfection of mind yet, this feeling of near invincibility, but I was lurking in its vicinity, strolling around its borders.

It is a feeling Gaby had helped build, as did US team coach David Johnson and psychologist Sean McCann, and the Colorado institute, where competition was stern and confidence hovered like a welcome virus. In the US centre I was treated on par with their stars and I responded to this faith. I had not won a quota place for the Athens Olympics yet, but I almost felt ready to win a medal there. I had shot good scores before, but now there was a difference: no longer were they a chance happening. I could, most days, make them happen.

The Americans were intrigued by my hunger for training and my ability to produce world-class scores. I was simply pleased to be an Indian causing so much nervousness to some of the best shooters in the world, including US world champion Jason Parker. In February 2003, a series of competitions was held in Colorado Springs. In the first match, I warmed up with a 598/600 and a 102.3 in the final for bronze. In the second match, on 22 February, I unleashed chaos with a perfect 600/600 in the qualification and then a strong 103.9 in the final.

The world record stood at 702.4 then; I had fired a 703.9. These were small competitions, the scores would not be ratified, but what happens in the mind is more vital than what occurs in a record book. I knew how I felt and it was like shooting in a trance. I could see the slightly nervous body language of the top shooters—what's with this Indian!—and it was satisfying. Order was restored a little in the third match as Parker, winner of gold in the first match, won again. I had a 597/600 and a sturdy final with 103.4, but Parker held me off to win by 0.6 points.

But then, on 22 March 2003, I did it again. Another world record score—not ratified because it wasn't an International Shooting Sport Federation (ISSF) event. At the Sportland NRW Cup in Dortmund, I shot a 599/600 followed by a 105.0 for a total of 704. It was 0.1 better than my score in the US. Every single shot hit the bullseye. Every single shot was putting me in a different league. For this brief, invincible while I was beating people by an entire point. By 2 points. These are remarkable margins in a sport of decimals. I was temporarily a machine of perfectly polished, synchronized parts. It was a performance that turned into a longing, a performance not so much accurate as pure, a perfection in execution yet also in feeling. It is a performance I still chase, a level I have never found again, not even 50 per cent of it. But a level I believe I will find again.

For a kid, sport is fun, it is pure release, it brings a smile. But innocence gets lost in competition, fun is obscured by results. You are not a child at play, but an athlete at work. It is a different kind of fun, an altered adult pleasure. But for those rare moments when you start performing well, and success flows, perfect 10s coming easily, sport returns to what it initially was. Unadulterated fun. This is how you dreamed it would be.

My family, watching, so invested in my journey, so supportive, was thrilled. They could see this inching closer to an Olympic medal. I still needed my quota place, but that was the future. For now the present was something to live in. Even the then prime minister, Atal Behari Vajpayee, took note of the situation during his speech at the closing of the 2003 Shotgun World Cup in Delhi. He mentioned my name in appreciation, along with Jaspal Rana's, for projecting a positive image of Indian sports to the world.

It was a heady time.

It was also a time for a fall.

I won a gold in Bavaria at their elite two-event air-gun competition with a 10.7 on the last shot of the final. Just another reminder that the sixty-nine shots before matter little if the seventieth is weak. Just another lesson about finishing strongly. A week later, in the second event, I lost gold because of a 10.1 in the last shot. But I was still flying, intoxicated by confidence. And then it happened.

I had returned to the US after my European sojourn to prepare myself for the World Cups in 2003. I needed the quota place. I was ready. The first World Cup was in Fort Benning and I actually believed, even in such a competitive atmosphere, a 600/600 was more than possible. It was imminent. It was a terrible mistake. I was so in love with my shooting, so certain of its greatness, that I fell for sports' oldest trick. The lure of overconfidence.

And I shot a 590.

I was in joint twentieth position, chastened and disheartened.

My instinct to attack let me down, for I hurried. My first series of ten shots was a 96. Just one poor series and my chance for the final was almost gone. Thereafter it was almost as bad: 98, 99, 100, 98 and 99. I was furious for forgetting that form was fickle. It has to be constantly nourished. Nothing is a guarantee, a given; every score requires hard work. I thought I was on auto-pilot and nothing could go wrong. I was completely wrong.

Five shooters had made the final with 593. I still had a chance to make it after the disastrous first series of 96, but psychologically, I was done. Suddenly, confidence had been stripped away. I was expecting a 600, I had put too much pressure on myself. I had forgotten my job, which was: shoot the best in the given circumstances and get the Olympic quota. But I had got carried away by my fabulous scores in the European circuit and my flawless shooting in training.

I just wanted to leave Fort Benning, flee this intolerable arena of embarrassment. At twenty, I was too immature to handle such a defeat. But my flight to Atlanta and on to Colorado Springs got cancelled. To stay a day longer was to remember the defeat, to travel a long way was like a punishment to the self. So I drove to Atlanta, flew to Denver, drove to Colorado Springs. It was faintly ridiculous, this literal running away from failure.

Losing bothers everyone. It's not unique. Roger Federer as a boy would sit under the umpire's chair and weep for half an hour. But I was particularly bad at handling it initially. It made me weep in the privacy of hotel rooms and howl down the phone to my mother. Losing made me throw things and led me to childish drama. I think my parents prayed for my success just to save themselves from listening to me vent my frustration at them. Dad, Mom, I'm sorry. For days I'd mope over the unfairness of life. Eventually I learnt, as the T-shirt says: 'Shit happens.' I took pride in my performance even if I lost. I learnt to focus on my plan. I learnt to let go. I grew up.

But not back then. My journey from Fort Benning started at 3 pm and ended in Colorado Springs at 3 am. I was tired and hurting, I slept, woke at 9 am and went to the range.

And I shot a perfect 600.

A month later, in the World Cup in Zagreb, I shot a 593 and missed the final by a point. Ten days later, at the Munich World Cup, my favourite arena, it finally came. I shot a 596, then a 103.9 in the final with a string of hefty scores—10.6, 9.4, 10.5, 10.5, 10.8, 10.3, 10.5, 10.4, 10.3 and 10.6—and won a bronze. And an Athens Olympic quota place, the second Indian to do after Anjali Bhagwat. I was pleased and satisfied, I knew I'd get it, yet it was confidence mixed with desperation.

Back home, people were thrilled. Gurbir Singh Sandhu, the president of the Punjab Olympic Association and a family friend, was generous with his praise. At a press conference in June 2003, he was categorical that I was capable of winning that elusive individual Olympic gold medal. And this was a man, whose son, Manavjit Singh Sandhu, was a trap shooting star with his own Olympic ambitions. My year got better when Samsung selected me for its Olympic Ratnas scholarship scheme with long-jumper Anju George, Anjali Bhagwat, athlete K. M. Beenamol, and weightlifter Karnam Malleswari. The company distributed Rs 10 lakh to each one of us and presented the Indian Olympic Association Rs 50 lakh. It was precisely the kind of support India's Olympic movement required.

Meanwhile, I missed a medal by 0.1 in the Seoul World Cup and was uninspired at the World Cup final in Milan. But there was a nice postscript to Milan. After I had finished last,

Amit Bhattacharjee said, hey, let's go buy some shoes, hoping that shopping would provide escape. Meanwhile, Anjali, shooting brilliantly, beat a classy field to win air-rifle gold. As we travelled home, I smiled at Amit: 'Some of us are going home with gold, some of us just with *jootas*.'

13

A GREEK TRAGEDY

a) Athens—*Ten Days Before*

The pain was cruel. I couldn't chew. I couldn't talk.

It was ten days to go for the 2004 Athens Olympics and I suffered my first minor setback.

A toothache.

Uwe Riesterer scouted around and found me a dentist, but a problem arose. I was paranoid about taking the wrong medication before the Olympics because so many drugs figure in the anti-doping list. So I said no to painkillers. Antibiotics were inevitable, but they weaken you, just drain a little bit from your battery. My mouth had stitches and once the local anaesthetic wore off the pain was even sharper. To complete my agony, a throat infection set in.

In the midst of this misery and growing panic, Uwe told me: 'Listen boy, this is God's will. We can't help it. If you want to go for the Olympics, you go, otherwise, you can drop out and nobody will blame you. This is a situation that is beyond our control. I am sure everyone will understand.'

I wasn't amused, but it brought clarity to my mind. You

don't win medals by being weak, by giving up, by letting go. Pain exists but it is manageable. It's like disappointment, you learn to shut it away in some cupboard in the brain. I knew I was not going to chicken out and I told him:

'I don't care. I will go to Athens.'

Uwe, a man of interesting contradictions, was also being clever. He told my mother he would be content if I came twentieth in Athens, which immediately unnerved her. Here we were talking about gold and he wasn't even talking finals! Was this coach for real? My sister, Divya, confident in me, even put a wager on my score: she told Uwe, 'Abhinav will shoot 597.'

But the German wasn't demeaning me, he was both needling me while taking the pressure off. The tooth was a distraction, yet he was cleverly attempting to bring me to that mental state where I might feel I had nothing to lose.

Maybe it was working because my training was superb, my skills sharp. In three days in Athens, I shot only a single 9. I even scored a perfect 600. In the pre-event training, my last ten shots were 106.5, an average of over 10.6 each shot. Like a racehorse, poised, pushing, I was ready.

I shot slowly in the qualifying, every shot prepared like it was some minor masterpiece of breathing and balance. Three times I left my gun and exited my shooting position, caught in my own private perfection, inhaling the air and contemplating the next shot to come. Everyone was taut, nervous. Amit was outside. Crying. Divya, my sister, later said: 'I was so scared when I saw your first 9, I had to go outside. I couldn't watch.' The room, she said, was suffocating with pressure and so she stood outside the range and kept asking people the score. She was right, of course; I shot 597, which was better than the Olympic record of 596.

Two Chinese were ahead of me. Zhu Qinan had shot 599

and his compatriot, Li Jie, was on 598. I had a series of 99, 100, 99, 100, 100 and 99 and was placed third. Third is good, it is medal position, but my third was still some distance away from first. I had to catch the Chinese. Jozef Gonci of Slovakia, who was one point behind me at 596, had to catch me. The game was on.

The final is a new start and it is a last chance. It is shooting at its most concentrated, it is ten shots to history. The final was in another hall, which was not unusual, for it offered more spectators a better view. Gaby—with me, as usual—was in charge of my rifle, which means she positions it and then takes a seat behind me designated for the coach. We could speak, but didn't. She didn't want to, she told me. I had to learn to be in my own world of silence and focus.

Professor Sunny Thomas, the Indian coach, came and spoke to me before the final. It is not a good time to talk to a shooter. It is too late anyway for advice, and chatter only clogs the brain. Still I cracked a joke. Soon I wasn't laughing.

Drama erupted, as it always does. Sport is rarely calm, it is so full of tense, highly strung individuals in their own zones, so full of lists, equipment, routines, that something is always forgotten. This time it was my bullets. It was like a footballer in an arena without a ball. The final range was some distance from the preliminary-round shooting arena and I thought I had everything with me. Except when I got to my position and started sighting and opened the ammunition box, there were only four or five pellets. Instead of 200.

Where were they, where was time?

Gaby's description of me then is of 'eyes like a football and mouth open and closing like that of a frog'.

Two minutes were left. She sprinted out of the range, past the jury, hoping to find the pellets in the changing area because the ammunition room was far away, found them in a bag, dodged and elbowed her way past security people who tried to stop her, and arrived with the pellets just as the judge was standing up to start proceedings. I still owe her a trip to the hairdresser because she insists she found her first grey hair two days after Athens.

And then, not because of the toothache which may have drained me slightly, not because of the bullets, not because of anything I could explain right then, I fell apart. From third I fell to seventh.

My form was strong, my mind was focused, my nerves had held under pressure. I was in the zone, but in the zone you shoot beautifully, not like this. Not a series of 9.4, 10.0, 10.0, 10.3, 9.8, 9.9, 8.8, 9.7, 9.6, 10.1. It was inexplicable. Later, Mansher Singh would say I looked devastated, and he understood: when you have that precious feel, and still you fail, it's harder. Suma Shirur could see it was killing me, aware that a golden chance was slipping away.

I like to deconstruct my shooting. But there is no time for this at big events, for before you can even contemplate what has happened, a microphone is in your face.

Why?

What happened?

Did you choke?

Understandably, these were journalists doing their job, but so many questions were absent of any logic and intelligence— sport being broken down into neatly packaged sound bites, which it never can be.

Everyone had a reason for my defeat, a theory. Some insisted the pressure had tilted my hand. I didn't agree. Some believed I had burnt all my energy in the qualification. I wasn't sure.

Coach Thomas told the media that since I battled through qualification, with many of the shots just a 10.0, I was simply 'lucky' to get into the final. I didn't agree. You don't get 'lucky' in shooting. You don't hit a target by fluke, like a shot off the net cord.

Some argued my parents had distracted me. I didn't agree. My parents can be present at an event, but I'm locked into another universe of focus. Anyway, their faith in me shakes me, moves me, it never pressures me.

Divya, who wept for days but never in front of me, said it was not meant to be, and was a warrior. When a journalist tossed a snide remark at me after my dope test—'very bad performance'—she defended me furiously: 'How many Indians come so far? You have no idea how hard he worked.'

The morning after my failure, I went to watch Rajyavardhan Singh Rathore at the trap range because I felt he had the best chance of a medal

He was inspiring, winning the silver, breaking the spell of bronze that went back to wrestler K. D. Jadhav in 1952, tennis ace Leander Paes in 1996 and weightlifter Karnam Malleswari in 2000. At his press conference, Rathore, responding to a query, said I would be a world champion one day. And Sharda Ugra, the fine writer who was then with *India Today*, was forceful in telling me my time would come, my gold would arrive. Later, some gentle volunteers tried putting the day in perspective for me. At the transport desk, going back to the Village, they asked how I did.

'Seventh,' I said.

'Excellent,' they replied.

'It sucks,' I countered.

'No,' they insisted. 'You are seventh in the Olympics. That is something.'

It is a beautiful thing to have people be gentle to you, to believe in you. I needed it because when I went back to India, the stories were all negative. Just another Indian who had buckled, just the same old story. You get branded, put in a box, and that's it. I was burning inside, with anger, with disbelief, with the ignorance of some of the views. But I had to shut up. You lose, you keep quiet, you swallow your excuses, it's the rule. Winning is the only licence to talk in sport.

b) Athens—*Ten Days Later*

My phone winked at me.

Message from Gaby. Message that would alter my life.

'DO YOU WANT TO KNOW WHAT HAPPENED TO YOU AT ATHENS, CALL ME.'

It was ten days after my Olympic final, I was in Delhi, it was 1 am, I hadn't been able to sleep. Not since Athens. Now my shaking hands dialled her number and a nightmare unfolded.

During my final in Athens, I had mentioned to Gaby that the floor felt a little slippery. Maybe I imagined it because I had forgotten it. In all my theories on my defeat, the floor never factored in because it is never supposed to be a factor. But Gaby trusted my instincts, she couldn't comprehend my scores either, and in her subconscious, the floor had registered suspiciously.

In an incredible coincidence, Valentina Turisini, another protege of Gaby's, had made the small-bore rifle three-position final. She was also on Position 3. Same as the position I used during my final.

What happened subsequently is what our phone call was about.

When Gaby was checking Turisini's equipment, she took

some extra time. Fired some dry shots. That's when the stand for the gun moved. Just a little, almost imperceptibly. But because Gaby knew about the floor, it registered. She looked closer, the floor was unsteady. She immediately reported it to the technical committee and they discovered the wood wasn't glued tight and a bubble had formed. It meant the tile had a *slight* bounce. *Slight* in shooting is fatal. *Slight* meant I was doomed the moment my feet stood on it for my art is about stillness. In a final, the concentration is total, the mind so much on bullets, sighting, posture that the floor somehow didn't register.

It wasn't just me either. I checked and my score was the best of anyone who had shot from Position 3 until then. Valentina eventually stood two feet to the left of that spot and won silver. But for me there were no comebacks, only shrugs.

When the phone call ended, I was stunned.

First, relief coursed through me like a river. It wasn't me, not my lack of skill, not some world-class choke which caused defeat. Athletes can't bear it when they err, it reduces them to a mediocrity they spend their lives escaping. Second, now at least I had an explanation, for the mystery of it had been painful. A fault must be pinned down for it to be rectified, though in this case the fault wasn't mine.

But then, I felt cheated and a frustrated fury rose within me. Four years of work gone in a moving floor. Would I ever be that sharp again, so ready. Was this a chance gone forever?

Sport, even in such distress, educates. Gaby used to tease me, 'Become a Catholic, learn to be on your knees.' She was trying to tell me that even the finest athletes need a helping of kismet. Or a good-luck kiss from God. In shooting, every 9 is only your own fault, so we try to control every second of competition. However, I had to learn that I could be fit, agile, concentrated, balanced, but that I couldn't control everything. The moving floor is like the deflected goal in football, it is beyond anticipation.

I decided to say nothing about the floor to the media except to a few who kept it quiet and coach Sunny Thomas. It would sound like an excuse, it would serve no purpose. The medal was gone.

I was struggling with myself, I wasn't certain if I had controlled the physical stress of the final well enough, and miles away a man could sense it. Uwe was trying to cajole me back to normality. He thought my 597 was world class and believed I exhausted myself on the journey through qualifying. So he wrote me a letter, a long one, six days after my event and before he knew about the floor.

It is a remarkable letter to an unsure young man, a letter of affection and understanding, of explanations and predictions, of hope and clarity. It is a letter I treasure for it showed great belief in me and it is worth reproducing extracts from it, even though some of his frank observations are a bit strong. But these are his thoughts, in his own words:

Hi Abhinav!

Believe you have reached home safely and first phase of recovery has set in! Enjoy this time... the next couple of months ... in your nice home, the best place to be after a long period of hard work and stress. Time to slow down and time to get the feeling for the (other) real and good things in life.

This Olympics is over... but you know... the one passed is the one before the next! And the next one is already in progress!

....Well... you put up the best fight of your shooting career and that is not only my personal opinion. 597-600 is the best score you have ever been shooting... not in terms of score!!!! but

in terms of quality in correlation of your physical, technical and mental skills and abilities. It is the first time in your already pretty long shooting career that you are able to maintain the highest level of attention. That's the kind of wood the lasting champion is made of!

Watching you so closely (facial camera and reaction), I realised pretty soon, that your batteries will be fully used by the end of your show. I hoped you could stand it'... and you did... even so it was up to the last couple of minutes (which you normally never do!). That is called fighting to the bitter end! And showing fighting spirit. A great experience and a feeling you will keep inside, memorise and mobilise when it comes to a showdown in another match. Great show... no sweat!

The next time the show will be familiar, not the same, not easy but that time you can activate your archives... you have been there! Most important... for your future performance excellence...

Watching your final... the first 2-3 shots, the facial expressions, that usual light in your eyes it was not there anymore. I told the commentator... "I hope he can plug into the reserves and rely on it at least for another 6–8 rounds...!"

Well... no fuel left! Nothing wrong with the technique, nothing wrong with the gun... just empty!

No need to analyse, no need to speculate on what went wrong, no hypothesis, only simple facts:

When the energy is gone, it's gone!

And you have used all of it when fighting up your way to the 597.

Well... many coaches would argue or even reason:

"... too nervous"

"...too stupid..."

" ... too cramped"

"... wanting too much"

...or as your chief coach has defended "himself" by saying:

"he was lucky enough to make the final... his 10's in the pre-competition have been already very shaky... etc. etc..." meaning (he should have not been making the final at all.. and the 597 was a lucky shot anyway...)

We read this on India news, asking ourselves if this guy has ever shot a single shot and/or if this guy is in the wrong sport anyway...?!

In any case: being in coaching for decades and having seen few shooters succeed and many being defeated (better: having defeated themselves!) I just want to tell you:

You are next in line!

World Champion in 2006

Olympic Champion in 2008

Don't count those "training" matches in between !!!! It's only those two matches which make you a " hero", a "legend", or simply "give you the inner satisfaction you are looking for".

But you have to work harder physically to build up the stamina which is needed to gain control and to be able to execute "automatically"...: put yourself on automatic pilot, when the fight to enter the final is draining too much of energy (which will happen more often the longer you want to stay up there!).

When you develop the skill of "switching to automatic pilot"... then you create the space, the room, the environment to execute your already well-developed mental strength, which is indeed the key to be on top.

The excellence of performance is based on "automatic body function" (execution of technical skills) and the skill and ability to gain mental control over the outcome of one's specific and final action!

Well... a lot of hard work to be done!

You have everything on hand:

* your own gym
* your own range

ultimate family support
no existential worries
well meaning support

Finally I would also like to mention:

You need to develop trust in what you do, how you do it, why you do it!

You need to learn to trust... not everybody.

Stay away from the gurus... it is destructive , not progressive and certainly not based on self critical evaluation.

Be focused but not intolerant.

Be flexible (and reassess!), don't be stubborn and self centred....

Know what you want and make sure you get what you want. Be a pro!

At the end: it's only a game but it is also the best school of life! Well... it's time to slow down, to recover quickly, to digest "post competition distress syndrome" (very close to post war distress syndrome... "I will sell everything... I won't touch the gun anymore... go to hell with shooting... etc. etc. etc.")

We have all been there!

Not much to worry! Just being burned up and out doesn't mean the world will turn the other way around.

Clean up the guns, put it aside, in a couple of months you will feel hungry again and you will ask for the challenge "of competing with your Chinese components and showing them that only one can be the No.1!"

I know it will be you!

Just make sure you believe it too!

Enjoy your home.

Will call you up when travelling the Indian Himalayas.

Never look back , always ahead.

Always

Uwe

The letter helped. My parents, so unyielding in their belief, helped. My sister's affection helped. It picked me up. Eventually, I had to shoot simply because there was nothing else I could do. Shooting is all I did well. So in 2005 I hired another coach, Stanislav Lapidus, just as a change, just as someone to push me on a daily basis in India. I also added an event, the 3P, or three-position rifle. It entails forty shots while prone, forty shots while standing, forty shots while kneeling—in that precise order—from a distance of 50 metres. It was change meant to invigorate me.

But I didn't compete for a while. For five or six months. People asked, where is he, but I needed silence, a break, and time to train in this new art. Eventually, I competed briefly in Europe and got selected for World Cups in South Korea and Fort Benning in spring. My results were decent, but my life was haphazard, I was drifting. My new coach, Lapidus, had to return home since his wife unfortunately had an accident. I skipped World Cups in Munich and Milan when my cousin suddenly passed away. I painted.

I needed something to drive me, just a change in luck, a fresh ambition, a win to halt my confidence from leaking. Something, anything. It came finally at the national championships in Hyderabad in December 2005. I hadn't shot there for two years and Gagan Narang was shooting superbly. He was also shooting at home and expectation draped itself across him. We were supposed to be enmeshed in a bitter rivalry, which was rubbish. We got on well, but the media needed a story.

It was one of the best 10-metre air-rifle finals I'd shot at a nationals. Three of us—Gagan, Sanjeev Rajput and me—were locked together on 595 after the qualifications. Then, in the final, my first shot was disastrous.

8.8.

Athens again?

But instead of depressing me, it drove me, it was as if the score was a tease, a test, and I shot the next nine shots superbly for a total of 103.3. It was enough for gold. Rajput got silver. Gagan got the bronze with 100.7 in the final.

It was the close to the year I needed, but when I looked in the mirror I saw another shooter. Not the boy before Athens, but an altered man of twenty-three. Always, I had been fascinated by shooting. *Was.* How do you, on different days, at different times, in different moods, under different pressure, find your best? It was thrilling, rewarding, addictive. Shooting used to move me. It gave me a kick. It triggered off what I call a chemical reaction of happy hormones. But Athens changed me. The emotion slipped out of me. No more happy hormones, no more positive feedback. That shooter was gone.

Never again would I be the same person, the same shooter, the same competitor. I wanted to win but there was a sense of detachment. I became process-oriented. Obsessed to the point where looking back it makes me laugh. Victory was nice but the elation had gone. Part of my passion would die and the person I became was colder, more clinical, a scientist on a mission, an athlete bent on redemption. It's hard to explain but I felt my performance in Athens was worth a medal. However, it was not enough for the world. I had to show people I could win. Of course, I could have waited four years, sailed through Silk Street in Beijing, and just bought myself a fake gold medal from its market. It would have saved me a lot of pain. But its heft, I guess, would be different.

14

CHAMPION OF THE WORLD

My talent is an opinion, an idea; I am trying to translate it into an unarguable fact. Coaches praise me. My mother is insistent I am gifted. I value myself as a world-class shooter. But dazzling myself in a lonely backyard, with flower pots as spectators, is insufficient. Eventually, I require proof of capability in the public arena, under the lights, cameras watching, the world judging, the very best in the planet competing.

I need it to convince you and satisfy me. As a sportsman, this is my job.

I was familiar with success. I had won World Cup medals, set world records and won fifty to sixty international medals. It was a fine CV for a twenty-three-year-old, but lacked a champion's defining moment. I had been shooting for eleven years and it was time to marry talent with occasion. I needed something big, desperately; I needed a World Championship or Olympic gold because that is all people remember.

Labels.

The best shooter in the world.

But 2006 did not commence like that, it did not appear to be the season of history-making I was chasing. Existential hurt after Athens was gradually being replaced with pure physical pain. My back had started to cause havoc. Muscle imbalance isn't unusual for shooters because our postures will never meet with orthopaedic approval: standing upright yet leaning back; the right side hoisting the gun and full of tension, the left side providing support.

Because I wasn't naturally flexible enough to get my left elbow into my left hip, and was compensating by overstraining and stretching muscles of the right side of my back, the discs in my back started to bulge.

Nerves would pinch and pain would explode in my lower region. Later, doctors in India would send a clear message: put down the gun, get under the knife. But I was fearful of surgery and explored further options before settling for intense rehabilitation in Germany, loosening some muscles, strengthening others.

The pain started to announce itself as we descended on a sprawling, beautiful Melbourne on a spring day in March for the 2006 Commonwealth Games. As cities go, this one smells of sport, as if the populace was born to run. Its stadiums glitter, its crowds comprehend competition. My redemption would not arrive here, for this was to become Samaresh Jung's personal Games, his haul so wonderfully rich (five golds, one silver, one bronze) that he could have been No. 12 on the international medal table himself.

Unwilling to be left out, Anuja Jung—in an echo of what Dana Zatopek did when her husband, Emil, won three golds at the 1952 Helsinki Games—interrupted this male procession to win her own gold in the women's three-position rifle. What a family.

My returns were more modest in this Games as I walked stiff-legged through an unspectacular venue in Port Melbourne.

Shooting as a team in such a Games is pleasant for the sport turns less lonely. For a brief while, your rival in the individual event is now your ally. You feel a different pressure as you are shooting for someone else, yet you feel the power of your partner's reassurance should you falter. In Melbourne, Gagan Narang would be that rock for his form was sterling.

In the Commonwealth Games air-rifle pairs, I shot a 591, Gagan had an excellent 598 and our total beat the 2002 record by 5 points. The Bangladeshis, a fine team, trailed us by eight points and got silver.

In the individual event, Gagan, now coated with confidence, asserted himself more strongly. His 597, with a 101.9 in the final, broke the Games record and subdued the field. I shot well, not remarkably but well, with a 594 and a 101.5. My focus still required a wrench and a pair of pliers to fix it for my last three shots of 9.9, 9.5, 9.8 allowed Zhang Jin of Singapore to walk away with the silver, leaving me with bronze.

A quiet event for me then took a dramatic twist in a familiar direction: If you play sport for a living, you know equipment will malfunction. But you are never quite ready for it. Daley Thomson, the legendary decathlete, once snapped his pole during an Olympic vault. Michael Phelps's goggles let water in during his run to eight golds in 2008. My gun, in the 50-metre three-position team event, simply fell apart.

I loaded a bullet. Fired. Nothing.

Loaded again. Fired. Nothing.

Every four or five tries, one protesting bullet at best spat out. The problem was the bolt. Coach Laszlo Szucsak said it was the trigger. Who cared, the bloody rifle wasn't working, but the clock was.

In three-position shooting, you get 45 minutes for forty shots in prone, 75 minutes for forty shots in standing, 60 minutes for forty shots while kneeling. Now time, in the prone section, ticked by. Ten minutes gone. Then twenty. Then twenty-five. But the gun, taken apart, screwed together, undone, redone, could not be fixed.

So Laszlo left the range, went to the armoury. Anjali Bhagwat wasn't there, but her gun was, her case was open, Laszlo grabbed it, ran, handed it over. I weighed its unfamiliarity and then began working at the speed of a Formula 1 mechanic at a pit stop. The butt place was unscrewed from my rifle and put on her gun. The sights were adjusted to my specifications. The trigger set-up was different to mine, but you can't fiddle with it, there's no time, damn it.

I lay down, put foreign rifle to nervous shoulder and fired forty shots in 15 minutes.

A 390 out of 400.

Not bad.

I followed with a 368/400 in standing and 386/400 in kneeling for a total of 1144. Ironically, it was a single point better than Gagan's score. Our combined tally easily outstripped Australia's to win us gold.

Gagan was not done either. He shrugged off his minor tremor in form and pocketed a fourth gold with a record score in the three-prone individual event. I happily took silver some distance behind to finish with two team golds, a silver and a bronze.

It was a wonderful Games to be a shooter for we could say, without embarrassment, that we 'saved India'. As an entire contingent, India collected twenty-two golds, seventeen silvers, eleven bronzes, of which shooting's contribution was sixteen golds, seven silvers, four bronzes. Yet a triumphant departure from the friendly Antipodes was laced with a sobering thought. If we concentrated our attention as strongly on our athletes as we did on the vapid 10-minute Bollywood dance segment at the Melbourne closing ceremony, we might have actually risen on the total medal table.

There was no flight home to applause for the shooters. We travelled straight to Guangzhou, China for the beginning of the World Cup circuit. My back was erratic, the competition was stiff, my results iffy. Gagan, on a roll, won gold in China and a quota place for the Beijing Olympics in 2008. In the World Cups, I was ninth in China, missed Brazil in pain, was twenty-seventh in Munich, forty-second in Milan.

It was June—hot, aching, optimistic. My scores told some stories, but within me an insistent voice said something else. I was calmer, more patient, unworried as my form inched forward, my attention focused on the 2006 World Championship. In Germany, I slogged with Gaby for two months. I fussed over equipment. Toned my body, ignored my pain.

I developed my own shooting shoes in tandem with a *mochi* and Drish shoe manufacturers in Chandigarh. After twenty days, we got it right: one shoe a millimetre higher than the other! From such small adjustments, whose efficacy is unprovable, comes strong satisfaction. Mentally, at least, I was ready. I cannot offer evidence, dissect it logically, but I felt I would shoot well at the World Championship. It is a sensation in the brain, a sudden prescient feeling. Confidence arrives without adequate explanation, but I remembered Uwe's letter after Athens, his insistence that I would be world champion, and I held that thought close.

The Indian team had already arrived in Zagreb for the 2006 World Championship, locked in camp again for ten days. I skipped it, for a repetitive camp made no sense. I arrived some days later, but my back quickly flared up. I missed official training, partly because of pain, partly because I just didn't need it, and earned official flak—on the night before my event!

It was poor timing and a poor response. Of course, we're moody beasts and occasionally high maintenance. But an athlete's pain cannot be seen by the outsider, cannot be felt, so it requires a quality of empathy, a sensitivity to the sporting world to appreciate how it affects us. It doesn't require a high IQ to know we're not normal people. Before major competitions we're highly strung, nervous, taut, edgy, plain freaked out. Pain disturbs the idyllic concentration we seek. An extra round of practice, when we're already tuned, just breaks a private rhythm. At that time we need the perceptive official, not the reprimanding one, we need people to understand what the athlete goes through just to perform. Forget about win.

Next day I began, against a field thicker than even the Olympics. At the Olympics, two shooters per country are allowed; at a World Championship, it is three. I shot strongly, aggressively, I felt no sense of struggle except in the last ten shots.

In the Munich World Cup earlier that year, I had shot 399 in my first forty shots, and then, tense, dropped 3–4 points in my last twenty shots. Here, I started again with 399 in my first forty shots, but a voice chanted in my head: *finish strong, finish well.* I did, with a 597/600, which left me tied first with three others. It was my day, but it wasn't Gagan's: his 592 left him in thirty-first place, while Sanjeev Rajput, a point further back, was in thirty-seventh position. Our combined total of 1782—in World Championships they simply add up the individual event scores—was three points from gold and two points from a team medal.

On shooting's best days, you don't even know where you are. You go so far inside yourself, are so one with your craft, that everything else fades. You hear nothing, neither advice nor heckle; you feel nothing, no apprehension or confusion; you see nothing but the target, and even then only the bullseye. It's the zone athletes speak of, a private perfection where no effort is required, no thinking, no conscious decisions, it all just flows. It is for these rare moments, a sort of athletic nirvana, a time when shooting actually feels easy, that you compete.

The moment doesn't last, it passes swiftly, but because you have been there you know it is possible and so you restart your search for it. For me this flow lasted for five to seven shots, and then it broke, and I was back to being a mechanical shooter, fearful and conscious of my actions. At my best in Zagreb, I had flow for 50 per cent of the time. Four years later, in 2010, I had it for 3 per cent; I was aware of the occasion, I was different.

Psychologically then, in Zagreb, I made a significant decision. There were five Beijing Olympic quota places on offer and after the qualifying I probably knew I had one. But I acted as if I didn't know, I didn't want to believe it; in my mind, I was still firing for that quota. There was, unusually, a gap of four hours before the final and intensity tends to fade. Creating this artificial challenge, this chase for a quota place that was already mine, was a way to keep my edge.

I returned to the hotel, showered, lunched with Amit and put on a T-shirt.

It was a fake Beijing Olympics shirt.

Later, in the preparation area where you gather 20 minutes before the final, I did not look down as usual, but around. I was searching faces, and found something. The Austrian,

Christian Planer, appeared nervous. The Romanian, Alin George Moldoveanu, looked edgy. Maybe I was imagining this, but it gave me security.

Three of us—Moldoveanu, Jozef Gonci from Slovakia and I—were on 597, one (Konstantin Prikhodtchenko from Russia) on 596 and four on 595. Olympic champion Zhu Qinan of China had a 595. We couldn't discount his ability to fight it out in the final. Of course, nothing could be taken for granted.

I was on Position 3, the same position as Athens. Everything registers briefly in the mind before training takes over.

Breathe, breathe, breathe.

Then I started. Beautifully.

10.3.

10.3.

10.3.

10.0.

10.6.

Nothing lasts, does it? Eventually a hand tilts, it shakes, a butt doesn't sit perfectly, an imperfection shows. From nowhere two 9s crept in, but they did not matter, what did matter was my response to those 9s.

9.3.

10.9.

9.2.

10.5.

One shot remained, one trigger pull from greatness.

What do people think at such times? Of parents? Of first days with flimsy guns under a Chandigarh tree? Of Olympic failure?

No, we're mostly too nervous to think of anything but survival. Yet you can't win by trying to survive, and it's a struggle to find that balance as you career between fear, anticipation, desperation, resolve.

The scoreboard glittered before me and the names were in order of shooting station, not according to scores. My name was listed third, I looked at it and beside it, it said:

1. *Abhinav Bindra*

Or wait, was it ...

7. *Abhinav Bindra*

I couldn't tell, which meant I had to be aggressive.

I was, in fact, 0.6 point ahead of Alin George Moldoveanu, 0.8 in front of Olympic champion Zhu Qinan. Victory was mine to take or leave. This time, I thought, briefly, about the Commonwealth Games in Manchester: '*God, I lost that on the last shot. Not again!*'

Five seconds of meditation.

Crack.

10.7.

I shook my fist. My fellow Indian shooters shouted.

I was Champion of the World.

I felt elation: at my execution, at winning from Position 3, at casting off some of the criticism aimed at me after Athens, for we are all fussy creatures. In some strange way, I felt more elation here than in Beijing in 2008. Because it was the first breakthrough, the first kicking down of a massive competitive door. You think, yes, I've done it. You think, finally, yes, proof has come for effort, reward for sacrifice, payback for pain. You feel pride, a sense of self-worth, that you trembled but overcame it, that you were challenged but mobilized your resources, that you were more perfect than anyone under the most perfectly unreasonable pressure. You feel, for an instant, a sensation of being the single best shooter in the whole damn wide world. I remember this. I remember giving the flowers which medalists received to the dope control officer. She was beautiful.

The medal in my pocket, I sat in my room, alone, quiet, reflective. It is my style. Then Gaby came calling, and Heinz, and off we went for dinner. A continent away, in India, there was admiration for my triumph over rivals and pain and the media began to display a finer understanding of both shooting and me. Neither is simple. I reluctantly allowed reasons for my Athens disaster to emerge in print. In 2004, it would have been an excuse. Now, as world champion in 2006, I could articulate it.

But all was not well. My back, the spine and vertebrae and muscles all felt like some shoddy construction that was falling apart. The pain reduced me to tears and my gun stayed locked in its case. The Asian Games in Doha came and I sat in the doctor's office. Five to six hours a day I laboured with a phsyio after that, balancing my muscles, strengthening them, relaxing them, alternating between exercise and therapy and acupuncture. My body needed recovery, but my mind had been restored. That night in Zagreb after the 2006 World Championships, over wine, Gaby was thrilled yet scared: no world champion had ever won Olympic gold—which beckoned in 2008—in the same cycle.

I didn't care, history didn't scare me. I needed redemption for Athens. This was a start. I was tired at day's end in Zagreb. My battery running on empty. I slept. But it was the sleep of the peaceful.

15

THE NEW SHOOTER

a) Forgotten Man

Sport, and this is its particular beauty and cruelty all at once, has no memory. Yesterday matters for it gives you confidence and yet yesterday is irrelevant. Athletes might say, 'I don't have to prove anything,' but it is bravado, often an irritation with the constant inquiry about their form and chances. Fact is, an athlete's life is an offering of proof.

Proof that we can be as good as yesterday. Better than yesterday. Better than tomorrow's new man? I owned a reputation now, but reputation becomes many things. It becomes a standard for yourself, a means of intimidation yet also a provocation for an opponent. You want to beat your best score and everyone wants to beat you. And no one, especially officials, remembers the past.

In 2007, quickly, a new hero emerged. That year, I had delayed my return to the circuit to March, skipping the World Cup in Fort Benning, but P.T. Raghunath had emerged as a startling talent there. He shot a 595, three points better than Gagan Narang. At the World Cup in Sydney, Raghunath was again the finest Indian with a 594, which left him thirteenth. I shot 591, Gagan a 590. The order of things was altering on the scoreboard.

In Kuwait, at the Asian Championships in December, it became evident. My score was a measly 592, but I was unworried. My shooting was low-key after a lay-off, my technique was fine. But my rivals made a statement. Gagan shot a 594 and finished fifth in the final. Raghunath was simply brilliant and won gold.

It meant the Indian air-rifle team was world class. It also led to talk among officials—that evening itself. Raghunath would possibly go with Gagan for the Olympics. I would not. Fine. But the irony was inescapable. I was working hard, plotting to be at my best at the Olympics when it mattered. I had a World Championship gold, an Indian first, just behind me from a year ago. And yet, it counted for nothing. The present in the form of Asian gold meant everything. The past I had was immaterial. Now I had to prove myself again for the future. I had to dig.

b) Learning to Dig

Dig. All great athletes do it. They find something when nothing should logically exist. Mark Kram, the *Sports Illustrated* writer, painted a raw portrait of this in his description of a drained Muhammad Ali at the end of the 10th round in his fight with Joe Frazier in Manila in 1975:

> (Ali's) head was bowed, and when he raised it his eyes rolled from the agony of exhaustion. "Force yourself, champ!" his corner cried. "Go down to the well once more!" begged Bundini (Brown), tears streaming down his face. "The world needs ya, champ!"

Ali dug, he found, he won. All athletes understand this. We're excavators, internal adventurers, we're always reaching into ourselves for something extra. More than we think we have, more than the next man has. Scraping the stomach and looking for some leftover courage, ransacking the lungs in the hunt for some last minutes of energy, rummaging through the brain in pursuit of the dregs of concentration. It's desperate, it's an instinctive refusal to lose. You dig to stay alive, to not go home early, to go a step or a shot further. You dig to leap from goodness to greatness and into the arms of victory.

Digging is important to who I am and where I come from. A publisher in Delhi once sneeringly suggested to me that my Olympic medal was bought. Paid for by daddy, like some parental birthday gift. Give the kid a top-class gun, build him a range, pay for coaches, and hey presto, it will come. I smiled thinly. I guess the Ambanis and Tatas never thought of this. Medal for hire for their progeny, that sort of thing.

It bothered me, not the personal accusation, but the facile idea that medals are for sale. As if there is some shop where you buy desire, purchase sweat, get resoluteness on sale. There is a lack of comprehension here, about digging, about how obsession is a disease that athletes like me actually want to get.

I don't underestimate my privilege, not for a single silky second, nor the advantage it has afforded me. Especially in a nation where the price of a gun can unsettle families. But I have one small, less evident, disadvantage. I didn't really need to shoot, my livelihood was never dependent on success with a gun. My father's business wasn't just a fund, but an escape route, a life to fall back on. Hardship didn't interrupt my day. This can be a problem, the fact that you can walk away any time can make you soft.

Arriving from adversity is not fun, or to be recommended. But adversity has one unintended benefit in sport: it occasionally grants you a chip on the shoulder to urge you on. It can make you hungry. I was shooting for personal pride, not much more, but others compete for something far more elemental. Like finding a steady job with a government institution, escaping hardship, living a decent life, providing for family. It gives them a different, deeper hunger. Their investment in sport is more meaningful, defeat for them has far greater repercussions. They cannot, sometimes literally, afford to fail. I could.

Life for some athletes in India has been so challenging that the demands of sport do not scare them. Milkha Singh, with his unflinching Mount Rushmore face, once told an interviewer: 'My experience made me so hard that I wasn't even scared of death.' He had—some say—seen his parents being killed in Partition riots and had slept starving on railway platforms in Delhi. Running and exhaustion and physical limits eventually held no fear for him. He was a man who had encountered hideous circumstances, but the one positive was the *aag* that flamed within him.

Something burnt in me, clearly, but just not as urgently as this. I had no idea how to reach far inside me to touch the reserves that a champion athlete needs. I had had no need to, no situation had demanded it. Life had been too kind. When a shooter, for instance, gets a new gun, it can be exciting, a source of stimulation, like a boy from the Brazilian favelas getting new football boots. But I was spoilt, a new gun brought only a mild reaction. I was comfortable and this is a sin in sport, it holds you back from the desperation that a medal demands.

So I had to learn how to dig deep.

No one likes to dig, by the way. It hurts, it drains you of everything and leaves you empty, a temporary shell of a man.

But you can't win without it. When I went to competitions I used to disintegrate, a bathroom visitor every 10 minutes. My mind was a mess, racing with insecurities—Was I good enough? Was I ready? To accept all this, to work through it, to find those reserves, you have to search within.

I am naturally competitive, but so is everyone at an Olympics. But for victory, to separate yourself, to be greater than even great athletes, you need to dig further. You have to find those leftover scraps of courage in the stomach. I guess it's what athletes call an edge, and it didn't come to me naturally. I had to learn it, I had to find a way to touch the minus part of the Duracell battery within me, the last dregs of my energy and courage. This you can't buy. It's why later it was hard for me to win events consecutively because it took too much out of me. Every week I had to dig and every week you cannot.

This was part of my journey after Athens, reappraising myself, reshaping myself as a shooter. This is when I cling-filmed myself in single-mindedness, the medal consuming me like addiction does. On reflection, my life then was unhealthy, an endless day of gym, range, running.

Wake at 5 am.

Gym 5.30 am-7 am.

Eat.

Range 9 am-1 pm.

Lunch.

Range 2 pm-5 pm.

Gym 5 pm-7 pm.

Dinner.

Sleep.

No other interest, just shooting.

Some days I shot 600 rounds, when seventy to hundred is normal. It's a lot, it's crazy. I'd be asleep and then awake with an idea, as simple as how to pick up the rifle smoothly from the stand, and I'd shrug off the sheets when the world was sleeping, go to my range and practise. My parents got so worried they started locking the range at night.

I invented a new word, I had become a new species, a negaholic, able to discover bad even in good. Athletes are expected to be extremely positive, creatures so swollen with self-belief that they see invincibility in the mirror. But doubt hung around me like a bad debt. Athletes shun thoughts like, 'What if I come last in the Olympics?' but they circled my brain.

But this was eccentricity with a purpose. I wanted to go into the 2008 Olympics having made it very tough for myself, so tough that nothing I faced would hurt. In 2008, at the Munich World Cup, I didn't sleep all night before the final so that I was stressed during competition the next day. It was practice for the night before the Olympic final when I presumed I wouldn't sleep.

I was right. I didn't.

16

THE EMBRACE OF OBSESSION

a) The Quest for Flawlessness

Obsession is the child of ambition; it is also born sometimes from the need for redemption. But obsession also arrives from the fact that flawlessness is possible in shooting.

600 out of 600. Done.

10.9. Done.

10.9, ten times in a final. Not done. Improbable really, but theoretically possible.

Flawlessness is a burden. In football, the flaw is allowed; of ten passes two may not be weighted exactly. In tennis, not every serve needs to dust the line. In shooting, flawlessness is measured, it is demanded; in shooting, inaccuracy is announced to you and the world over a loudspeaker half-a-second after your shot in a final. A 10.0 in a final is, in fact, a miss.

This need to be flawless becomes like a disease, every piece of equipment, clothing, breathing, stance is nit-picked over, it all has to be precise to the point where flawless isn't just a score, it's a feeling.

One week in Germany in 2004, I shot six consecutive, perfect 600s. Sixty shots into the bullseye. It is don't-mess-with-me shooting. But I was still irritated and even my mother was confused.

'What more do you want?'

My reply was curt:

'The feeling wasn't good.'

It is like winning but without rhythm, like a batsman hitting a four but the tremor of contact going from bat to hand telling him it isn't perfect, it is a shot without a sense of fulfilment. I guess it's hard to explain, or as Ian Thorpe once said in a different context: 'It's an athlete's thing.'

Obsession, in a way, is the journey to perfection. The bullseye is .5 millimetre, it is tiny, you can't even see it with the naked eye from 10 metres, which is where I shoot from. But the landscape that I traverse, geographically and intellectually, to hit that .5-millimetre black spot is vast. I will do anything to be better than the rest, I have to be better. It's a chant in my head, a tattoo on my soul. I am not shooting for fun, I am shooting to make a point in 2008. And so I go and get a lipo-dissolve done in Australia just to help my shooting, which my parents will first read about in this book.

I had love handles, which men dislike for it offends their sense of vanity. But my dislike for it was practical. If they were big enough, if I was hefty enough, they would work. Yet I felt my love handles were impeding my technique, that old problem of trying to dig my left elbow into my left hip. I felt they were giving me almost a trampoline effect and affecting my stability. So I needed to have them removed.

During a fitness camp in Australia in January 2008, I went to a clinic and a fat-dissolving substance was injected into my hip through a hundred very painful pricks. It felt like an army of ants on a picnic. It swelled up, I got a fever, but it worked. The second day I shot a 600 and I thought, this is it, I've got it.

The day after, damn, the 9s were back. So much for
Dr Bindra.

Failure of this experiment was hardly a deterrence. Timothy
Harkness, a sports psychologist with whom I worked closely
in 2008, once told a writer that 'Abhinav is an athlete who
will stop at nothing to achieve success.' You better believe it.
Between 2004 and 2008, I experimented like a hippie from
the 1960s. At one level, it was a pure pursuit of perfection, a
calibrated hunt for anything that could assist my quest for a
flawless performance by half a per cent. But it was far more
complicated. It was my natural sense of inquiry into technology
and spirituality, it was a counter to every insecurity that ganged
up in my brain. It was a need to isolate every variable, to control
every aspect of performance, to break it down into hundreds
of tiny, perfect parts.

It was also a break from monotony, for shooting can be a
mechanical nightmare and experimentation is a method to
keep the brain engaged and the spirit energized. Not every
vitamin injection I took, not every bottle of yak milk drunk,
bullet chosen, jacket redesigned, was going to help. I knew
that, but I was playing a mental game with myself. Even it
didn't help, if I believed it did, well, then it helped.

On my journey to Beijing, these are the places I went to in
an attempt to improve:

Dry Firing in Dark Room (2005)

In this blackness, like being imprisoned in a cupboard, I have
no visual sense, so I must function only on my instinct. I
sense my body more acutely, I am more alert and conscious
of my muscles. I stand in the dark, gun in firing position,
and concentrate, and it gives me awareness of my balance

and stability. To use a rough analogy, it is like rowers finding synchronicity by rowing blindfolded.

Samadhi Tank (2008)

During the time it takes me to shoot, maybe 10 seconds, maybe 75, my mind cannot stutter or shift. Samadhi means a state of deep concentration, which is precisely what a Samadhi Tank does. It is a flotation tank, a capsule, where you are deprived of light. You lie in 10 centimetres of water to which is added roughly 200 kilograms of Epsom salts to make it buoyant. You relax completely, tension exits like some unwanted toxin; it's a fine place to meditate and visualize. I found it in Germany and did about twenty sessions in Dortmund and Munich, many in the last month before the Beijing Olympics. I visualized being in the Beijing range, detached from everything, just doing my job. Which is shooting great shots.

Shooting Jacket (2005–07)

My jacket, pockmarked with holes, looks like it's been attacked by an irate grandmother with a knitting needle. My elbow bounces off the material, like with the love handles, so puncturing the jacket has erased that effect. I also got a tailor in Chandigarh to work with a luggage store (which worked with canvas and had the machines to stitch canvas) to design a jacket. I think the tailor went insane because I'd keep saying, '*Arre*, it's 5 millimetres off here, too tight by 3 millimetres here,' until he realized I was looking for an impossible perfection. I even have customized compression underwear, but let's not go there.

Floor/ Panels/ Light: (2004, Post-Athens)

Ivan Lendl had replicated the US Open court in his backyard in Connecticut. Coincidentally, he reached eight straight US

Open finals. Homework is never to be underestimated, like Sachin Tendulkar scuffing the pitch outside leg stump in preparation for Shane Warne's arrival in 1998. For shooters, the environment they compete in is crucial, from the solidity of floors to the quality of light.

Floors are like tennis surfaces, they differ, some are softer, some harder, and they activate different muscles. So in my home range, at various times, I had shooting stations made of wood, cement, sport flooring. Or just cement with differing elevations at each station.

At the Beijing World Cup in 2008, which is also a test event for the facility prior to the Olympics, I also noticed that the panels on which the targets hung were made of dark pine wood. I photographed them and had a similar backdrop created at home. The lighting in Beijing was also extreme because, unlike the norm, shooting would be live on television. At home, I replicated this as well.

Auditorium (2008)

Players who are unused to Centre Court at Wimbledon can apparently get unsettled not just by its aura but its size. The space behind and outside the lines is larger than in outside courts and this extra space can be disorienting. Similarly, the hall for the Olympic final in Beijing was unusually big and I needed to find a sense of myself within it. So I hired a marriage hall for a day in Chandigarh, set up a range in it and practised. It helped me get a sense of spatial awareness.

Ultrasound (2007)

Stillness is an art. Samaresh Jung, who won a bucketful of medals at the 2006 Commonwealth Games, once told a writer: 'Try standing still with your eyes closed and you'll find out how many muscles are at work.' Isolating and activating those muscles, especially in the core, which ensures stability, can be extraordinarily difficult. Then a trainer, functioning on the same obscure wavelength as me, suggested an ultrasound. During the procedure, while lying on a bed, I could go beyond an imagined mental picture and actually see the muscles as I tried to activate them.

Fitness (2006–07)

In 2006, on and off, I worked with Heath Mathews, a South African trainer. In January 2007, I went to a fitness camp in Melbourne and worked with Len Chong, a trainer introduced to me by the Mittal Champions Trust, a fine organization that is committed to nurturing future champions. It is run by Manisha Malhotra, a former tennis player and now a friend, who is inquisitive, interested, wonderfully pushy, reassuring when my head dropped, a keeper of the faith, and who constantly worked to discover the right expertise for her athletes.

Every day with Chong, up to six hours a day, we went at it. Twice a day I ran, 5 kilometres each time. I lifted kettle bells, did Pilates, worked on my lower back. I'd surf the Internet and buy equipment that could help. Once a Power Plate, a vibrating platform. Another time, a machine that assisted in core stability. Most was junk, but it indicated my dislike for the half measure.

If I had to put a number on it, I'd say the gym-work was worth an extra point or two in Beijing. When pressure seeps in during competition, the muscles tense or loosen, which is a problem, for there is an optimum tension that shooters seek. My extra strength and control of my body was valuable in this. The separation between winning and not-winning is infinitesimal and now I knew at least that exhaustion could be fended off, I wouldn't fade. I worked to the point where I believed no one was training like me. From my physical state I was gaining a psychological advantage.

Pellets (2008)

The Chinese shoot well for many reasons. One, I told myself, has to be ammunition. So in practice, I locked my gun into a vice and shot ten German pellets at a target. The grouping was 6.5 millimetres. Then I conducted the test with Chinese pellets. The grouping was 5.4 millimetres. In my sport, this was the difference between gold and nothing. I went to China but the patriotic manufacturer wouldn't be swayed before the Beijing Olympics (now they're available). No, he said, but no I wouldn't accept. I phoned a friend in Hong Kong and asked him to order the pellets. Weeks later I had 10,000 rounds.

Each box had 200 pellets. Every pellet I required was first weighed by me on a sensitive scale. If it was off by a couple of grams, out of the window.

Every pellet was then studied under a magnifying glass. If there was a bulge or scratch on the nose, into the dustbin.

This has an effect on accuracy. Trust me, I tested for it.

When I won gold in Beijing, I used those pellets.

b) Neuro-Feedback: An Experiment into the Mind of Greatness (2008)

At his mother's kitchen table in Durban, South Africa, a man told me he wanted to look inside my head. Place sensors on me, hook me to a machine and chart what my brain and body did when I shot well; what conversations I had with myself, how much I sweated, why my skin reached a particular temperature under stress; what emotional control I was capable of. Because in competition it is not just aiming that decides gold, but the capacity to be in sustained command of the emotional self and maintain a clinical focus.

Sports psychologist Tim Harkness—now working with Chelsea Football Club—wanted to discover all this, and so eventually did I.

Manisha Malhotra had met Harkness in South Africa in 2008. She called me. Meet him, she said, he fits your personality. I think she meant he was as single-minded as I was. Tim saw me as someone 'who can focus his own will'. He—both reassuringly calm and usefully articulate—understood: inessentials didn't interest me, not what I ate for dinner, not whether I sat in the front or back of a car. But if it was relevant to shooting, I was driven. Once, we sat across each other and for two-and-a-half hours just talked about focus. Nothing else.

A year later, in 2009, through Tim, I got a chance to visit Chelsea football club's training facility at Cobham, Surrey in England, replete with a Mind Room and sports science labs. Its gleaming facilities were only out-dazzled by the Bentleys and Lamborghinis parked within. Never, ever, have I seen such a parking lot. In the cafe, striker Didier Drogba sat close by and when it was mentioned I used neuro-feedback, he asked: 'Did it work?' I replied that I liked to think it did.

But to rewind, it was February of the Olympic year when I first met Tim, and by then I was a different Olympian. If it was Athens 2004, I would have refused Tim access, been too finicky to allow anything to distract me so close to a Games. But by Beijing 2008 I had learnt flexibility. If it helps, try it now.

Winning was all I thought about.

Durban had no shooting range we could use. So we improvised. An electronic target system was brought in from Germany and a rudimentary range set up in the basement of Tim's mother's house.

I was intrigued by neuro-feedback. If I was partly an adventuring boy, I was mostly an adult competitor who saw sport as a complex activity. A trigger was to be pulled but also felt, sport to be played but also understood.

In his book, *Half a Life*, V.S. Naipaul conveys some of what I feel when he wrote of being 'entranced' when he first looked down the barrel of a gun with his finger on the trigger:

> *It seemed to me the most private, the most intense moment of conversation with oneself, so to speak, with that split-second of right decision coming and going all the time, almost answering the movements of one's mind...*

I needed to examine this universe from every angle and Tim was my latest guide. To understand briefly in theory what we were attempting, I need to borrow some lines from one of his papers:

> *Psykinetic training uses a neuro-imaging technique called electroencephalography (EEG). It works on the principle that when your brain works, it emits small electrical frequencies. The harder it works, the higher the frequency it emits. By attaching sensors to the scalp we can monitor which parts of the brain are more active than others. Because we know what brain regions an athlete should be using (and not using) to fire a shot, we can use EEG to train the athlete to get into the right mental state to shoot. But the body needs to be tuned also. By using sensors to monitor muscle tension, skin conductivity and the link between heart rate and breathing, we can tell when you are in the right psycho-physiological state, and also train you to achieve this state at will.*

So, first, we enter my lungs and the heart. Sensors are attached to chest and abdomen and we listen into, and calculate, the most basic of human functions.

Breathing.

Try this. Borrow your granddad's walking stick and fit it to your shoulder. Think of a pea-sized bullseye you need to hit. Think of a medal on the line. Think your parents are watching with fingers crossed. Think that this chance you have, it comes again only four years later.

Then look, damn, your hand is trembling. Because your heart rate has accelerated, your breathing is erratic.

There is a fine connection between mind and body I am looking for. If I find the perfect synchronization between heartbeat and breathing, a state of calm arrives. I am not a footballer, I don't want reactive muscles, I don't want adrenaline produced, I don't want to activate my sympathetic nervous system, which creates arousal. I want to be in parasympathetic state, a more placid frame of mind, I need to control my heart rate through my breathing. If I can do so, I shoot a 10; if I can't, it's a 9.

So I am trying to breathe from a particular place. Not from my chest, not in a shallow, stressed way, but from deep in my abdomen, slowly, relaxed. Yogi with a gun. My respiratory rate prior to the Olympics was fourteen to fifteen cycles per minute, but I learn, slow down, slow down, and by the time I get to Beijing it is down to four to five cycles per minute. I need this because if the mind is going damn, damn, damn, the heart races, the breath turns ragged. I need to be stable, to hold my breath, stay calm, trigger.

Then we turn to my skin, which tells so many tales. Anxiety is always hovering and its calling card is sweat. The negative thought has a physical response on the skin, and it is so subtle it doesn't always register with me. But it does on a machine. So as I shoot, with sensors attached to my fingertips to measure sweat, I stay focused on a graph on the computer. The calmer

I am, the steadier the line. When I shot a 10.8 in the final shot in Beijing, Tim thought to himself, 'He must have done it with an icy finger.'

I have to remember this feeling from practice in Durban, replicate it, store it in a cabinet in the memory. Once I hook myself up to the sensors and watch a DVD of myself at the World Championship final in Zagreb in 2006. I see myself shooting a 9 and my parameters go haywire. This won't do, I need a constancy, an emotional control, where I can watch disaster and not be affected. I am trying to tune that impossibly un-tuneable instrument: the brain.

Every day we slog. Even Tim, a respecter of work ethic, is gently taken aback when I shoot eight hours straight till I run out of pellets. It leads to an interesting moment.

Tim ruffles through the Yellow Pages in Durban and discovers a shop that sells pellets. Off we go. The shop owner has advertised himself as a specialist in air rifle. He does not recognize me, the World Champion. This is hardly a big deal, maybe I am not photogenic. Anyway who keeps shooters pasted on their walls like kids do footballers? But it particularly amuses Tim.

It gets better and funnier. The owner begins, kindly but grandly, to offer me advice on shooting. When I ask for the expensive pellets, he suggests the cheaper ones. Presumably, the finer ones will be wasted on a shooting hick like me.

Then the owner asks me: 'Do you compete?'

I say: 'Yes.'

Whereupon, he asks: 'Where?'

Even though, right then, I can put him in his place by saying the Olympics and World Cups, there would be a certain hubris to it.

So I just say: 'I compete at home.'

This moment of levity done, we return, we load, we fire, we test.

Right up to the Olympics, I will carry a four-channel EEG (electroencephalography) machine with me. In the mornings I will test my skin, measure my breathing, try to find an athletic nirvana before going to shoot. In South Africa, during the testing of my brain, the machine is more sophisticated. It is a twelve-channel EEG contraption at the Sports Science Centre at the University of Cape Town. I am entangled in cables and compete against a few South African shooters. Machines blink, but I don't.

The brain's left side (T3 or Broca's Area) is responsible for generating language, from within it emerge the conversations that rattle through our head.

Am I ready?

Should I fire?

When I shoot very well, Tim can see evidence on the screen. My brain is quiet, relaxed, not lit up like a tree at Christmas. I am in an Alpha state and I need to keep rediscovering it for it shuts down Broca's Area, it stifles chat. It is a fragile state. Once, before I shoot, I find I have an Alpha drop and shoot a 9. Translated into English this means a prattling has resumed in my head, it means my triggering has been a very conscious attempt, not instinctive or from deep within.

So I return to Durban and practice, again and again, literally wired for greatness. If I achieve the right state of mind, I get a beep from the machine; if there is chatter in my head there is no beep. I want to be concentrated, pure, but the mind travels, it is filled with voices, and I need to silence them and fall into a trance. I am tuned to my body, to the point where Tim, generously, wrote of me in one of his papers: 'Abhinav has the best self-awareness of any athlete that I have worked with.'

It is not easy. As I quieten this one area of my brain, I must keep another part alert. The sensorimotor cortex, like a strap across the top of my brain, is responsible for my balance, for my gentle, precise act of aiming. It is the area that determines fine motor skills, like triggering, where my brain is allowing my finger to perform an act of delicacy usually associated with surgeons.

It is fascinating because I have to train both parts of the brain simultaneously, to be aware (motor skills) yet calm (no talking). I have to give my mind and body the best possible opportunity to execute a trained skill. Nothing must affect me, no thought must invade my consciousness, not about dinner, nerves, girls, medal. I train myself to make slow movements. Pick up the rifle slowly, load pellet slowly. In training I'd practise by looking at the monitor and only when I got to the right state did I pick up my rifle.

Tim is a considerate, patient teacher. He is attempting to transport me into a very precise mental state. If I'm not relaxed, I can't focus; if I'm not focused, I can't relax. However, he can't just order me to be relaxed, the brain does not simply obey commands; neither can he feel what I feel. But the machine is his ally, his investigator, he can measure my brain activity—and thus what I feel—through neuro-feedback.

Occasionally, tension is written on an athlete's face, a furrowed forehead, a taut look, a grimace. We can see it though the athlete himself is unaware of this delicate tension within. But the machine reads it, it provides me information, it assists me. One might say, Tim is not telling me what to do, he is in fact training me how to do it.

Neuro-feedback has a powerful effect. I start shooting unbelievably, not just the numbers (which were 600s), but the quality. I can feel the purity of my shooting. But I am nervous, I want to replicate in competition what I have learnt, but anxiety comes in the way. In Nanjing, in April 2008 at the Asian Championships, and then at the Beijing World Cup test event, Tim arrives and we train in the room, fine-tuning the mind. I shoot 592 at the Asian Championships and it is deflating. But it gets better, my routines are strong, and in the Beijing World Cup I rebound with a 595.

Tim, meanwhile, is still attempting to see how I function under stress. Sport is not a completely cordoned off world; even in shooting there is the murmur of talking, shifting, moving, phones, coughing. Distraction is inevitable, handling it is crucial. When Tiger Woods putted as a young fellow, his father would rattle change in his pocket. Tim makes that distraction look tame, he will stop at nothing to examine my focus.

He constructs a pulley so that suddenly, in my line of vision, a flag pops up. He shakes rattles as I shoot. He and trainer Heath Mathews stand inches away from me and shout 'miss, miss, miss'. They mock me, tease me, but the harder they sledge, the better I shoot. In Beijing, a few months later, when my sight went awry just before the final, Tim thought it was a 'massive favour'. It challenged me to perform under pressure. Or as he put it, 'Abhi's not a person to mess with.'

Not everyone believed in all this. Uwe used to occasionally watch from the sidelines and laugh. 'All shit,' he told me.

But I thought neuro-feedback was a fantastic tool, especially when my form began to splutter. It was terrific at bringing back a shooter's focus. But it's best to train on it, learn, and then forget. In competition, you're never going to be in complete control, suffering will never cease. Essentially, you have to call on courage because you are not a machine and you can't behave like one.

Or to put it another way, the machine will help you, it can't do it for you.

17

BEIJING: MISSION POSSIBLE

a) Leap of Faith

Discovery arrives in the strangest places. On the afternoon of 25 July 2008, I knew I could win gold in Beijing. I knew this while standing alone, at the top of a 40-foot pole in Munich, harassed by the wind and assaulted by fear. I knew because I had taken a leap of faith.

Shooters aren't usually found standing on poles. Blame it on Uwe and me. There's nothing weird we won't try. When I arrived in Munich, my technique had been polished by Gaby and Heinz. Yet preparation can never be enough, not with me.

So Uwe asked: 'What do you want to do?'

He understood the pressure that I was facing from back home as the Olympics approached. He also wanted me to understand that Olympic finals are won on technique yet also guts.

Because Uwe had been a commando once, he suggested commando training a week before I left for Beijing. I jumped at it. The only way to handle fear is to confront it. Uwe had taken a Brunei prince for jungle training with the Gorkhas and into the Arctic region as part of his grooming as a shotgun champion! His madness was not without method: he believed that when you had everything in life, you needed that extra challenge to 'go for it'.

I said, don't tell my parents. Eventually we decided to keep the information from my mother till the training was over. She would have killed him. My dad threatened to. He was concerned, but he put the responsibility on Uwe.

'If he fails,' he told Uwe, 'I will chop off your head.'

Dad was simple and straightforward: 'You take the responsibility and you take the risk.' Uwe grinned. My father and he were great friends, chatting for hours on the phone, two men operating on precisely the same wavelength.

Always the manipulator, Uwe brought his two sons along for the commando course. They were younger than me and he was using them to tease me. In effect, he was saying: the kids are here, Abhinav, there's no room for cold feet, no chance of backing out. Ironically, the only one taken aback initially was the commando trainer. He was probably used to testing the physical reserves of rugged hockey players, but a five-foot-eight-inch, not-quite-athletic-looking shooter?

Nonplussed, he took one look at me and then told Uwe: 'Oh, Jesus Christ, the guy is going for the Olympics. We have to be careful.'

'Careful?' said Uwe, 'forget it. No, push him, till he cries. Just make sure that no physical harm comes to him. I mean, that is clear. I need him in a week's time. He has to compete in the Olympics. I can't have him limping around.'

So I started. I walked a log of wood across a 50-60-foot divide. I walked a Burma Bridge, which is essentially a thick rope bridge that constantly sways. This one was 60 feet high. Panic nestled close by. The safety wires I was always attached to bring only faint reassurance.

I clambered up a rock-climbing wall, holds embedded in it, about 42 feet high. First time, I was scared. Second time, Uwe blindfolded me and sent me up again. I had a safety harness, but I thought he was insane. Yet he was smart, it was actually easier, I was more confident, less reliant on the people around me, more trusting simply of my senses. Touch, feel, hold, pull. It's what he liked to break shooting into: live or die.

And then came the pizza pole, fitted with steel rungs like on some telephone poles. It was 40 feet high, at the edge of a pool, and the higher it went the smaller it became. The top of the pole was tiny, the size of a pizza, hence the name. Uwe's sons clambered on top, the younger boy with a monkey's ease and elegance, the older son more carefully because he was bigger. They made it look simple, but it wasn't. Every rung I climbed, the wind buffeting me from the nearby sea, the harder it got. A crowd gathered. An interesting one. The more a climber shakes, the more they cheer you.

Halfway up, I said, no, enough, I can't. Fear had me by the throat, nerves had me by the collar. I yelled 'down', the crowd insisted 'up, up'.

The legs freeze, the mind quits. To just put one foot onto a higher rung, to lift, to pull, each step taking me further away from the ground that is our comfort zone, requires an enormous leap of faith. It is a leap of discovery, for it helps you locate physical and mental reserves you weren't sure you owned. It is not so much a conquering of the self as a journey to the limits of yourself.

As an athlete I understood this moment—it was simply a pressure to perform. Halfway up, Uwe told me, if you retreat, you will not forget this day because you will be a coward; if you continue, you will not forget this day because you have proved that you are your own hero. He was reminding me of the inner man that emerges during a final, when the competition is taut, when a voice asks inside you: what do you want to be today?

A hero?

Then go for it.

At three stories high, the last part of the pole is the most testing. It takes some manoeuvring to clamber onto this plate-sized surface, the wind whistling, the earth distant below, balance hard to come. Yet when I stood there, trembling, tanned face as white as a sheet of paper, Uwe knew, and so did I, that he had pushed me almost to my limit. And it wasn't over yet. Now I had to step off the pole into thin air. Just trust the wires.

For Uwe, this was a perfect lesson, stress managed without thinking. In sport, he insisted, you have to react immediately, intuitively, like a commando faced with a decision. In the Olympic final, when the last shot is called in a final, you have to just go, you just rely on your skills, you just shoot that 10.5 that is required. Think of the 10.5, dwell on it, and you lose. So I didn't think too long, I stepped off the pizza pole and felt serene and victorious.

Winning a medal, I told myself, cannot be tougher than this, it cannot be scarier.

That night in Munich, when Uwe dropped me back at my hotel, I said: 'This has been one of the best days of my life.'

He told me, write that down. Inscribe it in your mind. He prepared a worksheet for me with some pictures of my climb. He asked me to keep it in my pocket. When I ran into trouble, I had to take the piece of paper out and look at it.

A week later, I arrived in Beijing without fear. Faith was always an issue with me, but I had taken the leap I needed to find faith. On the day of the final, I thought back to Munich, to the pole, to that moment.

I wasn't sure I was going to win. But I knew I had the reserves needed to win because I had reached deep into myself and found them.

b) A Last Beer

It takes nothing to lose gold. A sudden spike in heart rate. A flickering loss of concentration. In Athens 2004, the brilliant American Matthew Emmons is leading the 50-metre three-position final. He's so far ahead he needs only an 8 to win gold on his last shot.

An 8! He could do it blindfolded and drunk and standing on his head.

But he goes from first to eighth in his last shot even though he shoots an 8.1. Because he shoots the wrong target. Someone else's target, just by aligning his rifle incorrectly. It happens, anything can happen.

So before Uwe, before I ascend the pole in Munich, I go over every detail, examine every possible eventuality, with Gaby and Heinz in Dortmund. I am living in their house and there are only two subjects of conversation:

Beijing and Athens.

What was, what will be?

Gaby, Heinz and I do one session a day in Dortmund. One long one. Ammunition is tested. Weighed. My scores are so strong, perfect 400s, perfect 600s, deep 10s like 10.5, that I paste a sign on the box of Chinese ammunition I am shooting with.

The sign reads 'Olympic final, Beijing.'

There is a tranquillity to my days. We sit in coffee shops on chattering sidewalks and discuss the world. Athens isn't put away in some box, it's taken out, put on the table. I knew that if I ever got to the Beijing final, Athens would come back, stare at me from the past. Better to acknowledge it now, than get rattled then.

We sit and manufacture exhaustive lists:

Which days to train in Beijing?

How many shots precisely will we fire on training days?

Which days will I play badminton?

Really.

I am like a method actor polishing my craft before a Broadway opening. I even practise how to walk into a range. In Athens, my arms are crossed, it is a defensive stance. I need to be open, absent of tension. I also have to walk to the final area in my ankle-high boots. It is a short walk but the boots tend to loosen up. So I practise tying my laces tighter so they stay snug. Nothing goes unnoticed.

We practise time pressure, firing ten shots in three minutes, just to see if I can manage the strain and find my balance and mindset fast. Heinz changes the sights on my rifle and simulates a final situation where I have to react quickly. Every surprise, if such a thing is possible, is being catered for. Dortmund becomes Beijing as Gaby holds 'finals' for me in the range. Announcements are made on the speaker like at a tournament. A mock introduction of shooters is done. At these fake finals, I shoot from every possible shooting point, one to eight. Before the last shot she distracts me: 'You're tied for the lead with someone else.' Four-five times she does this, demanding I shoot my best on my last shot. I love her for this because in Beijing it is exactly what happens.

Finally, they ask me: 'What do you wish to find in Beijing?'

I reply: 'I don't want to suffer.'

But they know, in shooting, suffering lines the insides of the sport. It is beyond escape. So a motto is prepared for Beijing. It is simple: 'Be ready to suffer.'

By the time I go to Uwe, I don't really need heavy practice. It's why we do the pole and go hiking in the Bavarian Alps. I do float therapy in Samadhi Tanks in Munich and take a 45-minute ride to the range. This is practice, too, for it takes precisely that much time to journey from village to range in Beijing. Everywhere, I am building a routine. Finally, there is one last thing I am practising—my favourite words in German.

Ein Grosse Bier Bitte. One Large Beer Please.

c) Time to Panic

It is 2 August, I am in Beijing. I am ready, I am hungry. I haven't won a World Cup all year, partially by design. In the Beijing World Cup, I shot a 9, deliberately, just to miss the final. It is not as absurd as it sounds. Some athletes want to arrive at a Games on the wings of victory, sharp with confidence. But not me. I want to shoot well at warm-up tournaments, but not win, to be in form but not satiated. I am playing games with my ego, dangerous games. I know how I react when I win, it makes me defensive, it brings expectation. For me to win in Beijing I need to be a wolf, hungry and on the hunt. It's a risk but it's like I'm storing all my desire for this moment.

In Beijing, I start cutting myself off. I sit in the final hall and try to feel the moment. I can't sleep and go and see the doctor attached to the Indian team, a sweet lady called Dr Sarla. Instead of giving me the sleeping pills I want, she tells me to go and meditate. So I go to the Italians and get pills from them! Next day I shoot thirty shots. Every one of them is a 10.

Opening ceremonies bring a colourful energy to an Olympics, but they also squeeze the energy out of you with all the waiting and walking involved. I attended in Sydney and it was enough. In Sydney, I felt honoured to be part of the 10,000-club, for only that many of the planet's over 6 billion people can be called an Olympian at one time. But my ambitions have altered since; now I need to be among the best of those 10,000. On one of my first days, as I exited the Village, a swimmer entered, gold medal around her neck. 'I want one' was all I could think.

A mail clinks into my Inbox from Tim Harkness, and it contains the positivity I need:

Hi Abhinav,
I just wanted to wish you all the best for tomorrow. As I have said to you before, I believe that your dedication and professionalism—the most important personality traits—leave you with nothing left to prove to anyone, including yourself. You have already achieved what really matters. Now all that remains is the shooting.
Tim

I hang out with trap shooter Mansher Singh and we hone our hand-eye expertise at video-game terminals. The Indian flag is hoisted in the Village, a tradition that produces an impromptu athletic moment from Suresh Kalmadi, the head of the Indian Olympic Association. When he realizes Sonia Gandhi has arrived at a different gate, he sprints there, in his suit and flapping tie, in impressive fashion. My parents haven't come. Despite early reminders to the IOA for hotel rooms, no reply arrived, but friends agreed to give them theirs. Then the IOA sent them tickets for the shooting: they were for the 14th; I was competing on the 11th. They stayed home.

I was calm, very calm, and a later reading of my blog from the Games surprised even me:

> *Instead of thinking about shooting perfect bullseyes... today I am going to think of the pretty women in the village, the weather, the great city of Beijing, and whatever else pops into my mind will be allowed to stay as long as it doesn't involve the words "rifle" and "shooting" in it. Hey all, it is a great time to be an athlete and this event is what we all live for.*

My serenity was rattling Gaby, it unnerved her, and she called Heinz and complained: 'He's too calm, he's too calm.' Heinz attempted to placate her: 'Relax, he's ready.'

She remained unconvinced and took a deliberate decision to scare me, to inject some panic into my system. It isn't illogical. Panic is never far away. No one wants a visit from it during the event, so earlier is better. So Gaby and I face each other, and she speaks like a counsellor:

'Abi, you realize tomorrow is the Olympics. All the work you put in depends on what you do tomorrow. It is judgment day.'

It's like she has flicked a switch in my being and a chemical reaction explodes in my brain and my body undergoes a rapid physiological alteration. On my neuro-feedback machine, my skin temperature readings would have gone berserk. I am suddenly seized by the enormity of what confronts me, this mission whose worth will be evaluated tomorrow. Butterflies tango in my stomach.

The answer is a McDonalds meal and a long walk. I am too wired to sleep, but then I've already practised going without sleep. I stand in my balcony at 3 am and look out into the dark nothingness, another athlete swallowing his fear in this dormitory of the strange and the gifted. But fear is not all I swallow. In Munich, before the Olympics, I was clearing out of my hotel room when I halted inexplicably at the mini-bar. I am not a drinker, yet I seized a miniature bottle of Jack Daniels. It was utterly out of character. Perhaps in a hideway of my mind I felt the pressure of the Olympics, as if a nervous breakdown was imminent, and I carried it with me. Now, on this sleepless night, I retrieve it from my toilet kit, I twist it open, empty it into my nervous stomach. As if it is an antidote to everything that assails me.

I sleep for an hour towards dawn and I awake fine, ready, rested. 'Have a good one,' David Johnson, the US rifle coach, tells me. Breakfast stays down, so it might just be a good day.

d) Goodbye Athens, Hello Gold

I envy cricketers standing in the midst of Eden Gardens, surrounded by a collective of 100,000 fans, heaving like one worshipful beast. My name has never been chanted, it never will be. I shoot in the sporting equivalent of an antiseptic waiting room, in front of family—if they're there—and a few fans. But Beijing is different, this is Zhu Qinan country, he is the defending champion, and a crowd has gathered.

I shoot next to him, but we don't see each other, we're about four to five feet apart but on separate planets.

Gaby is busy with another shooter, an Italian, so for the qualification phase Maik Eckhardt, a fellow shooter with whom I have often trained, is my coach for the day. My first shot in qualifying is a 10.9. Perfection. In the middle of the centre of the target. But this is qualifying, it only counted as a 10, yet psychologically it has a greater effect.

My first ten shots are worth a 100, then 99, a 100, 98, 100, 99, but by the end I am struggling.

'I'm losing it,' I mutter, and Maik reacts anxiously for he mishears me.

'No, no, you are not losing. You are second or something.'

But my feel is slipping away, my technique is edgy, and an error now is unaffordable. I become mechanical, like a mathematician going through his formula, yet I make a mistake. I get too aggressive, my last shot is a 9. It does not cost me my qualification for the final.

Laszlo and Gagan, who finish quickly, are standing behind me, shooters eyeing the shooter. I am conscious of them but undisturbed. I shoot a 596, Gagan a 595, I make the final and he doesn't. One lousy point after four years can break your resolute heart.

I am fourth after qualifying. Henri Hakkinen from Finland at 598 is first, then defending Olympic champion Zhu Qinan at 597, then Alin George Moldoveanu and me at 596.

I am also annoyed. Unlike the World Cup final, where four hours separate the qualifying round from the final, here the gap is 30 minutes to suit the telecast. Just half an hour to tune your mind to the next mission. But a Doordarshan crew, with no sense of place, no concept of sport, wants an interview. *Forget it, I growl.*

'Now the shit starts again,' I laconically tell Maik. He looks unimpressed by such idle chit-chat, he doesn't want a joke to release the tension.

'Got a job to do,' he grunts.

Amit comes to chat; Gaby, back with me for the final after her shooter doesn't qualify, wants a smoke. An edginess starts to build. Amit says my eyes are bright, not dull like in Athens. Competition is beautiful, you're in it, involved, on a high, it's the waiting that gnaws at the nerves. The guns are being checked again for legality. They can only weigh 5.5 kilograms, not more. You can't have a magnifier on your sight. The jacket can't be too stiff.

'Check the pellets,' Gaby says.

Done. In my pocket.

'Check the equipment.'

Jacket, trousers, eye glasses.

But no glove.

Everything takes on a slight hysteria at these times, as if time is fleeing. Frantically I dig, search, unearth, toss, where? Two searches later, it's there, in the ammo box.

Phew.

Gaby has been talking to me as if I have already won. How the ceremony would go, the drug tests, the press conference, not being presumptuous but preparing my mind for success. The last thing she says is like a mantra, a prayer, a reminder of why I am here, of who I am. After Athens, she was afraid I would take that trauma into every other final, so she pushed me constantly to be aggressive. Now, she says:

'Ok, Abi, I just want you to think for a minute about Athens, how they had stolen your medal. But for that stupid floor, you would have won a medal there. So stay aggressive, from first shot to last.'

I have five minutes of sighting time. And then, right then, in the final, disaster strikes with no prelude.

My gun is supposed to be ready, aligned, sights fixed. Except my first sighting shot, like a warm-up, is a 4.

A 4?

In the white of the target?

I shoot another.

4.2.

I am stunned I haven't shot a 4 since I was thirteen years old.

I look at Gaby, what is this? It should have been 10s.

A sighting shot is just a routine check, it usually requires only a marginal adjusting of the sights. This was like Rafael Nadal finding his gut tension was ten pounds off, when one pound is enough for a racket change.

I believe someone fiddled with my gun when it was left alone in the preparation area. Conspiracies don't attract me, but a sight cannot shift so much, or go so haywire, on its own. Gaby doesn't agree, she thinks on the walk up a narrow staircase, or in the crowded changing area, the sight was accidentally knocked. But that is irrelevant right now, I am adjusting my sight frantically, clicking away furiously.

Every click adjusts the gun sight, either .1 mm higher or lower, either .1 mm left or right. Usually you need two to four clicks to get your gun perfectly set. I need forty to align it that day.

Maybe something is broken. Maybe this is some deathly deja vu, maybe I have offended some Olympic God. Gaby can't speak, she, too, is thinking: 'God, not again. It cannot be this trauma again?' But she doesn't panic. She's been a shooter for twenty years, she understands the value of a competitor knowing he has a cool coach behind him. She opens her scope and studies the target. Is the target Ok? She speaks to the technical people, sitting beside her, who are in charge of the scoring system. They check. It's fine. She thinks that I look in control. She is relieved.

Moldoveanu, my fellow shooter standing next to me, can see what is transpiring. Later, I hear he thought: it's over for the Indian. One person less.

Tick, tick, tick. Thirty seconds left for the start.

My last sighting shot before the final is a 9.2. It goes high. I do some rapid math, calculate how much I have to click, do five or six of them, and tell myself: *it's too late, now just execute.*

My first shot of the final is a 10.7. I laugh inside.

Suddenly, wonderfully, I am in a perfect zone of calm, stability, balance, breathing. Panic is uninvited. This is who I am now, a child of competitive DNA, a product of neuro-feedback and commando training, a confection of practice, experimentation, courage, desire, will, luck, Gaby, Heinz.

Every drop of sweat shed, every trick tried, every pellet examined, every technical correction made, all of it has come together. I am shooting like a machine, shooting like a man in training. From the time my head tilts down for each shot, Gaby starts counting the seconds. Everytime I fire after precisely the same period. This was rhythm from a dream.

My next six shots are strong.

10.3.

10.4.

10.5.

10.5.

10.5.

10.6.

Gradually, I begin to move in on the leaders. Decimal point after decimal point, shot after shot.

Of course, I do not know this. I can see my score on the monitor before me. But the main scoreboard is behind me.

After the first shot, the 10.7, the standings are:

Hakkinen 608.1.

Zhu 607.2.

Bindra 606.7.

After the third shot, I have already crept into second place:

Hakkinen 628.8

Bindra 627.4.

Zhu 627.1.

After the fourth shot, I am closer:

Hakkinen 638.8.

Bindra 637.9.

Zhu 637.3.

After the seventh shot, I am in the lead:

Bindra 669.5.

Hakkinen 669.3.

Zhu 668.2.

Boxing hurts, you can see it, the geography of sweaty faces rearranged for a terrible millisecond as glove meets flesh, sweat flying like some painful rain. But shooting hurts, too, only it's invisible, like some internal medieval torture to the mind.

The anxiety about a mistake is like a scream building inside you, but you cannot let it out, you just stand there like some unmoved monk. It's unnatural. But the man whose control of emotion is the steadiest, the competitor who doesn't let disappointment leak into his breathing has the advantage.

I was in control. But for a second I allowed myself to realize I had a chance to win the Olympics. My scores were telling me I was close. I had to be close. A few minutes ago my rifle was faulty, I had nothing to lose. Now I was possibly the favourite, I had an Olympic gold to lose.

I couldn't see the scoreboard, it was behind me, but I kept at it.

I was digging and everything was put aside—life, medal, family, feeling—trying to find the discipline where the only words that echoed in my mind were 'Next shot, Next shot, Next shot.'

Then, suddenly, in the eighth shot, just a 10.0, like ice water on the face.

Hakkinen was now only .1 behind.

Then, in my ninth shot, I produced a 10.2 and Hakkinen and I were tied.

Posing for an advertisement for Walther, the gun company that has supported me as a shooter for 14 years.

At the 2000 Sydney Olympics, my first, where I was perhaps the youngest shooter in the fray at age 18. This is where I got the belief that I was good enough to compete at the highest level. With me in the picture are my mom (extreme left), Indian coach Laszlo Szucsak (middle), sister Divya (extreme right) and shooter Anjali Bhagwat.

Being crowned the world champion in Zagreb in 2006 was actually a more emotional moment for me than the Beijing Olympic victory in 2008. It was a moment of redemption for me after the defeat in Athens in 2004.

Facing page: In the finals I beat Alin George Moldoveanu of Romania (left) and Zhu Qinan of China (right).

PHOTOGRAPHS BY MIKE HECKER

Beijing Olympics final 2008. I am struck by panic (*below*) as I score a 4 in my sighting shot. I look back at Gaby with anxiety – is my gun broken? Do I need to tighten the screws? All this just 3 to 4 minutes before the final was to start!

Bottom: Relief after hitting a 10.8 in the last shot. I am happy that I have shot well, but I still don't know I have won.

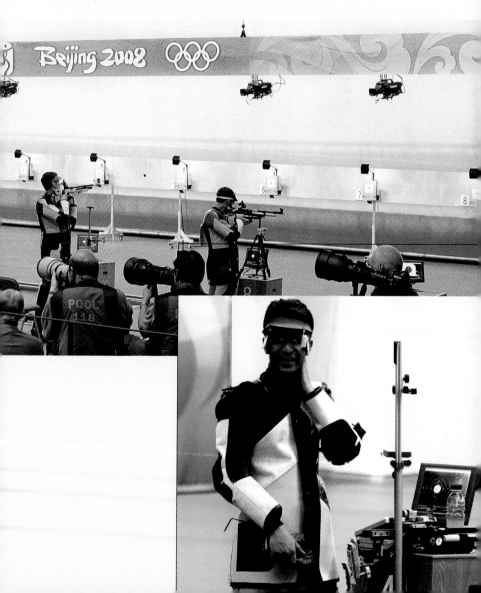

Facing page: Ever since I was a child, I had dreamt of being on the Olympic podium…and when the moment came in Beijing in 2008, I experienced a feeling of great accomplishment.

Below: I beat Zhu Qinan of China (*left*) and Henri Hakkinen of Finland (*right*) to take gold.

COMRADES IN ARMS: *Top*: I still don't know I have won gold medal as Gaby hugs me; I am just happy with the quality of my shooting.
Then Gaby does a thumbs up (*above*), and I realize I have won gold.

Below: Being congratulated by chief Indian coach Sunny Thomas, who has been a supportive figure and who has held the Indian shooting team together for a couple of decades.

Bottom: With Manisha Malhotra, administrator of Mittal Champions Trust, who believed in me when I didn't.

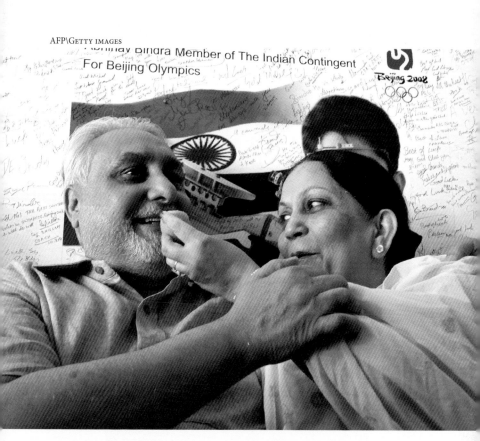

AFP\Getty images

Abhinav Bindra Member of The Indian Contingent
For Beijing Olympics

Beijing 2008

Above: It's time for laddoos as about 600 mediapersons and well-wishers descend on my house in Chandigarh on hearing the news of my win in Beijing.

With my parents (*facing page, top*) and sister (*facing page, left*) at Delhi airport on arrival from Beijing. It is obvious from their expressions how much the gold medal meant to them.

Calling on Congress president Sonia Gandhi (*above*) and President Pratibha Patil (*below*) after the Beijing win.

Right: Starting the baton run at the launch of the 2010 Commonwealth Games Queen's Baton Relay at Buckingham Palace in London.

Below: A moment of honour for me as I lead the Indian squad at the opening ceremony of the 2010 Commonwealth Games.

Above: Receiving the Padma Bhushan from President Pratibha Patil in 2009.

Facing page: Winning the gold in men's pairs 10-metre air-rifle shooting at the 2010 Commonwealth Games, with Gagan Narang, a fine competitor and a good shooter with whom I get along quite well.

An exhilarating moment as I get to fly in a US F16 IN Super Viper at the Bangalore air show in 2009.

About 3700 kilometres away, my family was praying. My sister, in Delhi, had spoken to me the night before. More a case of me saying, 'I'm sleeping, no talking.' Then she went to the temple. In Chandigarh, morning had just broken as my mother kept a cellphone to her ear and listened to a friend relay the scores of my qualification and texted them to my sister. The qualifying round wasn't shown on television, only the final was, so she listened, fingers and toes crossed, as she likes to say. My father had gone to ten gurdwaras the previous day. He dreamed I was standing on the podium; my mother always maintained I would win India's first gold.

Mother's instinct, she said. Who dared argue?

But I was somewhere else, in this place of reckoning that athletes eventually come to. This brilliant, terrifying place which you dream of on so many nights. A place where greatness hinges on a single shot, gold on one pull of the finger. A man alone with his future.

I picked up my rifle for one last time, looked at the sight, was aiming slightly to the left, corrected myself and pulled the trigger. Just touched it really. It was over fast. A few seconds. And it was as close to perfect as you can get.

10.8

I shouted when I saw the score on my monitor before me. I pumped my fist at the score, not victory, because it hadn't come yet. Hakkinen shot seconds later and had a 9.7.

But had I won? In my mind this wasn't clear. Gaby flashed me a 'thumbs up' for victory, but I misunderstood. I thought she meant a medal. When she hugged me, I was still asking, 'Did I win?' I couldn't see the main scoreboard, I was almost too scared to see the scoreboard. I desperately wanted that effort to be good enough for gold because I couldn't go deeper.

Then she said: Yes. Gold.

I laughed, and Gaby said, 'You're done with shooting. You've killed me, you've killed yourself.'

In Delhi, my sister wept. In Chandigarh, my mother had already sent someone to the mithai shop, but scared of jinxing me, had instructed him not to buy till she called after the final. I won, she ordered two kilograms of ladoos. The media poured in, eventually she needed 60 kilograms. In Beijing, relief flooded my brain. It's the first emotion that releases as four years of investment have been validated. Then exhaustion settles in the bones, satisfaction embraces you and for a second even ecstasy comes. Athletes are greedy, winning itself can be insufficient, how you win also matters. Because what we chase in our imaginations is an ideal, the notion of being your very best against the very best at your sport's very best moment.

Now I had won India's first individual Olympic gold *with the highest score ever in an Olympic final.* Dear God.

Later, I'd get a film of my performance from Germany and watch it, again and again. Every night, for seven or eight days, alone in my room. Like a boxer reviewing a fight. I guess I wanted to get a kick out of it. Damn it, done it. But there was no exhilaration, no pounding of the bed in delight. Yet it was not without pleasure. Those ten shots, they were magical. Stability, timing, execution, they were the best shots of my life. As I lay there, I knew: I could not shoot better.

Back at the stadium, people complained I didn't smile enough. Didn't leap in the air. Beat my chest. Collapse into sniffles. In fact, I did smile, I even looked at the video later to check if I did. But I had to wait for the judge to say it's over, there's no tie, no shoot-off, it's done. Till then, I needed concentration, not celebration. But even then, this is shooting, a hypnotic activity. When you finish, it's akin to exiting a trance and you take a while to adjust to the surroundings.

But winning is also a complicated feeling. At my first Olympics, in Sydney in 2000, I was entranced by victory ceremonies. The first one I saw was American Nancy Johnson's, after she won the air-rifle event, and the entire ritual and embroidery of triumph—the music, the flags, the anthems, the medals—was engraved in my mind. I felt something, almost an ecstasy. So I attended every victory ceremony at the shooting in 2000, imagining myself on the podium, how I might feel, holding close this fantasy.

As a kid, like so many others, I actually practised for these moments. I'd sit in my range at my home, in a small piece of shade reserved for dreaming boys, and construct celebrations in my mind. *Abhinav Bindra, Olympic Champion, World Champion:* it sounded as unbelievable as it was cool. In my boyish imagination I was jumping, yelling, and the mere creation of these fantasies brought me goosebumps. But my personality isn't really like that. I'm not a yeller, not a jumper. And this is shooting, dudes, not a World Cup-winning goal scored with a bicycle kick in the 89th minute.

In the Beijing hall, I felt a powerful peace. My hand was being shaken, my name said, the world was a daze. 'Olympic champion' takes a long while to become and it takes a while to wear as well. When it was my turn to ascend the podium, I didn't wait for the announcer to say my name. The moment he said 'India,' I walked on.

I felt the medal, it was heavy; I heard the anthem, I posed. It was sweet. Nevertheless, it was a trifle ridiculous when a photographer yelled, 'Start crying.' Just a reminder how staged sport can sometimes be. Later, a television reporter with no sense of sport or occasion, asked me: 'What are your plans for 2012?'

Who cared?

I jogged out of the stadium, wanting to keep on running, right out of Beijing. Just leave. I just wanted to move on. The journey was done. There was too much chaos and this wasn't my world. My world was the range, where the only sound was Gaby talking urgently and an air gun coughing out a pellet. When eventually a question did come, 'What do you want to do?', I replied, 'I want to go to the bathroom.' Really, I did. Then I wanted to faint. I took a taxi back to the Village with Mansher and even now he remembers me saying: 'What's the big deal, why are people going berserk?' I guess I hadn't understood what it meant for India.

Fabulous stories would be spun of my celebrations. That I downed fifteen vodka shots. I wish. That I took off my shirt and walked around Beijing bare-chested with my medal. Fortunately, that upsetting sight did not take place. My medal was in fact in my pocket and I dined quietly at the Peninsula Hotel with Manisha Malhotra, her mother, shooter Manavjit Sandhu and Amit. Then we retreated to a lounge, which brought a fleeting, sweet moment. Chinese television was showing the day's highlights and a waiter glanced up at the television, saw my face on it, looked back at me in front of him, and nearly dropped his tray.

Next day, the ambassador kindly brought me letters from dignitaries. The president was pleased, the prime minister was happy. Because of me? It was overwhelming. In a quiet moment, I flew back through time, wondering why it had taken so long for an Indian to win gold and hoping it would not take as long for another. Then I opened my phone.

Six hundred missed calls. I was famous.

And Athens was history.

18

THE DAYS AFTER

In a hotel in Bhopal, in a tidy room, on a neatly turned up bed, I finally fell apart. I just put my face in my hands and wept. My father gently left the room, it was the right and kind thing to do because I needed to be alone. I was swinging from euphoria to sadness. I was also overwhelmed, not so much by what I had done but by what I had become—even if temporarily—for people: this hero that I didn't recognize.

I was the boy who shot at paper targets under a tree, the man who wore a clumsy jacket, the competitor behind those complicated eye-glasses. I was a shooter, but a hero? Having roads named after me in Bhopal?

Coming home was intimidating, it was moving, new, amusing, exhilarating, draining, depressing. A shooter's solitary silent planet was turned on its head. For us, methodical, un-Stetsoned cowboys of an indoor range, a handful of spectators is akin to a crowd. We're just about sexier than lawn bowls competitors and they might even argue that. We're nobodies with little experience of how to handle fame. Now there were people at the Olympic Village turning me into the centre of attention because my face was on the front page of the *China*

Daily. Now there were crowds pushing to meet me at the airport in India. Now there were motorcycle-borne journalists chasing me home in Delhi late at night. I love cricketers, but they can keep this insane world of theirs.

From some angles, it was plain wonderful. In the days that followed, everyone wanted to see the medal.

Can we, they'd ask; *bhaisaheb please*, they'd politely request.

Touching it as if to confirm it was real; holding it just to see this foreign object that was tucked away only in the houses and bank vaults of distinguished hockey players; feeling it as if to understand why for so long we have clamoured for this small, spherical object.

The medal used to be in my mother's room. Now it's in a case with my Olympic bib (No. 1334) and score sheets in a room reserved for my trophies. People ask me if I like to touch the medal now and then. Not really. I went through the pain to get it, I won it, experienced it, felt the journey. The medal is for the moment, reward for two hours of shooting. But for the athlete it's not the moment of victory that matters, for it's taken him more than two hours. It's taken four years, probably eight, it's taken 250 international flights, 600 moments of 'I can't do this,' hundreds of technical changes, fifty tastes of defeat, four to five nervous vomits. It's taken internal struggle, psychology books, patient coaches. It's a dream taken and dipped into sweat to become reality. All that is more meaningful to the athlete.

On arriving in India, I realized swiftly how a life alters. You don't belong to yourself anymore, you stand for something, you become hope in jeans, an aspiration, you become that very Indian of things: the Chief Guest. All this at twenty-five years old. It makes you wonder how Boris Becker handled winning

Wimbledon as a teenager. As he was once quoted as saying:
'When you are thrown onto the stage at seventeen in such an
enormous way, it becomes living on the edge because every step
you take, every word you speak, every action you do, becomes
headline news. And it became, for me, life or death.'

My situation was not as dramatic, or excessive, but I quickly
understood I was not just a winner of a sports medal. Ordinary
folks were wonderfully gentle with me, inquisitive, proud,
affectionate. But for others my victory had morphed into some
massive public relations exercise that everyone wanted to be
a part of. I was both winner and actor at official functions,
smiling like a Miss World contestant and performing from a
tattered script: the happy, grateful hero in this new artificial
universe of constant applause.

It was dizzying, fun, harrowing, humbling. At the United
Nations, the Chinese premier gifted Prime Minister Manmohan
Singh a picture of me. When someone tells you this, you shake.
In Delhi, a politician told me, nicely, that a controversy was
building about his non-appearance at the airport on my arrival.
'Please say that you were happy with the welcome,' he pleaded.
I felt for him, for how does sport become this madness?

I began to see the Olympics differently. For me it had been
a goal, a challenge to see how far my talent stretched. Now I
began to understand its wider power, the effect a medal, *this
medal*, was having on people and my life. Walther, the legendary
gun manufacturer, presented me with a golden gun that really
shoots. Then the US ambassador invited me to take a ride with
a naval pilot in an F-16IN Super Viper. This is the adrenaline
equivalent of being asked to take Halle Berry out on a date
and the one word you don't say is 'No.'

Of all the toys that attract boys, fighter planes often come
first. Something about the flight suits, dark glasses, cocky

walk, sheer speed (yes, I know, too much *Top Gun*-watching) confirms our sense of masculinity and is seductive. I wasn't disappointed.

First, a five-hour medical, where my heart, cardio-vascular system, brain, eyes, and the pressure that they can take, were tested. I was fine. Second, a meeting with forty-seven-year-old Paul 'Bear' Randall, whose log book said 4200 hours in the air. Third, a trip to the simulator to acquaint me with the basics. Finally, the G-suit, because the F-16 can go up to 9Gs (we did 6.97, which is higher than what a Formula 1 driver does).

I was in Olympic mode: nervous and focused. And stuffed into a cockpit that made a sardine can look like a suite. Then we were gone, down the runway, the speed felt in the stomach, the acceleration pushing me back like a bully. We did flips, rolls and manoeuvres whose names I didn't even want to know. I felt like I was in a glass globe, turned upside down, sideways, moving almost at the speed of sound (Mach 0.96). I took the controls and the joystick was like a rifle trigger, responding to the slightest touch. It was 55 minutes in heaven.

It was a lovely moment, but not the best moment. That was when the postman lugged sacks of mail into my Chandigarh home every day. Telegrams, thousands of them, from my fellow Indians. Roughly 380,000. Some just addressed *Abhinav Bindra, Chandigarh*. Some containing marriage proposals (I still get them), even calls to my mother. Gold, I guess, makes even me eligible. You sit, tear open the telegrams, the letters, and listen to yourself read out affection from a stranger. It is beyond description.

This was foreign to me, even unsettling. Cricketers constantly feel the connection between athlete and nation, between success and worship: they taste it daily, in airport departure halls, hotel lobbies, restaurants, parties, fields. Even when they lock out the world, it's hard not to hear the murmur of a nation praying. But shooters rarely perform in grand arenas, nor do we peel off our shirts to show off pale chests in victory. We're never sure who watches, who cares, who reads the stories of our deeds in the sports pages. But now, for once, I could feel India's response, and it was beautiful and staggering.

Long after I'd come home, a driver who picked me up at Mumbai airport, turned around in the front seat and told me: 'Sir, my family and I are very proud of you.' In Singapore, an Indian gentleman stopped me on the street and asked: 'My mother is a big fan, will you please speak to her?' I did. Fortunately, I was not swayed by the adulation. My ego neither shrank nor inflated: I had seen defeat too often for one victory to turn my still head.

Winning gold gave me an unusual opportunity, a chance to see India. I got, and responded to, invitations from Kerela, Bihar, Maharashtra, Assam, Madhya Pradesh, Uttaranchal, Karnataka. Everyone wanted to shake my hand. Hours in the sun just to grip a young man's palm. This power to make people smile, as simple and profound an act as that, affected me and helped me. It forced me to peel off a layer of my insularity and become more interactive; it reminded me, a person not instinctively given to displays of emotion, to turn into a more welcoming man.

In Bhopal, thousands of people lined the street and a five-kilometre journey took three hours of *maalas* and mayhem. It humbles you instantly, this reaching out of a nation to touch you, it makes you want to weep.

And so, in the hotel room, I did.

Emotion from people had overwhelmed me. Exhaustion from victory had not left me still. And depression was lingering on the edges of my being. Winning is complicated, not just the art of it but the accepting of it. My mission, to which every fibre of my being was dedicated, was done. The mountain was climbed. Now what? It seems uncharitable almost to speak of emptiness after such a fulfilling victory, but such are the contradictions of achievement.

Heinz described winning 'as a big crisis, a real disaster', for he appreciated both the neurotic quality of the shooter and the dilemmas of a mission accomplished. At least four of the Olympic champions he coached suffered after winning, with heart disease, diabetes, hormonal problems. Whether this could be directly linked to winning is impossible to say, but it stood as a strong coincidence. Certainly when I won in Beijing, Heinz telephoned Gaby in China and said: 'Be prepared to cover him, to pamper him.'

I took a long while to comprehend this feeling. Gaby and Heinz came to India, so did Uwe, who wrote me the most sensitive and perceptive letter after Beijing, which in part read:

> *Now you will enter 'another' world and the world 'out there' does have expectations. You are the only 'white Bengal tiger' left in the universal Indian circus. Depression: indeed this is called 'post victory depression' and in fact symptoms are very similar and closely associated to 'post war syndrome'. Your 'war' is over... nothing more to fight for! Batteries are done, head is empty, been left 'alone' and inner emptiness is prominent... Like sitting in the movies trying to look at your own film and not knowing the script... Nevertheless its part of your 'new life'.*
>
> *Peace and quietness associated with some relaxing physical activities will create the environment of limiting the depressive moods... If you feel its getting too much consider a*

'time out'.... Don't try to match up with the Indian society's
hopes and expectations! They will 'eat you alive'... and I do
know a good number of people which did never recover from
that experience.

I spoke to them, to friends, coaches, past medallists, and
they did not view my bleakness as uncommon. For fourteen
to fifteen years, I had woken up every morning with a single
purpose:

Winning. Winning. Winning.

District events. State. Nationals. Asian. Olympics.

Now I had done it? Now what?

Now I could sleep late, but I didn't know how to. I was
dressed, but with nowhere to go. In my range I found myself
lost, my gun I didn't want to touch. I had gone from 100 per
cent obsession to zero obsession, like someone had put a brake
on my accelerated life.

The journey that had consumed me had ended. Medal
wanted, medal won. Fulfilled yet empty. This is the inner
conflict only athletes know. Few people live their entire lives
focused on a single deal. But this was precisely my world. At
twenty-five, people are starting their lives, I was done. I was
asking, what do I do now? Am I good at anything else?

Shooting is pastime, obsession, bliss, but it isn't a living. Now
I had to make one. At least I had done my Bachelor of Business
in the US, at the Olympic Training Centre in Colorado, and I
had fall-back options. But what about the others who speckle
the training camps in Bangalore and Patiala, young men and
women who chase glory in their country's name? No one cares,
there are no resources to guide the twenty-eight-year old who
retires. Or the twenty-two-year-old whose injury stifles his
dream. In some countries, athletes are taught to manage their

finances, to learn a trade just in case, to prepare themselves for lives beyond the lines. Not here. It is why athletes in India are so focused on finding a job, it's their security, the one guarantee in a sporting life that offers none.

People helped me, they listened, they offered answers. And in a time of internal conflict, I could have done with a call from a sports official saying: 'We understand you've been on a long journey, but it would be great if you could shoot for the country again. It will be good for the team, we will support you.'

I wanted this, but it never came. Then again, my critical comments over the years, which agitated officialdom, may not have helped.

So I took 2009 off, put the gun away, locked the range. I explored business opportunities and worked with a few grass-roots athletes. I spoke at schools, seminars and conclaves. Everyone wanted solutions to Indian sport, some secret recipe to Olympic success, and I was like some grand wizard of the gold. Sweat and desire is never a sexy answer, but eventually, if you distil greatness, often this is what it is.

Practice, practice, practice, want, want, want. Like you have taken some holy vow.

I remember writing a speech for the India Today Conclave. I took three months over it. Agonized over every sentence. Showed it to friends. Practised it in front of the mirror. It is the fear of failure, the fear of a silent, uncommunicative shooter whose words had suddenly become a sort of sporting gospel.

But I spoke because I wanted athletes to believe. I wanted boxers in dimly-lit municipality gyms, badminton players in small towns where the lines are fading into the cement, young runners on dusty ovals in forgotten districts, wrestlers in muddy akharas, to believe. That struggle is worth it. That dreaming is imperative. That winning Olympic gold is not beyond us.

Earlier, when we went to the Olympics, athletes rarely looked beyond bronze, for it was the best we had ever done. This century, silver through Rajyavardhan Rathore became a possibility. But now I sensed a gentle shift. In ranges, conversation went further, now they said: *gold toh lena hai.* Gold had a mystique, it had been far and foreign, like a Wimbledon title, a Masters green jacket. Now it was touchable.

No one person breaks a barrier alone, no one arrives at a sporting moon alone. It happens in stages. Rathore, who won India's first individual Olympic silver in 2004, demolished one part. So did Leander Paes (tennis, 1996), K. Malleswari (weightlifting, 2000), Khashaba Jadhav (wrestling, 1952), Sushil Kumar (wrestling, 2008), Vijender Singh (boxing, 2008), all of whom won Olympic bronze. And Milkha Singh (400 metres, 1960) and P.T. Usha (400 metres hurdles, 1984), who came fourth. And Gurbachan Singh Randhawa (110 metres hurdles, 1964), who came fifth and Sriram Singh (800 metres, 1976), who came seventh. Each one dismantled one bar of this enormous Olympic barrier, every feat clearing a pathway. I just climbed on their collective shoulders and shot off the last piece.

Rathore changed me, his silver ensured that gold became my possibility. It's what Indians need to do, feed off each other's success. After the Olympics, Gagan Narang—shooter, friend, colleague—and I spoke for three hours. We're at the same level; he can win just as I can. We spoke about his preparation, about what I felt he might do. But I don't hold all the answers.

People talk to me. That's change. They watch me in the range, how my shoe laces are tied, how my trousers are worn. I think they ask themselves: 'What's so damn special about him?' They ask me about motivation, the setting of goals, the technique of triggering. They're all very nice and they all want to beat me.

In the Netherlands one day, when I returned to shooting in 2010, a Dutch shooter produced his personal best and then told me: 'It was because I was shooting next to you.' It was a compliment; it was also a warning.

19

A NEW YEAR, A HARD YEAR

Clarity arrives in the strangest places. Mine finally came while sitting painfully cross-legged on a mat in a Haryana village. As befitting a shooter, my ten-day Vipassana meditation course in Rahaka Sohna was wrapped in silence, stillness and suffering. The food was vegetarian, the bed basic, misery my early friend for two days before I could find delight in a simple glass of cold water. On 40-degree nights, I slept with no fan for it only churned out a hot, sticky air. On calm days starting at 4 am, I sat in halls and dark meditation cells and searched for equanimity. It was June 2010 and I was still confused.

In November 2009, after an entire year of drifting and indecision since Beijing 2008, worn out and worried and distracted by my father's health, business issues, federation hiccups, my own ambivalence, I had finally returned to my art. Opened my range, unpacked the gun, returned the butt to the indentation it had made in my shoulder. I was shooting because of the most elemental of reasons: how do you walk away from a talent? How do you reject a skill? Especially since it is the only skill you know.

But I was an athlete with a dilemma, teased by various options. I decided, rather dramatically, that shooting must give me pleasure; I told myself that winning was no longer to be a 24-hour infection to my brain. Adventures must have new routes to stay interesting. My pursuit had been crazy, but committing to that craziness had given me pride. The medal had arrived only because I had chased it with persistence. But could I mimic that evangelical approach again, could I repeat that ardour? Did I want to? Did I have the physical resources within me to do it again? Could I submit again to marathoner Bill Rodgers's world, of which he once said: 'If you want to win a race you have to go a little berserk.'

So I trained, intensely, but not unforgivingly.

No training for two days? Fine.

No training for a week? No panic.

I convinced myself that not winning was acceptable; I told myself to enjoy the little delights of competition. Some days it worked, some days it didn't. In Germany, in early 2010, I shot a 586, 10 points off what I should have been scoring. Pleasure be damned, suddenly I wanted to win another gold medal. Activated by my low scores, my ego was swollen in annoyance and in the next few grands prix I won a couple of golds with scores of 596, 596, 595.

But I would keep battling between the new cool approach and my instinctively demanding self. I wanted to shoot without obsession, compete without a sense of mission, become an athlete whose priority was not just gold. I didn't want winning to define me, yet I wasn't quite deaf yet to an insistent voice in my head telling me: no shooter has ever won back-to-back Olympic golds in air-rifle shooting.

My early scores in late 2009 and early January 2010 impressed me after a year off. But the NRAI was still insisting that foreign scores were irrelevant (now they've altered their tune), that only trials mattered. But shooters don't operate like this, we need competitions to test ourselves, competitions to peak, time to train. If each competition becomes vital, it turns stressful.

Controversy flared. I said I had little chance of success if I didn't train; a newspaper spun that into a headline suggesting I was on the edge of quitting. So I skipped the trials for the first three World Cups, only relenting when it came to the World Championships. In Pune, with people watching, I shot poorly, a 591 and 594, but it was enough for me to qualify.

Emotions ricocheted inside, from hurting, to confused, to unhappy, to unsure. And so, always the shooting wanderer, I took the dusty road to Sohna village in June. It was not salvation I sought through Vipassana, but lucidity. I found it. When my mind shifted away from meditation and wandered, it only took me to one place: shooting. I saw it as a reminder, a calling, a rejuvenation. It told me I couldn't quit.

I let go of things. Of my issues with the federation. Of my fear of failure. To win a World Championship and Olympic gold is beautiful, but as with all such ascents, a fall is inevitable. A climbdown and a starting from nothing. But I realized that it was more than winning or losing, that I loved this sport. It was who I was. And so I began again.

I wasn't a great shooter. Not an elite shooter. Not anymore. It was humbling but invigorating. I was a 595, 596 shooter, I needed to be a 598 shooter by London 2012. A few points translate into thousands of hours of practice. But I had direction, eagerness, resolve. It was a beginning. My style was also changing. Once I was the fighting shooter, gun up, gun down, gun up, gun down, using every minute to struggle. Now

I was clearer, faster, less anxious. Part of it was my Lasik surgery post the Olympics. Better eyes, better focus.

In Munich in July, at the 2010 World Championships, I tasted fresh pressure, as the presence of a defending champion from 2006 brings media inquisitiveness. The new background music to my shooting was a repetitive symphony of the 'click, click, click' of the camera shutter. Even at the Commonwealth Games in Delhi later in the year, , when I stepped back to speak to my coach during competition, a hundred photographers took collective aim.

My technique was decent in Munich at the World Championship, but my desperation was absent. I'd forgotten how to dig, I didn't yet have an adequate cause. For Beijing, there was always a mission to drive me, but not here, so I tried to manipulate my mind, trying to convince it that I was desperate, but it didn't work.

My first forty shots (397/400) were reasonable, but I stuttered with two, fatal 9.9s in the fifth series. I finished with 593, my reign as world champion was over. I had been dismissed: thanks for coming, buddy, but goodbye. It breaks you a little, it annoys, you smile inwardly at your misery, you pull on your actor's face. 'It was fun to shoot,' you say. Bullshit. It hurts like hell. It was depressing, yet a tutorial. Physically? Fine. Technically? Fine. But under high pressure, my mind wasn't muscular enough. I wasn't in that place where the subconscious takes over, where it just happens. Intellectually, I understood: sport is so competitive, so wide, so harsh, athletes so monstrously driven, you can't just put down a gun for a year, pick it up, and rediscover a persistent excellence. Yet emotionally, having been at that level, to not be able to switch it on, on command, is destroying. Faith, I told myself. Just keep the damn faith. It will come.

I was trapped in a paradox. In some ways, I had to forget what I had been, take a hoover to my brain and cleanse it of the past. Great? Was. Olympic champion? Was. Good shooter? Am. My past gave me no free points, it wasn't tennis, where greatness offers intimidation, or football, where reputation can freeze an opponent's legs. But in the Indian universe, with no other individual gold medallists, this wasn't easy, for the past was everywhere, in every story, honouring me yet hounding me, a past hard to erase. Yet, ironically, the past was also my friend, it offered me security. As I chased London 2012, I knew at least that I'd been there in Beijing 2008. What I'd achieved wouldn't help me achieve it again, yet what I achieved told me it was possible.

By now I accepted that my fleeting need to find pleasure from shooting, win or lose, wasn't going to work. I wanted excellence, and excellence demanded obsesssion. The level I aspired to again required that I submerge myself into the sport again. I wanted that level and if I found it, well, then that would be the pleasure. So Claudia Lepera, a South African trainer, arrived at my home and we worked. Crunches. Cardio on the treadmill and bike. Wobble boards. Swiss ball workouts. Bio-mechanical corrective exercises. Weights for every part of the body.

Don't look back, I told myself. Don't.

Don't drop the flag either, I told myself at the Commonwealth Games in Delhi in October 2010. Don't mumble during the oath (I even went to a rehearsal and this time I demanded I get to practise the oath). Shooting is hard, this was terrifying. Fortunately the pole was light, luckily I spoke clearly. As a rule, I dislike opening ceremonies. Primarily because my shooting event usually arrives early at a Games. Of course, it was an honour, but ask me if I'd sacrifice that for gold, and I'd say yes.

But this had an altered feel. It was a home Games—I'd never get one again—and it reminded me of my journey, the seventeen-year-old rookie in Kuala Lumpur 1998, my first Commonwealth Games, now an Olympic champion and flagbearer for my nation. This symbolic act, leading a nation, was also my parents' dream. I kidded to my mother, if it's such a big deal, I'll get a flag and parade up and down your garden. She was deeply unimpressed. But I, not given to ceremony, practical in my pursuits, was surprised by my reaction. I was moved that Indian athletes gravitated to the flag, each one asking for a picture with it and me, till I had taken close to 700. Then I walked into the stadium and was assaulted by a roar that defied the blasé athlete in me. The ovation, the enthusiasm, was staggering. I felt proud, not necessarily to be carrying this flag, but to be part of this team. I had struggled to care, but now I did.

The Games had started chaotically, but ended triumphantly for India with 101 medals. The venues shone, the food was superior to the Asian Games in Guangzhou, the transport was fine. Home advantage laced with expectation. There was a comfort to not travelling and being in a familiar environment; there was an edge of tension to volunteers at the Village saying, 'Gold toh kal aa hi jayega' (gold will come tomorrow).

But the preface to the Games, disturbing and embarrassing, lingered. Athletes were calling me from abroad, will it happen, should I come? I found my room at the Athletes' Village layered with mitti, the toilet leaking, but some quick housekeeping fixed it. Of course, television channels insisted I had thrown a tantrum, hurled keys and demanded a single room, refusing to share with a wrestler. Admittedly, from some angles, shotgun shooter Mansher Singh does look like one, but he was my roommate. The TV story was disappointing yet almost predictable, for much of television journalism in India is nothing but an excitable dance with facts. I respect the media, I enjoy thoughtful writers who care to look under the skin of both the athlete and his sport, but occasionally there is a sensitivity missing.

At the Commonwealth Games, a writer called: Can you talk about Gagan Narang and your rivalry?

At 10 pm? On the night before my event? No way. But don't answer and you're arrogant.

But Gagan and I have no rivalry. We get on just fine. We shoot at targets, not at each other. We see bullseyes, not each other's faces. I was in a good state of mind, he was perfect. I had a 595 in the individual event at the Games, he had a 600. He had been striving to get to that level and now deserved to be there because of the effort he invested. I had individual silver, and team gold (another 595), and a hundred queries on how it felt to lose to Gagan. I was, and am, happy for a decent man. I wanted to prove myself, I wanted gold, but I wasn't ready yet. But I had in my phone a text message from Rajyavardhan Singh Rathore that I cherish: 'The world will keep asking for more proof of your skills, but you just have to play for yourself.'

Two days later, I was back in Chandigarh. Training. Looking for consistency, looking for a quality of execution in every single 10.

Stripped figuratively at home of some of my armour, in China this stripping was almost literal. After landing in Guangzhou for the 2010 Asian Games, and clearing immigration, a few Chinese officers—customs or security, I cannot tell—asked me to come with them. They offered me no explanation and we were divided by language. They took me to a room, put me against a wall, patted me down. They checked every piece of my baggage. They confiscated my phones, took away my iPad, and put them on a machine whose purpose eludes me. They rifled through cheques I had carried from Chandigarh to Delhi and had forgotten to give my office and appeared bemused. An hour later, without comment, they let me go. I didn't read too much into it, it certainly didn't affect me, but it was, in retrospect, rather inhospitable.

The Athletes Village was far away from a rambunctious city centre, where its spitting drivers, with their nonchalant disregard for driving lanes, made me feel at home. Its rooms were large, comfortable and hygeinic. Is it just fastidious me, or do all athletes crave hygiene, so fearful perhaps are we of falling sick on the eve of an examination that we have invested entire calendars in.

I went down for a swim in the unusually large pool available for athletes, nervously splashing away, holding onto the sides, valiantly trying not to drown. I can swim, in splendidly ugly fashion, but the freedom found at home in Chandigarh in my pool was absent here. At home I am alone, here I was surrounded by these rather leviathan-looking creatures, like Indian swimmer Virdhawal Khade, who stroked powerfully and easily across the pool, making it seem as if we were ungainly impostors in their fluid water world.

In the range, my arena, I have Khade's measure; in the range, for a while during the Asian Games, I had almost everyone's measure. In a dim arena, where I had shot before, with light filtering in from the back, I started strongly. 100. 99. 99. 100. Did I look at the scoreboard? I can't remember. But China's 2004 Olympic champion Zhu Qinan and I were joined at the hip. Leading.

Then, in the forty-second shot, disaster.

A 7.

I look at the monitor and recoil within. I have never, ever, shot a 7 in competition in my adult life. To be immodest, like Olympic champion divers who don't quite score 5s, this is not a world I exist in. Maybe only with a large fistful of vodka shots could I get to a 7, but not here.

Yet the monitor is immoveable.

The score says 7.

When shooters trigger, we know, more or less, what we have shot. In our terminolgy, we *call* a shot. I *called* that as a 9, possibly a 10. But the computer was unblinking: 7, it still said.

My being went numb, like every system within my machine was shutting down in shock. With a 7 you can't win, with a 7 you're holding back your teammates, for a team competition— with China, who else—was concurrently going on.

I put my rifle down and turned back to Indian coach Stanislav Lapidus. If we wanted to protest, we had to do so immediately, before the next shot.

'Did you see it?' he said.

'I am not sure,' I replied.

'Should we protest,' he countered.

'I'm not 100 per cent confident.'

On the first day of practice, I had mysteriously shot an 8. I called it a deep 10, it turned out an 8. This incident was at the back of my mind. Was there an issue with the gun? An issue with me? Or was it an issue with the target, which is not unheard of? I knew that if the protest was not upheld, I'd be docked two points which is huge, not necessarily for me, for I was already in trouble, but for the team. Ironically, we lost team gold to China by a single, cruel point.

So, I didn't protest. Of course, in retrospect, I should have.

Behind the target is a roll of black paper. Every time you hit the target, it is punctured and then unscrolls an inch. So you have a new piece of paper to puncture. The target is set on a frame and it takes about five-six shots for the paper to unscroll enough to emerge from behind the frame. Only then you can see the holes, only then you can tell if your shot was high, low, left, right, a 7 or a 9. Later I checked, it was a 9, but the moment was gone.

Individually, I knew a medal was gone, for amidst such talent as Gagan and Zhu a 597 was a minimum requirement to be in serious contention. I concentrated, I fought. In the next eighteen shots, I dropped two more points to finish on 593, still good enough for a shoot-off to get to the final. I'd been scrapping for the team, but now that was done and my desire leaked to the floor, I was vacuumed of intensity and caring. I had come to win, not to make finals, and I laboured unsuccessfully through the shoot-off for the final. Sanjeev Rajput, who also missed the final, and I laughed ruefully at our misery and focused on the elegant Chinese hostesses with their rather amusing wigs.

Disappoinment is natural, yet I didn't allow it to flood me, I had no room for too much of it. The negaholic I was before Beijing, always searching for what could go wrong, the dissatisfied perfectionist, was out of place now, it was unaffordable. So you scratch defeat from the memory, don't let it linger and corrupt the thought process or flatten the spirit, you find little victories and small happinesses where once you saw only mistakes. One gold, two silvers at the Commonwealth and Asian Games 2010. Not bad, I told the mirror.

When I had flagellated myself before Beijing 2008, there was a purpose to it; I was shooting superbly and desperately pushing the envelope of my talent. But now, uncertainty hovering, form imperfect, my stockpile of self-belief and confidence still thin, I had to give myself some credit. I was growing again as a shooter and needed the tonic of excitement to fuel me. I had found greatness, lost it, and now I had resumed a search for this faint, intangible edge, this sliver of genius, if you want to call it that, that allows me to be consistently excellent. It's excruciating some days, this chase, this consistency that comes, leaves, flickers, but I believe in hard work, I relish it, I know no other way.

As the year concluded, my mind was alive with purpose. I needed a new rifle after ten years, another jacket, more gym work, as I sought to qualify for the 2012 Olympics. The harder I pushed, the more robust my mind felt. It's what I did that day in Guangzhou at the Asian Games. Empty-handed in the individual event, I travelled to the Village, tossed my bag into my room, and went to the gym. Whatever residue of rage, whatever dregs of disappointment still remained, required release on a treadmill.

I started running. One kilometre, two, three, four, till weariness set in. Which is when I saw her. Two or three treadmills down the line, the brilliant Saina Nehwal was running. Fast. So I pushed on. Maybe it's just guys and their silly egos, but I wouldn't quit till she did. Sneakily, I kept looking sideways at her. But I was not looking back.

20

MR INDIAN OFFICIAL: THANKS FOR NOTHING

At any Games, I am conscious about who I am shooting for. Myself. My family. My coaches. My country. Who I am, an Indian, is written on my face, it's in the Indian Olympic Association emblem on my blazer pocket, it's in the three letters (IND) that stand next to my name. People who don't know me, will identify me simply as this: 'Oh, he's that Indian shooter.' I kind of like it.

Shooting for India is both pleasure and privilege. But some people make it a pain. The irony of sport in our country is that officials don't assist, they hinder. Not all, but many. Ignorance is worn without embarrassment, incompetence continues almost without interruption. It is a failure to learn that sets us back, a *chalta hai* attitude that mocks the idea of any culture of excellence. Too many Indian personnel in my sport have no clue about shooting. No clue about the rules, the developments, the training, the sophistications.

Champions have to be built. Talent found, skill sandpapered, techniques tuned, minds strengthened. It requires a detailed and relentless pursuit of greatness. Think of it like a military operation. But it doesn't exist in India. If producing champions was a degree, most officials would fail. It's why so much of what is achieved is in spite of officials. It's a pity. So much of this nation has changed around me, so many strides taken, but attitudes worn by sporting officials still arrive from another archaic century.

They are often like some royal, pious granters of favours. Sport is about deserving, about earning. But athletes in India, irrespective of performance, are often made to feel grateful. As if some extraordinary accommodation is being made for them. It is a belittling, tiresome exercise for the athlete because by the end he is often begging for money which, ironically, has been allocated for athletes like him.

In 2006, I attended a meeting at the ministry of sports to request funding for training through the National Sports Development Fund (NSDF). It was the year I had won the World Championship. Yet I walked out of the meeting completely disillusioned. Every request for funds for coaching, for equipment, for training was questioned.

Kya beta, do you really need this?

Questions are fair, accountability is necessary. I even got some funding then, for which I am grateful. And post-Beijing, the unnecessary questions began to decrease as the association and the sports ministry started to sniff professionalism. But it is how you are questioned, it is the identity of the questioners sometimes, that I objected to.

The tone is patronizing, the manner feudal, the atmosphere unwelcoming. *I* am their job, but I feel like *their* burden. These are bookkeepers, who look like they feel a physical pain in parting with money that is not really theirs, who have little understanding of sport yet will interrogate us suspiciously on why a sports psychologist is necessary. It's like going through the ABC of sport all over again. It is humiliating, it is tiring.

Preparation for any sport is precise, thorough, different. Runners plot their marathon training to the last kilometre, tennis players chart their weekly schedule carefully. Everything is exact, it has to be for this is a world where just a plane ride can alter the pressure of my trigger. But an understanding of, and an interest in, what it takes to *chase* a medal—forget *winning* one—the hours, the technical foundation, the science, the coaching, the number of pellets, the equipment, is too often absent in India.

What, you can't use normal shoes to shoot?

What is a jacket?

Once, an official, on being told a jacket/trouser can cost 1000 euros, says: *You must be wearing only an Armani or Versace?*

Eventually, I received some funding, but the experience stays with you, it fuels a sense of distrust, and you go into every meeting feeling uncomfortable. I was bloody lucky anyway that my dad could support me, but what about athletes who had no backing, no families who could afford guns and equipment? How do they explain to men ensconced behind a desk that even if you spend their/your precious money—a lot of money—there's no guarantee of a medal because sport can't be scripted, because you can't prepare for luck and chance? Of fifty shooters at an Olympics, one wins, but the others don't necessary fail. How do you convince officials of this?

It is why athletes often touch the feet of officials in India. I am a traditional Indian, but that seems plain wrong. As if the athlete is accepting his future lies in official hands, instead of in pure performance. As if the official believes he controls the athlete. It sets the wrong tone for the relationship. This is supposed to be an equal relationship, not a deferential one. Eventually, only scores must matter, not patronage.

In the West, they get this right: the athlete comes first, the administrator second. I never touched anyone's feet as an athlete, but if I had, my life would have been easier. Maybe then they might have got my name right. A senior official called me Anwar Sultan before the Sydney Olympics. The Indian Olympic Association boss, Suresh Kalmadi, referred to me as 'Avinash'. I am a shooter, hardly a household name, but you'd think he'd know who I was, considering I had just won Olympic gold in Beijing.

The day after winning gold in Beijing was as revealing. I went to see Colonel Rajyavardhan Singh Rathore perform. Four years earlier, in Athens 2004, he had won a medal, India's first individual silver in any sport. He is both a fine man and a fine shooter, but more importantly for us, he was a pathbreaker, a pioneer. He was proof that the world could be challenged, a medal could be won. You have no idea how liberating that is.

In Beijing, Rathore struggled. It happens. Perfection is an elusive, untameable beast and so it was with him that day. On such days you need support. You want to believe in this time of terrible loneliness that you are not alone. Just a silent, consoling pat from an official on the back. Best is just a respectful silence for it conveys an understanding of the fickleness of sport.

But in India there is often blame or regret or quibbling or contempt and it demeans the shooter. When I broke the Olympic record in Athens, a senior Indian shooting official refused to believe it. As if I was simply not capable. After I lost the final, he happily told the media that I could not take the pressure. From them comes mockery not inspiration.

When Rathore finished in Beijing, I heard the then president of the National Rifle Association of India and the secretary general ripping him apart, listing a series of absurd reasons why he lost. That he was lucky to have won silver in Athens, that he had too much attitude. I wasn't surprised by their reaction, I wasn't disappointed, I was simply sad. I realized that irrespective of performance, few people in the administration really care for shooters and shooting.

When athletes win a medal, the first reaction is usually one of relief. Simply because winning is exhausting, it warrants the confluence of so many elements. It is why a professional environment is essential within a team, it protects the shooter, it keeps him calm and rested. If everything functions, he feels, so can he. If everything is in place, the mind has no distraction.

But in India, we must swim through chaos on the way to a medal. It almost feels as if our medals are more meaningful, considering what we go through to win one. At the 2002 World Championships in Lahti, Finland, overburdened with coaches who wanted single rooms, the athletes had to share. I found myself in a double room with six people for three days and then shared a single room with coach Thomas for two days. Maybe some of the coaches got confused and thought they were competing.

Coaches who travel with us are sometimes not even coaches. Nice guys, sure, but inadequate coaches. If they knew their job they'd know that detail is everything, it is the foundation of victory. Sport has enough of an element of luck for anything additional to be left to chance. So athletes and teams are almost painfully fastidious in their method. Tactically they might gamble, but in preparation they are precise.

Andre Agassi would stack his rackets precisely, the most recently strung ones always at the bottom. Footy players in

Australia sometimes fly back to their cities at lower altitude because they believe it assists with the healing of injuries. At the Beijing Olympics, the Americans spent US $3 million to set up a high-performance centre for their athletes at Beijing Normal University.

Such detail is what separates athletes, what helps them find that extra centimetre in a jump, cut off .01 of a second in a race, and they go to extraordinary lengths to find it. We go a long way, too, but sometimes in the wrong direction. In 2002, the flight from Delhi to Busan for the Asian Games should have taken roughly 10 hours. The connections we took resulted in a 29-hour trip over two days. Tired athletes are not ready athletes. Two years earlier, in 2000, officials had forgotten to send my gun details to the Olympic organizers. So I turned up, had no clearance, and spent the night in Sydney airport getting it.

Underestimating the small things is to misunderstand the psychology of sport. Playing well often comes from feeling good. Even, sometimes, from looking good. Appreciably not every athlete is lucky to get sponsored equipment. The dignified Abebe Bikila, a poor farmer from Ethiopia who enlisted in the army, won gold at the Rome marathon while running barefoot. That's fine. But when administrators in a modern age, when everything is sponsored, sent me a left shoe that was size 11 and a right shoe that was size 8 before the Beijing Olympics, it's not fine. Just hilarious.

We used to laugh off official incompetence in India, just grin and bear it, but it's shameful. Walking out in front of the world at an Olympics in shabby uniforms is embarrassing. It makes you feel second class. The only thing that caught attention was the saffron turban, and foreign athletes often asked for it. But begging for an Olympic uniform, as my mother literally did one year because I was overseas, is humiliating. In Beijing,

I turned up on the victory podium in Bermuda shorts not necessarily out of choice. I discovered that the track pants I had been given were size XXL. If you've never seen me, I'm just slightly bigger than a short toothpick.

All this is part of an old story. Teamwork. It's hard to win without it. In Andre Agassi's autobiography, *Open*, he repeatedly dwells on the powerful role his fitness trainer and protector, Gil Reyes, played in his life. Athletes understand this. We're complicated creatures. We're selfish, self-obsessed, we tend to live in our own worlds, we want the world to revolve around us, yet we need to believe we are not alone. Even in individual sports, we require the reassurance of a sense of team. A team whose expertise you can rely on. Except our idea of expertise was an armourer who often travelled with the Indian team but could barely open a screw.

The world has changed, but Indian sport is slow to learn. At the 2010 Vancouver Winter Olympics, the Chinese contingent apparently arrived with eight foreign coaches. To be the best, they got the best. It's always been their way. Greatness, they understood, comes only with humility. They are not alone either. The English have had Australian swimming coaches, the Australians have had Chinese diving coaches.

But Indian sport tends to hesitate in accepting world-class help from outside. Sometimes we look for the cheap deal. Or they're good coaches who are compromised quickly by a bureaucratic system that expects them to conduct an orchestra with tied hands. Or coaches are simply overburdened. Athletes need individual attention and a coach shouldn't work with more than ten shooters. In China, it's even less than that. In India, the fine rifle coach we have from Kazakhastan, Stanislav Lapidus, is saddled with 150 shooters. Of course, he can only concentrate on a few, which means many feel neglected.

We need more coaches because shooting has caught the middle-class imagination. At my first nationals, in the mid-1990s, there were 300 competitors. In 2009, there were roughly 3000. Shooting suits us. Indians tend to have a fine motor control and a preference for the contemplative in sport over the physical. From wood craftsmen to magicians such as P.C. Sorcar, India has had a colourful history in hand-eye coordination. In sport, this alchemy of timing, wristwork, elegance, idea was provided by batsmen, hockey players, badminton legend Prakash Padukone and tennis maestro Ramanathan Krishnan. It might be too glib to say that Indians, arriving from a land replete with gods and gurus, are accomplished at finding inner peace. But certainly the shooter resembles a motionless sage caught in meditation, controlling his breathing, emptying his mind, banishing emotions.

Young Indian shooters—who own this calm and stand as still as unsmiling footguards outside Buckingham Palace—need support. They require ranges spread all over the country and coaches to clean up their technique before mistakes get cemented. Experts from abroad need to be supplemented by training Indian shooters, who are approaching retirement, as coaches. The more expert an administration gets, the more it dilutes the shooter's stress. Experts, for instance, understand schedules, peaking, planning. The inexpert official just wants his way. The way 2010 started was a perfect example.

A shooter's schedule is key to his performance, especially in a year like 2010, a year of the World Championship, Commonwealth Games, Asian Games. A schedule is a step-by-step, tournament-by-tournament, pathway to greatness for us. This sport is too hard to be perfect in too often. The difference between a final and oblivion is marginal, just three points, but those three points exhaust you, they demand every part of you.

So the shooter must decide when to peak, when to experiment, he must tread a fine line between learning and performing. He must use events to test minor changes in technique or even adjust to the fit and weight of a new shooting jacket. He must refine his tactics. Competition is invariably interrupted by critical moments which one can only survive by addressing them tactically. Sometimes you shoot aggressively. Then it doesn't work. So you choose patience, sometimes raising and lifting your gun twenty times for a shot.

Administrators need to understand this. If they don't know a sport, feel it, taste it, then they don't understand us, they can't make champions. Yet in early 2010, incredibly, yet predictably, they demanded trials before every event all year. Form for them became irrelevant. In the seven competitions post Beijing, I averaged 596/600, the best I've ever done. Big deal, attend the trials, they said. Trials before every Games. Trials all the time.

Double-trap shooter Ronjan Sodhi had won two World Cup medals in 2009 and won gold at the Asian Clay Shooting Championships. His fine form was evident, he'd proved himself in the intensity of international competition. But he was told, too bad, buddy, attend the trials. Demotivated and demoralized, he came fourth in the trials. It qualified him only for the minimum qualifying score (MQS) category in the Acapulco World Cup – these shooters compete outside the main competition and are ineligible for a medal. Furious and brilliant, Sodhi proceeded to shoot a world record score at that World Cup. Proved his point, right? Nope. Next World Cup, he was still in the MQS category.

Only in Indian shooting!

But I am still a believer, I have to be, this is my sport, my country, my life. Change is always possible.

We should temporarily stop holding large, multi-event Games. No Asian, no Commonwealth, no nothing. Playing at home, against strong competition, is a privilege but it is not a persuasive enough reason for a Games. If a city craves beautification, if it desires roads, a shining airport, a sparkling Metro, it should not require the excuse of a Commonwealth Games to do it.

Such enormous sums on a single stadium is foolish, for eventually they rust with underuse, lying in the sun as mute proof of limited wisdom. Instead, we must build smaller stadiums across India, let district boys know what it feels like to be enclosed in an arena and hear a chanting crowd. Sport has to be more accessible and more respected: kids require a place to play and a backing to play.

Investment is required, not just in flyovers but in the athlete. Chasing a medal isn't a dreary task of shuffled papers, it is an adventure and a commitment. The issue is not just money, it is enthusiasm. The finest ammunition is within India's financial grasp, it is the will to deliver the ammunition on time to shooters, the ability to take a Sunday morning drive to the customs shed 30 kilometres away, which is the issue. But even though things are changing, not enough of a sense of urgency, of even just doing a job professionally, permeates so much of Indian sport. Athletes not playing cricket could well qualify for second-class citizenry.

We can start with a clear separation between administrators and experts, for sport has a managerial aspect and a training aspect. Former athletes don't always understand organization and babus can't fathom the intricacies of sport. Each must know his place.

The manager must market his sport, grow it, build its image. He must ensure funds are delivered fast to shooters, the range is in order, tournaments smoothly run, flights perfect, accommodation sound. It is as if he's running a corporation. But the shooter's daily life must lie with the expert, who knows science, technique, talent, who can look at a junior and see that despite decent scores here is a kid who needs support. He sees the grey in sport, where the babu only sees black and white.

Both are accountable, but a coach cannot be unless he has freedom, for he is an artist and his team a creation. Stanislav Lapidus had plans, but in 2010 roughly 5 per cent were implemented. Which makes it impossible to judge him. It frustrates experts; this kind of treatment led Indian hockey coach Richard Charlesworth, the great Australian, to walk out and his successor, José Brasa from Spain, to dramatically tell *The Times of India*: 'I have lost. Your system has won. I tried my best to change it. I pleaded, I cried, I did everything. But it won't budge.' The federation officials cannot be allowed to defeat the coach. One funds the plan, the other makes it. One picks the team, the other sends it abroad. When officials start picking elite teams, the system starts to fall apart.

Plan is sports' favourite four-letter word. We did it for the Commonwealth Games in 2010—funding, camps, support— and the medals were encouraging evidence of it. States like Haryana and Punjab offered their athletes cash awards, and such incentives push athletes, drive them, offer security. Medals look pretty around the neck, but you can't eat them.

But sporting progress in India is often followed by disappointment. In December 2012, the IOC suspended India's national Olympic committee. For a democracy with a long Olympic history, this was embarrassing; for a nation that just ended the London Games with a record six medals, it was sad; for an Indian sports system that limps along, it was inevitable.

In May 2013, the sports ministry asked me to join their delegation to the IOC to make a case for India's readmission to the Olympic family. One faction of the fractious IOA went, too. So did the national sports federations, who rumouredly had a meeting one night in the corner of a Lausanne bar where, for a while, the subject was me.

As in: Don't let this outspoken shooter fellow, who will criticize us, speak.

One of them even proposed a deal: 'Beta, don't say anything here (to the IOC). It's an internal matter that we should solve at home. We only want to be back at the Olympics.'

No, nothing is being solved at home. No, it was time to speak. No, it was more than just being back at the Olympics.

Even then, even after the suspension, they didn't get it. This wasn't about the fragile, fake pride of red-faced officials. This wasn't even about me because I'd been to four Olympics and had luckily won a gold. This was about every Indian athlete who I happened to be representing. This was about boxers, runners, hockey players, wrestlers, some who'd never been to a Games but live just to get there. This was about an exhausted tribe of athletes who were tired of being pushed around.

And so I told Jitendra Singh, the sports minister, that if I am not allowed to speak, then I'd like to return to India. I wasn't going to be an Olympic champion put on mute parade, I wasn't going to be a front for clandestine back-room deals that I didn't attend or agree with.

To his great credit the minister said, go ahead, say what you want.

I did.

I spoke to an IOC commission of three people for roughly

10 minutes and left them an even longer note. Athletes are creatures of actions, and deeds, but sometimes even we need words. One paragraph from the document I left for them encapsulates what I feel:

'We deserve federations that are professionally run, which have the necessary structures in place, that genuinely care for athletes and sport development; we deserve mechanisms which are accountable and transparent. What we need is a clean system with results being the only determinant. The issues that have never been effectively tackled range from grassroots sport development to having a fair and free electoral process to having independent ethics and dispute tribunals to athlete representation in decision making.'

Our lives as athletes, I told the IOC, are unusual, because they are short. Maybe ten years, sometimes fifteen. When our athletic bosses in India are inept, or slothful, they have a massive impact on our aspirations. They are effectively shortening our life spans and they are amputating our dreams. And sport is nothing without dreamers.

I spoke about things that people have said before and we have to keep saying till someone listens. Am I hopeful something will happen? Yes. Only because I am an athlete and I am conditioned to hope.

21

WINNING AND LOSING

Winning is no one's birthright. There are no born winners, natural winners, destined winners. Look at me. I was a chicken heart. I am not a natural competitor. On the starting line, I am scared. There was a time I even wanted to cry. Don't believe the movies because my life is not a sports film. I am not *Seabiscuit*, I am not *Cinderella Man*. There is no uplifting soundtrack when I perform, no beautiful blonde watching, no last-minute, dusty, bleeding heroics that leave me victorious. But I learnt enough to win Olympic gold. Learnt to go deaf to everything, including my pounding heart; learnt to go blind to everything, except the black blob of a target before me; learnt to find calm amidst chaos. When the time to win comes, it's as if a mutiny begins within your body, but if you've suffered in practice, you don't fall apart. Pain brings trust. When I shot a 4 in the Olympic final during sighting shots, it was numbing, but I overcame it because in my mind control had not flown.

Now I'm suffering again, I have to, for no one has won Olympic gold in the 10-metre air-rifle twice. I want to be that person. I am ready to be stripped naked in front of the world, which is what it feels like when competition comes. I want to win also because I don't want to lose. I hate to lose. Because losing—some days, important days—is like a slow bleed within the chest.

People think I'm cool, in control, unperturbed, but they have no idea. My face is a lie. Losing is hell, losing turns you into a performance artist. From the moment you shake hands with the winner or go mumble a few words in his direction. Gestures matter, this is only fake war after all, but an intriguing theatre is being played out. The winner has a glow on his face and you wonder, is he empathizing with me? Probably not. And are you, the loser, really happy for him right at that moment? But you don't want to show yourself at that moment, don't want to allow your skin to be peeled away and reveal yourself.

So you wear a mask, it's like a shutter that descends with defeat. You don't want to get overwhelmed in public, you don't want to show disappointment, you don't want to show weakness, you're like some robot in pain. Everyone is watching you. The spectator is a suddenly interested student of body language, he wants reaction, you don't want to give him any. It's a contest between voyeur and actor. Inside you're falling apart, but the mask imprisons emotion, it won't let it out. The ego won't allow it.

I don't want to talk when I lose, I've already retreated to my private planet. I don't want to say a word, not to my parents, not to anyone. Yet small talk, offered kindly, gently, nibbles away at me as I walk to the locker room.

'Bad luck.' 'Next time.' 'Well tried.' You smile, you act, you walk.

At the press conference, questions come in a flurry. 'What went wrong?' 'Are you disappointed?' 'Is this a setback?' The questions are fair, but you're in no mood to give an explanation, you don't even have an explanation yet, because clarity comes with coolness. So you fall into cliché. You keep the mask on. But then in the privacy of your room, it comes. A physical pain. A useless feeling. The mask is off, the mask is only a postponement of hell.

But losing is the driver, it's like a kick with a steel-toed boot to the ego. I didn't like losing the Asian Games and Commonwealth Games in 2010, yet I was not there really to win the Asian Games and Commonwealth Games. Only the Olympics, because the Olympics is maximum proof. Whatever else you win, even a World Championship, next morning you awake and the Olympics still lies before you. Beckoning, calling, teasing. There is a great German shooter called Sonja Pfeilschifter and her story is both inspirational and melancholic. She's won multiple World Championships, she's won World Cups, she's set world records. But no Olympic medals. So she goes on, and on, the lure of this medal too powerful to resist, as if her very self-worth depends on it.

She knows, I know, winning is slow, laborious, excruciating. It can't be hurried. The athlete, especially when young, leaps, then stalls. You rise, plateau, rise, plateau, the further you ascend, the harder improvement becomes. To shoot 590/600 is quickly achieved, then every additional point can take months, a year, three. Then one day a 593 is found, it is pleasing but caution lurks: an Olympic medal requires at least 597.

So you start again, and you get stuck again, rooted to a score, improvement unavailable. Every day at the range, at the gym, hour adding on hour, days into months, but nothing. No progress. Some days you feel like breaking the gun and wanting to leave. Some days hopelessness grips the body like an ache. Some days it's as if a sudden truth has washed over you. My God, I'm not good enough. You fail, fail, fail, the target telling you scores that are like wounds to the spirit, but stubbornness won't allow you to let go of patience and persistence. You can't stop. You just can't. Because there has to be a way, a solution, some hope.

And then, without warning, it comes. Suddenly you shoot 597, then an entire sequence of 597s. Exuberance arrives, it's akin to a feeling of weightlessness, the most profound, private, unfathomable triumph. But even here, anxiety is creeping through the brain. Will it stay? Next morning, will it be there? Will you focus too much on one element and forget the rest? By now, both frustrated and fascinated, you've understood, there's no finish line to greatness. The high score has to become routine, it has to be found on fever days, lethargic days, lousy days. One year at a World Cup in Bangkok, food poisoning sent me to a hospital for a night on a drip, but next day, pale, unsteady, I shot a 595. On my worst day, I found a good score.

Winning demands honesty, a sneering at the short cut. It allows no fooling of the self. I wear one fact like a badge: I have never been late for practice. In the gym, in the range, lying is easy: Ah, what the hell, today we'll cut practice by 10 minutes. Body's feeling weary. Just not into it. I'll do an extra 10 minutes tomorrow. Anyway I'm fit and shooting well. No big deal.

It is a big deal. It's about 10 minutes more, not less. It's about swatting away excuse. One day, a trainer miscounts the repetitions in my crunches and says, good job, ten done. I am in pain, there is no one else in the gym, no audience, no media, no competitor, only the mirror. Yet I say, No, I only did eight. Two more to go. This is being true, this makes me feel strong, this is the extra bit that might bring me my medal. Later, hours later, I walk out of the gym and inhale the sun with a victorious weariness. This is the unseen world of the athlete, this only athletes understand. It's been a good day.

Winning remains for me an inquisitive undertaking. But it's not everyone's way and this is the democratic beauty of sport. There is no single route to gold. Presumably some athletes function primarily on instinct, not given to overthinking, and it's a gift. They practice, they play, sport distilled to its most uncomplicated. But I want to roam the boundaries of shooting and comprehend the viscera of my sport. I want to grasp weaponry, absorb technique, break down balance, examine the sporting brain. I want to unscramble shooting, I want to turn greatness into an experiment. By being interested, shooting remains interesting to me. It has also rescued me.

A shooter can explode into form, his mind and mechanics in perfect synchronicity, his gun turned into a detachable fifth limb. But form is always on the edge of betrayal, it never stays, eventually body or mind or technique rebels and a slump is upon you. This is when the athlete who relies purely on his coach, who has not examined the machinery of greatness, who has rarely concerned himself with fit of jacket or angle of elbow, struggles. But if shooting has been approached like a scholar does a classical text, then it's easier to identify which element is falling apart. Knowledge is more than an ally, it is a weapon.

Winning, in shooting, demands I have to be at full, undiluted throttle all the time in competition. I cannot play at 80 per cent, I cannot cruise, I cannot just play the big points well, I can't wait for a lesser bowler to come on. I have to find this best of mine from start to finish. I also know I cannot win all the time, no one can, so even in defeat I take something positive away. Yes, my balance was strong. Yes, my breathing was not ragged. Yes, my triggering was sharp. Athletes need this internal comforting of the self because externally, the world, especially in India, reduces sport to its basics. *Medal or nothing. Winner or nobody.* When you win once, you must win constantly. When you don't, you're dumped as a fluke. Criticism we wear, carry, shrug off, it's our daily bread. I am not searching for acknowledgement, aloofness is my protection. But younger athletes need reinforcement from the community, to hammer them is to hamper progress.

Elation over winning is easy, but respect for effort in defeat, for the hard journeys made, is often what athletes crave. It's why, when asked about my favourite athletes, I have no names that you know, yet I have many heroes. You'll find them speckling the fields of Patiala and Bangalore and Pune where national athletes train, endeavouring in anonymity. They warrant respect because winning is fine, but it is an outcome, it is the pursuit of it that is fascinating. It is in committing to discipline, in offering sacrifice, in wearing disadvantage, that heroism lies. It is in the boxer waking at dawn to punish himself, the weightlifter scraping her throat as she hauls up a bar over her head, all of them, every morning, trying to be that simplest of things: the best they can be.

The hero is the district winner, the state conqueror, the national champion, for every medal, of any weight, requires effort. The hero is the athlete who won't even win any of this, for not everyone can. Because they still strive, he running for family, she swimming for country, sometimes not given a lucky break, missed by a selector, bereft of sponsor, absent of mentor. But unshakeable from their task, taking the leap, confronting shortcomings. This is man at his best, invisible, unacknowledged, still pushing to do the deed amidst hardship. This athlete is never irrelevant, he has still won. He has pride and it is only found with everything given.

This hardship Indian athletes face, the once-frequent but now-reduced traumas of equipment, coaches, facilities, toughens us. Mentally weaker, we aren't. Mental strategy, perhaps we lack. When inevitably pressure arrives like a G-force, like a tractor sitting on your chest, how do you handle it? Indian athletes have the potential to manage it, we're not always taught how to. It's a skill undeveloped, it hasn't been planned for, a psychology not adequately worked on.

But raw resolve we own, it is apparent in the shooting ranges, in the tone and volume and frequency of chatter. India has changed, there is an irresistibility to the confidence of the young, even if the brashness is occasionally disquieting. My generation was defensive, the new one is unfamiliar with the word, and I am almost envious of them. In the old days, if asked, how's it going, we slipped into timidity. *Arre, ok, yaar, not bad, chalega.* Now ask and they don't look away, they stare you in the eye, and say: 'Great.'

Now they have to win. Now I need to beat them. Now no chicken-heartedness will do. It won't be easy. Just qualifying for the 2012 London Olympics wasn't easy. By the time the Munich World Cup arrived in mid-2011, my second-last chance to qualify, I was still struggling. Had gone back to my old gun. Didn't even want to go to Munich. Couldn't sleep. By now the qualified were a separate species. They were free, relaxed, the burden of London lifted; the rest of us were tense, taut with pressure. Through the months of unsuccessful labour, I spin a positive out of my temporary failure to qualify:

This is harder than even winning in Beijing.

This relentless pressure is fine practice for London.

Those already qualified will lose sight of reality which will strike them abruptly in 2012.

It is just the normal voices in the athlete's head. Finally, in Munich, I am caught in a five-shot shoot-off with nine shooters for two Olympics places. I find courage. I come second. I am on my way to London. I don't know if I can win there. But I now have the licence to dream, at least, that I can win there. My form needs work, but it's OK. I am learning. I am learning to suffer again.

22

LONDON 2012: UNDERSTANDING DEFEAT

At the Athletes' Village in London I saw the Queen in the dining hall and for a second contemplated having a word with her. Your Highness, a pleasure to meet you. Oh, by the way, the food here is awful. But to complain—which the world did rapidly at Delhi's Commonwealth Games—seemed in poor taste. Even if pizza for breakfast one English morning, the only remaining edible food, hardly qualified as athletic fuel.

Already, I knew: in Rio 2016, I'll sequester myself in a hotel (already, I firmly believe I'll be in Rio). No more Village, no more thin walls, late roommates, distraction. Laughter in London among the Indian shooters made for a great atmosphere, for it eased the pressure, but was it good for me? Some athletes are solitary beasts, some unwind in company, some need the edginess of pressure. Some just age differently. Anyway, even Roger Federer opts for hotel room service outside the Village. Yes, I know, he's hounded for autographs by fellow athletes and I am not. But we share a common truth: into my thirties, like him, I am just older, fussier and more fastidious.

The food was not quite why my form hiccuped in London. It wasn't why I shot only 594, wasn't why I had three 9s late in my last series, wasn't why I missed the final. I didn't win, in sports' simplest terms, because fifteen competitors shot better. But it's never enough in sport to just say 'not good enough', for that is far too philosophical for me. After London I had to regurgitate every single detail of a year gone by and then comb through it like a forensic investigator.

If victory requires investigation—how? why? what the hell?—defeat needs an even finer analysis. What did you miss? Where did you stumble? You peel back the year and look for those bullies called errors and bad luck and circumstance, which you can never quite recognize while they're ganging up on you. Failure has to be owned. Failure is no one else's. No one steadies your body as you fire a perfect 10 under stress and no one jiggles your hand to cause the 9 under tension.

I screwed up. Only I.

Because of my sabbatical after Beijing, and my struggles to qualify for London, I experimented less. No dry-firing in a dark room, no cocooning myself in a Samadhi tank. If I was slightly less neurotic then I also found fewer quaint rituals or scientific exercises to flirt with. But I was still me, still curious, still inquisitive, and I continued investigations into myself as a competitor. This time my journey took me to hypnotist and healer Radhika Kawlra Singh in Delhi.

No, she didn't have a pocket watch on a chain which swung like a pendulum. No, she didn't peer at me like Kaa the snake in *The Jungle Book* and hiss 'trust in me'. You've seen too many movies. In real life, there wasn't even a couch. Just a chair, relaxing thoughts of gardens and beaches, and ideas planted like seeds into my subconscious. In an inward sport, I was trying to convince my insides.

Between April 2011 and May 2012, Radhika and I struggled. I am, as a person, rarely relaxed, increasingly analytical and thus an imperfectly malleable subject. She wanted me to see myself as a 'superhero', bristling with confidence, but I scowled and said no. That's not me. I am no shooting Superman, more a willingly sweaty Clark Kent. She suggested I visualize myself standing on the podium in London. This didn't work for me either, it is too confident an image for me to wear.

But over 200 hours of probing conversations we made progress. She helped me forget the last shot, erasing the immediate past just like a windshield wiper does with falling rain. She helped me create a fresh, hungry feeling after every shot. Instead of clutter there was clarity: I want the next shot, I am going to shoot it well. Together we forged a superb pre-shot routine. It's as if the concept of slow motion had been applied to my world and I was responding to a different clock. Everything was slower—the movement of my rifle, the movement of me, and it was a valuable tool in helping me focus. It was as if I was lulling myself into a trance.

But I did not do hypnotherapy in the two to three months before London.

Was this is a mistake? I don't know.

Not having Gaby next to me in London wasn't a mistake for I had no choice here. In this I was defeated by circumstance. Sometimes you can't appreciate the value of a voice next to you, till it isn't there. In Beijing, she coached the Italian team but somehow we found time to interact. In the road to London, having polished the Italians into a superior squad, she was unavailable. Heinz, her husband, was my necessary guide but I also missed her familiar and harsher tone. He was gently analytical, she is like sandpaper. He guides, she bullies. I needed both voices, not just one.

Gaby understood greed and I didn't have enough of it. To win again, and again, and again, you have to be relentless. I had a great moment in Beijing, I think for periods I was even a great shooter. But athletes like Carl Lewis (four successive Olympic long jump golds), Michael Phelps (eighteen gold medals across three Olympics) and gymnast Larissa Latynina (nine Olympic golds over three Games) are exceptional athletes.

Shooting is different from tennis and swimming, it is not structured towards repetition, it allows for few brilliant encores. I am not undermining myself either. I have a fine set of roughly 85 international medals of my own, which include World Championship gold, Commonwealth Games gold, Asian Championship gold, Olympic gold. Even so, as I returned from London, a defeated defending champion, I was in awe of Phelps and his breed's ability to reproduce form. Over time and at a precise time. Phelps' natural, physical gifts are like a cosmic kiss and they are a distinct advantage. But the rest is hunger, greed to the point that it resembles an athletic version of an obsessive-compulsive disorder.

Phelps sees a black line at the bottom of the pool, I see the blurry black blob of a target. We see it hour after hour, day after day, year after year. This is our focus, this is our self-centred world. But Phelps just wants it more, this greed that pushes you through the boredom, through the limits, through the pain. I've spoken to Michael Diamond, the shotgun shooter with successive Olympic trap golds in 1996 and 2000, and I can feel his greed. And I say this in the nicest sense. After all, with a hundred shooters arrayed down a line with similar skill sets, it is this greed for gold that takes you past them.

I didn't know it, but my tiny mistakes were collecting like pieces of rust weakening my iron. My greed wasn't enough, my gun wasn't as efficient. If my rifle can be categorized as a performer, then it was half of what it was in Beijing. Heinz tested ten to twelve rifles for me, stripping them down, aiming, weighing, balancing, and this gun was the best of them. But it wasn't the best for me. Maybe there was a disharmony between pellet and barrel, an imperfect marriage between lead and grooves. Maybe the pellets were less accurate, maybe the barrel was worn and torn. It requires luck and time to arrive at the perfect combination of rifle and pellet. In Beijing, the Chinese pellets saved me before the Olympics; here, I was less fortunate. In Beijing, with the rifle put in a vice, the grouping of 10 pellets was 5.4mm. Now it was 6mm. It's not an excuse, it's just a shooter's everyday irritation.

Psychologically I had changed from Beijing, yet psychologically I still needed to shock my nervous system like I did before Beijing. I needed to replicate my nervous ascent of the pizza pole in 2008, and I chose to sky dive in Cologne two weeks before London.

I didn't tell my mother. Later, bewildered, she asked: 'Are you mad?' It was a rhetorical question. She knows I was and I am.

I needed a jolt before the Games, a confronting of my fears, but the sky dive had little effect. The pizza pole took a while to climb, enough time to be flooded with anxiety and enough time to learn to conquer it. Here, I fell from a plane and in 60 seconds it was done. Fear arrived and disappeared too quickly, before I could learn to negotiate it. On the pizza pole, I was also alone, the solitary shooter, untied to anyone, unaided, but here I jumped in tandem. I was strapped to another man. Another man who could not pull the trigger for me. This was no leap of faith.

All year in 2012, Tim Harkness, the sports psychologist, and I were in constant conversation, trying to find a state of mind for the Olympics. Mails flew across borders, ideas were fenced with. We discussed the notion of 'price', about how much I was willing to 'pay' for every shot. Paying the price is doing everything required for a shot. No short cuts. No digression from the established path. No 'bargain' shots, but paying the 'full' price, paying any price. Paying the price hurts, it is being disciplined about every movement, every breath, every thought, every ritual. But paying the price is worth it because the pain won't last forever. I know this and Tim reminded me of it: 'You have done it before! You can shoot 70 good shots at the Olympics. You have never died from shooting 70 good shots.'

I also carried with me a printout of a triangle which reminded me of my geometry homework as a boy. Formulated by Tim and me, it was called a 'perspective triangle'. It was a protective device, a reminder that in the spotlight, bathed by sweat, assaulted by anxiety, the first thing that often flees is clear thinking. This is how it worked:

On one side of the triangle was EVERYTHING, on the second was ALWAYS, on the third was ME.

At an Olympics, for instance, in a final, stress is inevitable, dilemmas that spike the blood pressure are inescapable. Balance, aiming, triggering, breathing, pellets—there is always imperfectness.

At the moment, pounded by pressure, I might think this final, this moment, this is EVERYTHING in my life. It defines me, I am nothing else but this.

At this moment, when I'm uncomfortable and out of control and bullied by stress, I might also think that it's ALWAYS going to be like this.

If I think all this, it means I've lost direction, I've abandoned my focus.

It's when I have to think of ME.

I have to remember this is not EVERYTHING in my life, which is built of so many other fascinating parts.

I have to also know this is not going to happen ALWAYS, this is just today, it will pass, I can fight it.

And I can fight it, and find perspective, because of ME. Because I have time to solve this problem. I have the experience. I have skill. I have mastered these problems before and I can do it again.

All year I have also been fighting the past and its expectations. Beijing is like background noise that won't go away, the ribbon of my gold medal now like a silk noose. I've never been in this position before and my head fills with useless thoughts: a silver medal in London would be fabulous, but after Beijing would it match up? As my brain wandered, I decided I required a clear attitude to take to the Games. So Tim and I came up with this approach to winning in London:

'I DON'T NEED IT, BUT I WANT IT.'

It is a statement that is a combination of two realities.

Fact 1: I want this medal as athletes do. But I don't 'need' this medal, not because I already have one but because I am alive, healthy, loved, happy. This medal is important but it can't define me.

Fact 2: Pressure affects every shooter's aim and his scores, which is why perfection in practice is rarely replicated in competition.

Put these two truths together and we get this: By convincing myself 'I don't need it' I am reducing the pressure, which increases my chances of shooting better.

Tim has done me a service by dampening the pressure. He knows being realistic is my style. He also knows that hype is not. Hype is an inaccurate perception of reality and it never improves performance. Yet for all that common sense, on the rare, odd day after London I did think: Maybe I was wrong. Maybe I can't win unless I 'need' it, unless I am wrapped in urgency. But it's only the second-guessing of the defeated.

Strangely it wasn't a faulty year running up to London. Medals matter, but so do scores. I had both at January's Asian Championships with a 597 and a gold. Two 596s followed at the World Cups in Munich and London. In France, as a warm-up to the Games, I shot a fluent 596 and 598. It seems counter-intuitive, but maybe I was shooting too well, too early. Shooting without suffering. Just one of those shooting weeks when it just flowed. Not quite like Federer in his prime—shots that just come instinctively, casually, unthinkingly—but close. But flow is dangerous in a way for I couldn't presume that in London my form would flow again. Only a masochist craves a crisis but perhaps a crisis in France would have toughened me. Because in London, as in any Olympics, a crisis was inevitable.

Meanwhile, I was still trying to be my methodical self. I wasn't sure if I was going to be chosen to carry the Indian flag at the Opening Ceremony, but I pre-empted it with a letter to the Indian Olympic Association asking not to be considered. Two days after the opening was my event and so my letter wasn't presumptuous, it wasn't rude, it was just me being practical. It was a smart move, but I then outsmarted myself. After three previous Olympics, scheduling should have been second nature, but I erred in my arrival programme into London.

In Beijing, I arrived early from Europe, eight to nine days ahead, primarily because of the massive time difference. In our sport of fine balance and tiny precision movements, my body has to shake off every trace of jet lag. In Athens, 2004, I went three days earlier. Here I overcomplicated it with a double-trip to London.

I ventured into the Village just when it opened. No Indian had arrived yet. Early meant a silent Village and an uncrowded Village. Early meant familiarity. I found my room, visited the cafeteria, checked the transport hub, figured out bus timings, did my accreditation and practised for three days in an uncongested range. Think of it as a dry run.

I was comfortable and flew back to Dortmund with a ticket to return four days before the Opening Ceremony.

My logic appeared sound: If I stayed in London for one long trip, say eight to nine days, the Village would be bustling, noisy, boring. Every day my only companions would be other athletes with tight, nervous faces that spoke of a gathering pressure. This way I had scouted the Village and yet escaped.

Dortmund was quieter and better; Dortmund was a mistake. Two trips was a mistake.

One visit, just four to five days before the Games, is what I required. Unfamiliarity with the Village has its value for it makes you edgy. And edginess for just a few days has a benefit. It sharpens your senses and increases your awareness. You're a bit skittish, you realize you're part of a Games, you know this is the point of no return. You enter what one might call a survival mode.

Instead I was comfortable. Too comfortable. Edginess might have helped. Might have got me a point. Might have.

The shooting range at the Royal Artillery Barracks was a bizarre, pre-fabricated, boxy structure. It was cool design but scarcely shooter-friendly. In April, during the test event, it froze my insides and destroyed my perfect jacket. Kept outside in a container for equipment, the jacket absorbed moisture and wouldn't pass the stiffness tests. I was forced to tear off a layer of the jacket to make it legal. I'm not as superstitious as athletes who will re-use lucky underwear—sometimes unwashed—but the jacket was like a second skin. It offered me a comfort that goes beyond fit, it makes me feel all my parts are working. Now, like the gun, it was an annoyance I had to block out.

By the time August arrived, it was still cold for an Indian but I was ready with a skier's thermal underwear and hand warmers found in golf shops. I thought I had considered every competitive probability and every possible sporting mishap. But, of course, I hadn't. The swollen, turbulent crowd in London was a surprise—in the long-term it's what we need, in the moment it was an unanticipated distraction. Over a hundred people gathered behind me and I was flattered by their interest, but unbalanced slightly by their noise. Shooters prefer to compete in tombs, but this was a lively arena. Spectators are usually sworn to silence, yet now phones chirped and expressive fans ignored any volume control.

Every shot they went 'Go for it, India', and every shot I heard it when I should have gone deaf. In my last series of 10 shots, a spectator encouragingly shouted, 'Abhi, do it for Mother India' and even though I was not aiming at the target yet, my finger twitched and I almost shot a zero. The entire ritual of the shot was restarted but my finger had become tentative and I shot a 9. It was not the fan's fault, it was completely mine. Focus is my responsibility.

This animation of the crowd was strange yet charming. This has to be shooting's future for all sport is driven by spectators. Of course, competitors require respect and each sport requires its particular atmosphere and specific identity. In basketball it is almost mandatory to hoot during free throws yet in contrast tennis stadiums morph into hushed chapels when a player serves. Booing a shooter would be unseemly and dancing cheerleaders might make us flinch. But shooting isn't heart surgery either. It is sport, it should be fun and it must engender emotion and involvement. The enthusiastic fan brings colour to a pale sport. He also taught me a lesson. Perhaps I should have shot in the Bundesliga (the German shooting league), where noise is customary, for five of the London finalists had coincidentally honed their art there.

Still, I was close. I finished my London qualification at 594 and failed to make the final by two points. Two was nothing, yet two was the end of my defence.

I started the qualifying round strongly with 99, 99, 100, 100. After four series, I was second on the table. I had a 99 in the fifth series and needed a 100 to finish.

At 497/500, I was precisely at the same score as Beijing.

I needed 10 more perfect shots to make the finals.

Only the first three were perfect. They were deep 10s. Then I stumbled with three 9s in the next four shots.

Only the first 9 really mattered for with it hope had flown. It meant it was too late for a medal. I failed to fight to even get into the final and this was a new, strange me. In Sydney 2000, I would have fought even for a ninth place. But my scale of measurement had altered. Ninth place was now meaningless. A final was not enough. And it was a fundamental flaw. A younger, desperate me would have fought—fought to just get into the final, fought because anything is possible in a final. I had always believed I had to be 'in it to lose it'. Now I hadn't even given myself a chance to lose in a final.

I was incredibly close in London but impossibly far. Of the three 9s I shot in my last 10 shots, two were 9.9s. They were closer to a 10, but counted only as 9. They were in fact .1mm away from a 10. You know how tiny .1mm is—it is less than the dot that precedes the 1. If I was .1mm closer in those shots and my 9.9s turned into 10s, I would have finished with a 596. I would have made the final. These are the margins I worked with and so did everyone else on the London range. It's heartbreaking, it's scary, it's skill.

I was not the shooter from Beijing. Then I could feel my heart hammer and race, but in London I was more placid. Maybe too placid. Every tiny hiccup all year, the gun, the jacket, the crowd, nothing was insurmountable, these were all just the usual travails of sport. I could have overcome them all if I had found within myself a more raging desperation. I felt no frustration, but a gentle regret. In Beijing I had clarity, in London I lacked certainty. The lost medal of Athens gave me hunger in Beijing; the won medal in Beijing brought me distraction in London. This sport, it's a funny business.

Yet I was strangely calm in London and even proud of how I coped. Disappointment washed over me but my perspective was intact. A journalist asked, 'Are you going to retire?' and my response was cool: 'I look old but I am still pretty young.' Another writer approached me with such a mournful face that I asked, 'What happened, did somebody die?' and he was taken aback.

It was a flat day for me but a shining one for Gagan Narang, who won bronze in the air rifle, while Vijay Kumar grabbed silver in the 25 rapid fire pistol. With the final hall stuffed with spectators, I watched Gagan on television and I was impressed. His coach, Stanislav Lapidus, was ill but he was concentrated enough to not let it get in his way. It was a worthy medal for a worthy talent.

I returned home to Chandigarh enthused with shooting. Rio was already in my head. I was driven to continue shooting not because I failed in London but because my year has been another bright, learning adventure. I understand that all these possible mistakes, all this brilliance of hindsight, it could be nonsense. Maybe nothing hurt me, and nothing could have helped me. Maybe I just wasn't good enough on the day for reasons I'll never know. Maybe I needed a little kiss from luck. Maybe the very appeal of sport is its idea of randomness, where reward doesn't quite perfectly match investment. Maybe this is just the new philosophical me. All I know is that I had to review London, make notes and move on. The past is just excess baggage after a while.

My life had altered and it was made amusingly and abundantly clear to me. Four years ago, in 2008, carrying gold, a poor elephant stood outside Delhi airport as I was swallowed by an army of people when I arrived home from Beijing. Now at Delhi airport in 2012 there was no one waiting for me in the vast halls. No garlands, no questions, no placards, no interest. Nothing and nobody. Sport is a uniquely lonely place for the defeated. Yet I was not alone. Waiting for me was my family. Always, win or lose, there is my family.

23

BEFORE RIO, UNDER SIEGE

Terror comes after lunch. Quietly and without warning. Suddenly, the right side of my body stops working. My shoulder freezes, my neck locks, my arm and jaw are knotted in tension. It's too fast for me to make sense of it as half of my body begins a mutiny I don't understand.

I start shaking, I quiver, my right side caught in some painfully jerky dance. I am in a place where I've never been, which is the absence of any control. On an April day in 2014, in the solitude of my room in Chandigarh, a nightmare has unfolded. I am scared, my bladder has emptied involuntarily, I lie drained on the bed.

I don't know it yet, but I've just had a myoclonic seizure. An epileptic episode wherein my brain is having an electrical conversation that it shouldn't. I have become the shaking shooter.

I call my mother, a doctor is summoned, and a first MRI done. No lesion. No one mentions epilepsy yet but I can already feel confidence in my body slipping away. In purely sporting terms, there's little worse than the unsure athlete.

Two years later, after Rio is done and I've retired, I'll keep saying that no Olympics was more meaningful for me. It's because it is my last goodbye and my career closing; it's because—and this is the key reason—I invested myself entirely into pursuing a second medal; and it's also because of this. The seizures.

This epilepsy syndrome will become my challenge for a year. I must learn to absorb it, deal with it, ignore it, shoot with it. I must meet my body's rebellion with equanimity and not be defined by these occasional electrical impulses in my brain. I must not cart around fear like useless luggage and yet it is there in the beginning: When will a seizure come, will it happen during a competition, in public, at an airport, what will I do, will it be embarrassing, who will help? The questions wash across my mind like a depressing tide.

I am booked to travel on a training trip in the next ten days and uncertainty settles on me like the night. Athletes are creatures of control, we want to be in charge of everything— competition, emotions, routines, equipment. We seek equilibrium but this is disturbance. As an athlete I have been fascinated by the workings of the brain, but not by these frightening parts. I can repair form but this is beyond my tool kit. There will be no easy fix to the slight tremor in my hand.

I enter a strange world where I am tiptoeing around myself, constantly conscious of my body, alert to every twitch, almost waiting for it to happen again. And then it does. This time on my physio Digpal Singh Ranawat's table in Chandigarh. Involuntary contractions of my upper body and right leg that leave me in an exhausted daze.

My Pilates teacher in Germany, Tina Hense, uses her contacts to arrange an appointment for me with the head of neurology at the Evangelisches Krankenhaus, Klinik for

Neurologiea, in Herne. It is the beginning of my medical tourism adventure through Europe. Every specialist wants an MRI, a blood test, an EEG. They confirm that I am having myoclonic seizures, yet I am trying to find a doctor who won't treat me as a patient but as an athlete who is a patient. I have a medical condition, I am struggling, but I am still a shooter.

The medication is playing havoc with me and its side effects unbalance me. My head feels heavy, as if it's been invaded by clouds. Dizziness arrives, headaches come, listlessness appears. My energy depletes and fatigue hugs me. In France I shoot a competition and I have double vision. I win. Don't ask me how.

If I am not standing up to shoot, I am lying down in a doctor's room. My soundtrack is the bark of pellets and the metallic bangs of the MRI machine. I change doctors and medications. I try vitamins and minerals and learn about magnesium levels. I have these 'auras' where I feel an uncomfortable sensation in my abdomen, a sort of tightness which is a warning that a seizure is coming.

My medication is altered but my hand still shakes. Every day it shakes. Some days I drop a spoon, some days I film my hand shaking, some days I want to stop shooting and go home and crawl into my bed. As if I've been defeated by my greatest ally—my brain.

It will be a year of OK days, workable days, terrible days, but there are no good days. I see life through a tired lens. In the staggering beauty of Slovenia one day, I cannot feel any pleasure. I'm on the planet of the numb. At practice one afternoon, I am so spent that Heinz has to help me leave the range. One competition day I cannot even rise from my chair and get to the firing point. Another time a friendly French shooter, probably disturbed by my lack of coordination, helps me put my shoes into a bag at the range. The simplest task is an ordeal.

My body feels foreign, as if it belongs to someone else, and my exhaustion—often just because of the medication—is like a thick drape that pins me to my bed. It's an effort to rise but I do and just this simple act helps me. I am looking for hope, anything to convince me I will be fine. Some medicine, some cure, something to rid me of this condition which feels like an obscenity. Nothing is working yet just getting up, and searching for answers, and visiting doctors, tells me I haven't given up. In my brain, my resolve is at war with my epilepsy.

I get an appointment in June 2014 with the sports medicine guru Hans-Wilhelm Müller-Wohlfahrt. I am desperate and yet I am very cautious. Every substance that goes into my body is very carefully checked. I know the WADA (World Anti-Doping Agency) code and I deeply respect its struggle for clean sport. If something goes into my body which shouldn't be there, I can't blame doctors, physios, agents, parents. It will be my fault.

I may be an Olympic gold medallist but in the celebrity rankings I am at the bottom of Dr Müller-Wohlfahrt's client list. If you flick through the internet you'll find that through his doors have walked Usain Bolt—who I saw twice when I was there—and reportedly, footballer Steven Gerrard, golfer Jose Maria Olazabal and boxer Wladimir Klitschko. Müller-Wohlfahrt is a sort of a star healer, and I land in Munich at 7 am, get to his clinic at 10 am, get five MRIs done and see him at 3 pm. Only for him to send me to a neurologist. The hand is shaking, a tiny quiver, but it's linked to my brain.

A few days later, I return to Dr Müller-Wohlfahrt's office and he gives me fifteen to sixteen injections of a homeopathic medicine in my spine. My finger stops trembling. For a day, then two, then three. Then it starts shaking again. The injections are a band-aid to the brain.

All my life, discipline has been my weapon and now it is my saviour. It makes me get up and shoot. It is bewildering but a most intriguing irony is unfolding. The range will become my refuge, the target my distraction, the shooting my therapy. By forcing me to concentrate, shooting is rescuing me. I am fighting for a medal but also for my sanity. And by thinking of a medal I am keeping my sanity. Shooting calms me, it forces me to focus, it offers me a routine, it leads me back into a world of triggers and pellets and stance, and away from fear and insecurity and self-pity. Heinz understands and tells me, you can't give up shooting because shooting is keeping you together. He tells me Julius Caesar had epilepsy—which is now being contested—and yet he built an empire. I smile. Heinz is my Roman pillar to lean on.

In July I win my first Commonwealth Games gold—the fine Indian shooter Ravi Kumar came fourth—after being third in qualifying. No fuss, no twitch. It's a victory meaningful to me in ways I can't easily explain. I spent the morning doing hand exercises with a rubber band, just taking my mind to another place. Because I didn't know what would happen, when a twitch might interrupt me, I shoot exactly as the textbooks prescribe: one pellet at a time. If it's an error, move on. It's a clarity that works for me.

In hindsight, I think I shot with gratitude. As an athlete at a certain level, you expect to compete, you almost take it for granted that opportunity will come and major Games will be visited. But now I saw my world differently, I was grateful for the opportunity to shoot and to compete. I was grateful not to pee in my pants.

In Granada, Spain, in early September 2014, before the world championships, I have another seizure. Since we live in a fidgety, gadgety world where everything is recorded, I even have a film of it. On the floor of my room I lie, twitching, jerking, scared. I can't stitch sentences together and sit there empty and flustered. Later I use Google to navigate through a foreign world, reading on epilepsy, making sense of my shaking hand, researching medicines. I'm like everyone else you find on an epilepsy thread, looking for comfort and solutions, reading accounts of 'overcoming fatigue post-seizure', finding reassurance from my new tribe.

I come fifteenth in Grenada with a score of 624.8. It's an average of 10.4 per shot and still not enough. Weeks later, in Incheon, South Korea, I grab my first individual medal at an Asian Games. It's bronze but it's heft feels different to me. It is proof I can still shoot. The reason I seem to exist is still valid.

I am exhausted after the qualification in Incheon, and merely carrying my bag to the finals is an effort. My questions to myself do not concern complex issues on shooting but the most basic things: Should I carry my rifle with my bag? Can I manage the load? Focus, I tell myself. Focus, and don't drop it. There are no excuses, this is life and I am hardly the only one with a story behind me.

When you look at athletes it's possible you only see tuned machines, but scrape away that polished exterior and there lies a human tale. Funding vanishing. A father lost. A marriage failing. Shooter Matthew Emmons battling thyroid cancer. Never do I have to look far for perspective, for if I peel away the past it puts me in my place. There's Lou Gehrig, who so bravely fought and died from amyotrophic lateral sclerosis; there's Wilma Rudolph, who had double pneumonia and scarlet fever as a child and wore a leg brace and yet sprinted to three golds in Rome 1960. Shooting itself is flush with its own suffering, for depression eats its way through the field. So many in shooting are struggling and yet so many find respite in shooting. I am not alone and yet I am on my own.

The injections to the spine are too expensive and it is just too difficult to get an appointment with Dr Müller-Wohlfahrt. So in August 2014 I find another ally, Dr Joachim Schubert. He lives close to Dortmund, which becomes my training base. Dr Schubert will 'care' for me, and I use that word advisedly: he will show interest, expertise, compassion and even stay in touch with me on WhatsApp.

My seizures are more in control but my hand quivers like a gently nervous debutant. Dr Schubert, whose speciality is sports medicine, links me with Dr Knut Lesniak, a neurologist who cycles to work. He's a lovely man but, sigh, he wants more tests. He suggests a new drug, Oxcarbazepine, but I am sceptical and scared of the side effects. I wait. The finger shakes.

During all this I don't reveal my condition to the National Rifle Association of India (NRAI) for various reasons. Since this is a medical condition, I can't speak to just anybody, I can't merely tell a bureaucrat or official, 'Hey, I have seizures.' I need to deal with a doctor attached to the shooting federation who understands my predicament and the need for privacy, but there is none. I am chary of speaking to anyone else in the federation because Indian sport has a disrespect for confidentiality and information drips out like water from a leaky tap. I am shaken, confused and I need the comfort of privacy. There are people who know, even journalists, but they gratefully hold my secret. Disclosing my epilepsy now, publicly, for the first time, has not been an easy choice. But it's been my choice.

I also believe everything in sport must be earned and I am not blocking anyone's place by not divulging information. If

I shoot poorly at trials I won't be selected, if I keep shooting erratically at major Games my form will be evident to everyone, if I don't find my best self I cannot qualify for the Olympics. There is no hiding from the mark a bullet makes.

Throughout my struggle, one necessary person is aware of my condition: Dr James M. Lally, chairman of the medical committee of the International Shooting Sport Federation. The American physician is knowledgeable, kind, reassuring, thorough, and keeps my confidence even as he always knows about my medication. He is the expert in my corner.

Early on, Lally's committee gives me a Therapeutic Use Exemption for a year, from May 2014 to May 2015, purely for safety purposes. Initially, I am trying various medications, in different combinations and dosages, and this is just to cover the remote possibility of drug interactions resulting in a false positive. It never happens. But there is no real fear about a banned substance because medication to manage seizures has a negative effect on shooters. For instance, when I eventually change to Oxcarbazepine in late 2015, my trembling finger is better but I am inviting other trouble. If you go to the Mayo Clinic website, these are the more common side effects of Oxcarbazepine:

- change in vision
- change in walking or balance
- clumsiness or unsteadiness
- crying
- dizziness
- double vision
- false sense of well-being
- feeling of constant movement of self or surroundings
- mental depression

- sensation of spinning
- uncontrolled back-and-forth and/or rolling eye movements

I struggled for a long while about whether to write about my epileptic episodes in this book. My family, whose first instinct is to protect me, thought I was asking for unwarranted scrutiny by revealing it for they know people can be cruel. *Salaa paagal hai?* But for all my many flaws, I've never been scared of life or failure or challenge or people's lazy opinions. I don't care if people look at me differently. I only asked myself, is it worth sharing?, and the answer was yes.

Why? Because human beings everywhere are touched by illness, in its various forms, and yet in Asia, instead of compassion, we often hide our conditions and shame people into silence as if we are concealing a wrong. Ignorance about physical conditions sits like a stain on a culture and needs to be erased. Epilepsy, for instance, isn't a madness or the inhabiting of a human being by spirits. It's not a curse, it's only a condition. As Hippocrates is believed to have written, it's just another natural disease, to be treated with medication.

I'm incredibly lucky because as an athlete I have a platform and to not use it on behalf of the other 10 million people in India—or as the India Epilepsy Centre estimates, 1 per cent of the population—would be unforgiveable. I am proof of life with it. With this condition you can play music like Neil Young or be a sensational athlete like Jonty Rhodes or hit bullseyes now and then or just live an able and productive existence.

In 2015, finally, everything begins to stabilize and the seizures pause. Stop is too final a word. In the suburbs of my brain, epilepsy lurks. But quietly. I am, right now, one of the lucky ones. Only once at a World Cup in Munich does a full-muscle-twitch lead me to an 8. But it's an aberration. In the meantime, I've built a tiny wooden ledge on my rifle near the trigger where I rest my finger. It doesn't shake so much, if anything it's now a little rigid.

By the time I reach Rio for the Olympics in 2016, my disease is not a factor. It's controlled, monitored, bearable, workable. I don't come fourth in the 10-metre air rifle because of a twitch or a tremor or a medical condition. I come fourth only because I am not good enough for third.

24

RIO: DEATH BY DECIMAL

'Hello Heinz, can you roll me a smoke?'

It's Rio, it's over. Just like that a career ends. No fanfare, garlands, speeches. I lose, I leave, as undramatically and wordlessly as I first came to shooting. If I shoot .1 better in the final, I will win bronze at least. This is death by decimal. I dismantle my rifle, shrug off my jacket and pack away my entire shooting life. I pick up my suitcase and leave the arena that was my church. No hymn plays.

I want a cigarette even though I've never smoked. I want it, perhaps, because it's a symbol of everything ending. I have done everything possible to be great all my shooting life, which includes not smoking. But now the quest is over. I can be everybody else now for two minutes. Normal. Silly.

So right there, in the final hall, to my amusement, Heinz begins rolling a smoke. Humour is our glue. Across the hall sits his wife, Gaby, whose shooter, the Italian Niccolo Campriani, is about to win gold. When it's over, dope test done, hands shaken, Heinz and Gaby and I will stand outside the shotgun range. Friends blowing smoke into the Brazilian air. I am not as cool as I look.

Fourth!

On the plane home, I'm sitting next to the president of Slovakia and we are kindred spirits of a sort because politicians, too, know loss in public and the wearing of masks. I stare out the window and don't see clouds but a .1. Medal gone into thin air. It's possibly the first time I've had a chance to consider how close I was, and disappointment spreads like pressure in the chest. Failure has an uncomfortable weight of finality.

You can't change the .1, you can't go back, you can't rewind shots. But 'what ifs' dance uselessly in the brain and later I go running in the gym to sweat them out. I've just found out that both my parents were ill during Rio but protected me from the news. For all our perceived toughness, athletes are indulged babies.

I'm not emotional but I am exhausted. I don't reprise my career in my head but only the last four years. Even to the end I am a pragmatist, examining my preparation, surfing through a list of equipment, coaching, training, thinking, planning, asking myself the question that will decide forever how I see myself.

Did I do enough?

Yes.

.1 of a point in terms of width is somewhere in the vicinity of a wood shaving or a capillary. Millimetres are too big and, so, micrometres, used to measure bacteria, might be better. This is the size of defeat after four years.

Decimals became my obsession because shooting, the sport, had fallen even further in love with them. Earlier, decimals mattered only in finals where shots were graded from 10.1 to 10.9. In the 60-shot qualification, only whole numbers—10, 9, 8—mattered. A 10.9 or 10.1 in qualification was only a 10.

Now, post the London Olympics, the scoring system had changed. Decimals counted for every shot even in qualification.

Deep 10s (10.7 and higher) were necessary, shallow 10s (10.1, 10.2) were average shots. Just hitting the bullseye wasn't enough. Even with a magnifying glass you could barely tell the difference between 10.5 and 10.6. But if you added up that .1 of a difference, over 60 shots, it adds up 6 whole points.

This is what I was searching for. .1. Anything that could edge me closer to the bullseye. Life lived in a tiny pursuit. Trying to improve on every shot by a distance smaller than a human hair. There is no sport without purpose. Or madness.

I'd do anything for this .1. Anything. Change my technique, even. My style was to align my rifle at 12 o'clock, just above the target, slowly lower the rifle to the bullseye, lock on, breathe and fire in one or two seconds. Even if I was a little left of the bullseye I'd fire because I was only chasing 10s and this technique was sufficient for that.

Now I needed 10.5s and for this I needed a more efficient aiming process. Now I had to keep the gun fixed on the bullseye for at least 4-5 seconds. It seems a tiny change, just 2-3 seconds longer on the bullseye, but it took a year to master. All those millions of shots I'd fired before, all those endless hours, all that had to be scrubbed away. I was writing a new code, I was reconfiguring my machinery, I was rewiring my instinct. This takes time.

Anything that can get me .1 closer to perfection on every shot is worth experimenting with. Even hiring a sixty-plus-year-old gunsmith from Turkmenistan, Anatoly Fedorchenko, to work on my grips. His teeth were gold, he ate *daal* by the bowlful, did 200 push-ups a day, spoke no English and yet insisted on being called 'coach'. He brought me hard bread from his homeland and claimed that chewing it would ease my nervousness. His grips were good, this theory was not. Yet I listened to him, for knowledge arrives from the strangest places.

Decimals would have to be found everywhere. People, equipment, places. Even from body parts. For the first time, I hire a full-time physio, Dr Digpal Ranawat, who monitors my older, fraying body.

If there's muscle tension in my trapezius it will pull my scapula down, which will make me aim lower. If the hip flexors are tight, the superficial muscles of the back will overwork and the deep core muscles and the gluteus, which is actually supposed to fire to stabilize me, will be inhibited and eventually disturb my balance. A perfectly unstressed body might be worth .1.

So every morning Digpal will take five minutes to assess my physical state: shoulders and trunk, rotation and flex, alignment and tightness, stability and sway. He's like an engineer inspecting a complex machine. If I've slept badly, he'll know; if I've travelled poorly, he can tell. Only once he's relaxed me, will shooting start.

My team and I aren't reacting to mistakes, we're working to prevent them from happening, we're in search of solutions. So Heinz and I will change the stock of my gun.

.1?

We experiment with ten to fifteen types of sights, from their shape to their colour, to find one to suit the light and conditions in Rio's range, which we visit during the test event in April. We're trying to design greatness, we're ensuring no detail is insignificant. It takes ingenuity and labour and trial and error.

The front sight is round and we build a square box around it. It's a bit like the target, which is also round and sits in a square box. When I aim, the straight lines of the sight square and the target square offer me a good reference point. Think of it as a small square inside a big square. You can tell when you're not aligned.

We rely not on feel but data. Heinz films me every day and the results with the square sight are superior. My quality of balance is significantly different.

.1?

I recreate the Rio range in my home in Chandigarh, even down to the Olympic logo and the background colour. This is homework, this is to reduce surprises in Rio. To sharpen the realism I give the three lanes—or 'points' as we call them—in my range random numbers: 27, 28 and 29. When I get to the Olympics, I am assigned lane 28. It makes me smile.

.1?

Everything can't be solved, but there's no panic. We rest, we take a step back, we return to the problem. At day's end we're exhausted but we sleep well. Effort is the best satisfaction and sedative.

One day I build a fake rifle, which in effect is a pipe half-filled with water. It is exactly the same length and weight as my rifle. When I hold it horizontally and aim, it becomes a brilliantly simple test of my stillness. If I move, the water moves. If my hips are misaligned, the water moves.

.1?

In practice, I make Mark Wahlberg, the sniper from the film *Shooter*, look like a guy who should go pop balloons with kids with an airgun. The world record in qualifying, over 60 shots, is 633.5 and in practice I'm outdoing it. 634 one day. 635 another day. Shooters chase flawlessness and yet we're never intoxicated by it because we know it never stays. And yet we need these days of flawlessness to come, we need to know it's possible, we need to believe we're not chasing ghosts.

I'm travelling between Chandigarh and Dortmund (where my coaches live) and I am a fortunate shooter because I have access to expertise. But in a perfect world I'd never leave India for a single day except to compete; in a perfect world, much like Germany, every shooter in every small town has a range, a gym, a physio, a sports medicine doctor.

Travel wastes time; jet lag wastes time; finding sponsors to fund trips, as many shooters have to, wastes time. Time that is being used by other shooters to practice. This is the efficiency that Indian sport has to be searching for. One day we won't be flying out of India to find experts. One day people will be flying in to find our experts. That will be progress.

In Dortmund, I squeeze triggers nonstop from 8.45 am to 1 pm. I am so familiar with this city I could run for office. Certainly the cab drivers, immigrants eager for a conversation, are generous to me. One, an Afghan, says, 'Hey, aren't you the rifle shooting champion from India?' Another, a Turk who drives me now and then, gives me a Borussia Dortmund coffee cup as a memento. The decency of strangers is a beautiful thing.

I am a child of routine because it soothes me. Routine ensures I stay true to my mission and don't drift. It offers me a sense of comfort and direction. And so every day is almost a Xerox of the next. I wake at 6.30 am, am assessed by Digpal by 7.15 am, buy lunch on my way to the range and then work. You don't 'play' shooting like you 'play' football, it isn't joyous, or playful, or whimsical, or fun; it is, in fact, labour. More than medals, what we seek is mastery over ourselves. For me, so many years later, so many shots later, so many Olympics later, this is still my pleasure.

And so I work, and work, and these days and weeks, when I push myself to keep going, when I labour and polish and repeat and grind and try and hurt, are sometimes my greatest victories. This intensity, this devotion, this clarity of cause, I will never feel again. There is a complete honesty to my effort, a truth to my sweat. At my worst times in Rio this will help me: I will always feel, it will be alright.

At 1 pm Digpal reassesses me, stretches me and we head for Pilates, where Tina works on me. Her studio is in the middle of an art gallery, and I am like an object she is reshaping. Balance requires a certain sensitivity, an ability to understand and activate the small, deep muscles which keep you stable. It's like figuring out the intricate wiring within your body, and Tina's exercises help me do that. I need this because even though I am not running a mile or dribbling a ball, my art requires a finely tuned body. Irrespective of the strength of my mind, it cannot compensate for faulty balance.

After Pilates, we grab dinner on the way home. On good days, Tina, Digpal and I will reward ourselves with a piece of cake. Like ascetics, three people share one piece. Spinach cake is my favourite. Yes, shooters are strange people.

My mind, in the last few months, is full of clarity, not romance. Saying farewell to shooting in Rio sounds like a sentimental journey, the last chapter of a story that began with a boy and gun. Yet my heart beats for 10.6s, not for idle drama. I am too busy to be sad, too preoccupied to think of goodbyes. Instead, through the year, my mind will enter various states. Before the Games, I am fuelled by desperation. I have to find my best. I have to do well. When I enter the Games, emotion is replaced by process. Is everything in order? When the Games begin, my mind won't wander anywhere beyond the shot I am about to fire. This is not romantic, it's real.

In April 2016 I visit a fitness expo in Cologne and am introduced to a revolutionary company named Tecnobody. I am so impressed by their technology—used to train athletes and for the rehabilitation of people who suffer strokes or accidents—that I later become their distributor in India.

Athletes like me want to comprehend our bodies as we might a rifle: we want to know every part, appreciate its role and fix it if it's faulty. Both rifle and body are delicate, precise instruments which require feeling. If I can tell a rifle is imbalanced by a gram, then I have now found a machine which tells me the same about my body.

When I stand on the round metal plate on Tecnobody's stability device, a string of sensors measures the minute oscillations in my body. It tells me where my centre of gravity is and which way my body is leaning. If I shift left by a gram, it will tell me; if my balance is imperfect I will immediately know. It is helping me fine-tune my stability with real-time feedback. I bought a portable version, weighing 40–50 kilograms, and carry it with me on my travels, using it to awaken my muscles and find my early-morning balance.

How much could it help me?

.1?

All my life I've been willing to venture into the periphery of sport, to its remote corners, to find unusual ways to squeeze the best out of my myself. This time it involves a sports dentist. In Germany, some believe that the misalignment of the upper and lower sides of your jaw can contribute to bio-mechanical errors and the misalignment of your body. So I visit a dentist, who X-rays my jaw and makes a splint for me—as apparently he has for football players—to wear while sleeping and training. A sort of plastic denture. The result is incredible. When I wear the splint the range of motion in my neck improves by 15–20 degrees and helps me perfect my alignment.

.1?

On 17 June 2016, I leave India for my last shooting trip and my family cuts a 'good luck' cake. All my life I've lived out of suitcases but this is the last of those journeys. Everything ends. Especially sporting talent.

This last journey will take sixty-two days and it is meticulously planned. Days of training and then travel. Alone and yet always with Heinz, Digpal and Tina. One tribe together pursuing excellence. I shoot for myself and also for them. Never in sport do you let only yourself down. I journey through Baku (seventh in the World Cup, 627.4 + 102.3), Dortmund, Moscow, Hanover, Munich, Bergammo and then leave for Rio on 30 July. Form never stays but right now mine is excellent, my training scores high, my technique sharp.

Rio is familiar because we had a test event here in April where I'd roomed on a floor with North Koreans. Terrific guys. Never smile and always smoke. This time I am carrying 200 kilograms with me, including two intriguing items. The first, an emergency kit which a Luxembourg shooter had gifted me and which included toilet paper (for nervousness), chocolate (as an anti-depressant) and a miniature bottle of gin (for courage). The second, as I will explain, was the Mandala.

In July, I went to visit a well-known Austrian artist, Ernst Handl, who is Tina's brother-in-law. Taking a break from training for me is not a simple process because I am a difficult man to keep amused. I find nightclubs too loud but my brain needs to be stimulated, and this was an ideal distraction. With guidance from the artist, I build a Mandala (see photo insert), a diagram which reflects my mindset and my plan for Rio. I hang it on my wall in the Village as inspiration and it can be interpreted as follows:

The gold leaf: The goal, the gold.
The line of green and yellow: Defines gratitude for the opportunities I have been given and also acceptance.

The black area with power cells: Signifies discipline and determination.
The parts of the phone which are like coiled electrical parts: Represent resistance which is always there, the idea that there will be pressure from within but that I have the mechanism to deal with it.
The red stones: Expresses energy.
The cell phone boards on the outside layer: Stand for the mind-body connection.

Of all the Games I have been to, the Rio Village is my favourite. My apartment is neat, clean and my taps work. Complaining is tiring anyway, being grateful for shelter is better. What I admire most at the Games is the professionalism of nations. Singapore, for instance, with only twenty-five athletes, has a Singapore House, which is 7,600 square feet of home-cooked food, pool tables, foosball tables, a TV with Netflix, PlayStation, not to mention physios, psychologists and trainers. The Germans, meanwhile, have bread delivered to every athlete's doorstep. India has lessons to learn.

I usually skip opening ceremonies at major Games to rest myself and because ceremonies don't connect with me. Only competition does. But I know that my dad's dream has always been for me to be a flag bearer. I had regretfully declined that privilege in London, but here in Rio I agree. My father hasn't asked me but I want to do something for a man who has been unflinchingly devoted to my endless dream. Fortunately, my event is three days after the ceremony. The Opening Ceremony is exhausting: we leave the Village at 4 pm and return only at 2.30 am.

Practice is more fun and the practice range is where I am among the last to leave. Every session. Every day. One day we get into the bus to go home and find that training time has been extended. We get off, open bags, re-assemble the gun. Practice.

I am happy in Rio, my team protective, our energy infectious. I awake in the dark on competition day, take the 6.30 am bus, wait for the sun. I have to walk from the qualifying hall to the final hall to find a toilet. All are taken. In the preparation area I lay my rifle on a table and then sit on it.

I am relaxed... and then I am falling.

Boom. The table collapses. I land on my bottom and partly catch my falling rifle but the sight breaks. My carefully chosen sight. Ten years ago I'd be in a panic but I've learnt acceptance. No excuse, no drama, just change the sight.

Before Rio I've been shooting 10.5 and above regularly, but at practice at the Olympics my scores fall. Two-three points lower than normal. I take a microscope to my technique and nothing makes sense. My aiming is fine, my triggering good, my follow-through perfect, my rifle in order. It's a mystery. But shooters constantly talk to each other and we figure out that many of them are registering lower scores. Maybe it's the lighting, or colour, but the cause is the range.

The answer is recalibration, not of the sight but of my mind. I expect 10.5s, but now I lower my expectation to 10.4s. I have to adapt else I will be frustrated, which will annoy me, which will distract me, which will ruin me.

Calmness is my friend as I start. My first three series of 10 shots—104.3, 104.4, 105.9—are strong. My fourth dips to 103.8. I take a break and lubricate my dry eyes. My fifth dips to 102.1. I have only shot above 10.5 in that series.

One last series remains, possibly the last 10 shots of my life. I don't know where I am in the qualifying ranking, I just know it needs to be a superior 10 shots. My 56th shot is a 10.8. My 57th is a 10.8. My 59th is a 10.8. My 60th a 10.4. My total is 105.2. This last series is the reflection of my confidence: I believe because I have worked.

I still don't know if I am in the final till Ronak Pandit, the former Commonwealth Games champion who is sitting in the stands behind me, does the math. You're in, he tells me. Out of fifty shooters, I am one of eight finalists. In five Olympics, this is my third final.

In the hour or so before the final, in a freezing room, my mind drifts to gratitude and acceptance. Gratitude for the opportunity to shoot, to be in a final, to compete and train and travel, to be at the Olympics, to have a chance at a medal. None of this do I dare take for granted.

The other part is acceptance, to meet every situation in the final as it comes. To accept reality, not resist it. There's pressure, fine; I'm feeling uncomfortable, it happens; my body's not relaxed, I'll get over it. To focus on the task is to find a solution.

The eight-man final begins with two series of three shots each. And I have to make a choice. A hard choice. Choice that could determine my final. Choice between two strategies, both of which are high risk.

A choice in a standstill sport which is about speed.

'To you,' Heinz tells a journalist later, 'every shooting range looks the same.' Not to us. Everything matters. How much light is there on a target and how much in the background? What's the temperature and the quality of the air? What's the height of the target, the colour contrast of the wall, the hardness of the floor?

The final range in Rio is the same for everybody but it's not the same as the qualifying range. The background is dark and it creates a conundrum. In training we measured that the longer I aim the lower my heart rate becomes. This is good. *So I should take my time with every shot?* But if you aim for too

long with a dark background you can lose balance so it might
be better to shoot quicker. *So I should not take my time with
every shot?*

I need to make a decision. Take my time. Or not. My choice
is about to affect my decimals.

Since everyone's heart rate rises in the early part of finals,
I decide to start patiently. First 10 shots slowly, then shoot
faster. It makes sense, but it doesn't work. I take my time but
I don't shoot straight enough.

10, 9.7, 10.2.

Average. I am joint fifth.

9.7, 10.1, 10.4.

Ordinary. I am seventh.

I won't give up. I can't. Elimination doesn't even cross my
mind. If you were watching maybe you were cursing under
your breath. Nervous. Crossing your fingers. Not me. Seventh
place doesn't register with me. Emotion doesn't pester me.
My mind is almost in perfect control. All it is concerned with
is the next shot.

This is one of those moments you see on television, when
the athlete is slipping, when skill eludes him precisely when
he needs it, when he's running out of time. It's frightening
and yet fascinating, for it's a test. How do you react, who do
you look to, what do you remember? When you're young,
you drown in panic; when you're older, you trust in instinct.

I attack, I shoot faster, I take a risk, I find a solution.

10.7.

10.4.

After eight shots I am in fourth place.

10.8.

10.7.

After 10 shots I've leaped to joint third.

10.7.

10.1.

After 12 shots, I'm still in third place.

Without over-dramatizing it, my shooting life, career, reputation, legacy is changing every shot. Another medal? No medal? This is why we compete, to just be in this lunatic place of possibility.

Then, suddenly, a flurry of inconsistent scores. 9.7, 10.5, 9.9, 10.2. Millimetres are my enemy. It will appear later that these shots fatally wounded my medal chances, but it's an incorrect assumption. Any fault or flaw lay not in the end but in the start. In my first six shots I lose the decimal I need, the .1 which will put me in a three-man race and assure me of a medal. But .1 had gone before I even knew it. I do not mourn it, for this is sport and a medal is not yet fully lost.

Now there are four shooters left and I'm joint third. Tied for bronze; .3 from silver; .7 from gold. It's time for an elimination shoot-off against Serhiy Kulish of Ukraine. In the 2008 Olympic final I am tied after the 9th shot and shoot a 10.8 and win gold. Here, in 2016, I shoot a 10.0, Kulish shoots a 10.5.

No medal.

For an hour I've given India a little drama. Maybe made a few people watch shooting for the first time. Maybe made them admire the skill of my tribe. Maybe made the odd kid want to pick up a peaceful rifle. It's been tiring. Where's that cigarette?

I pull my mask down and speak to the media. I portray a satisfied man, which isn't untrue at all, but something's tearing inside which I disguise. How do you put your hurt up for public display? I am leaving sport in fourth place and for an athlete chasing perfection this is the most imperfect place.

Later, weeks later, months later, when I am no longer the process-oriented athlete who coldly evaluates his actions, but the retired athlete who sometimes indulgently rewinds the past, the outcome of Rio can make me emotional. Proximity to a medal is both a privilege and painful. So close, I think. So close. So close. Regret clings to me briefly and then it evaporates.

That final day, I finish my drug test and shooters shake my hand in farewell and congratulation and this matters to me. Respect. The media is extremely kind to me and for hours they gently question me. They are almost as disappointed as me and it is touching. In India, my six-year-old nephew weeps for an hour.

I have prepared myself for retirement and there are no tears nor second thoughts. There are no pellets left in me. Heinz, Digpal and I sit late into the night and talk shooting. Not with regret but with affection. It's been a fortunate life, a tough day, a fitting finish. Fourth is hard, fourth hurts, but fourth I can sleep with.

I am uncertain about what closure means but for me it translates into an absence of regret. More than medals this is the athlete's gift to himself as he leaves his sport: The truth of effort, the memory of deep commitment.

If my last shot in the final in Rio, before the shoot-off, had been a 10.3 instead of a 10.2, I would not be tied, I would have a medal. For four years I'd chased .1, chased it from before dawn to after dusk, chased it in small towns and big cities, chased it with eagerness and fastidiousness, chased it because perfection is always worth chasing. And yet .1 is what I have lost by. I've done enough and yet it is never enough. It sounds cruel but maybe it is fitting. My life of decimals has finally been decided by the smallest one.

EPILOGUE

Only once in the four months since Rio do I visit my range. I take my nephew there but I feel like an intruder. The range for me is associated with clarity, goals, motivation, purpose, but I feel nothing. I am the casual visitor out of place in the terrain of the competitor.

I spent thirteen years in that range. 250 days a year. Six hours a day. Even on my rare days off, I'd go in and fiddle with equipment. Now I've lost my religion and this is no longer my temple. My mother could turn it into a vegetable garden for all I care.

But she won't. My last practice session in that range, in June 2016, was a personal best. 634.9. A world record. She's framed it and hung it on the wall alongside my certificates and scoresheets. A short history of me.

I am finished as a shooter but my mother has my range cleaned every day. Pellet boxes dusted. Targets neatly stacked. Gun cases wiped. All of it ready. Waiting.

Just in case

CAREER AT A GLANCE

Olympic Games

Venue	Year	Score	Rank
Sydney	2000	590	11
Athens	2004	597 (OR*) + 97.6	7
Beijing	2008	596 + 104.5 (Highest final shot in Olympic air-rifle history)	1
London	2012	594	16
Rio	2016	625,7 + 163,8	4

* Olympic record

World Championships

Venue	Year	Score	Rank
Barcelona	1998	574 (jr)	44
Lahti	2002	589	40
Zagreb	2006	597 + 102.1	1

Venue	Year	Score	Rank
Munich	2010	593	25
Granada	2014	624,8	15

World Cups (Top Performances)

Venue	Year	Score	Rank
Munich	2000	596 (Equalled Junior World Record) + 101.7	4
Munich	2001	597 (New Junior World Record) + 103.5	3
Milan	2001	594 + 102.2	6
Atlanta	2002	595 + 102.7	5
Munich	2003	596 + 103.9	3 + Quota
Changwon	2003	596 + 103.2	4
Sydney	2004	593	9
Bangkok	2004	595	9
Guangzhou	2006	595	9
Bangkok	2007	595 + 100.9	7
Bejing	2008	595	18
Munich	2011	596 + 100.7	7 + Quota
London	2012	596	10
Munich	2012	596	14
Munich	2015	627,5 + 122,4	6
Baku	2016	627,4 + 102,3	7

Commonwealth Shooting Championships/Games

Venue	Year	Score	Rank
CSC Auckland	1999	1160 Team	3
		584 + 98.5	4
CSC Bisley	2001	594 +102.8	1
		1176 Team	1
CG Manchester	2002	590 +101.4	2
		1184 Team	1
CG Melbourne	2006	AR 1189 Team	1
		594 + 101.5	3
		3P 2287 Team	1
		1151 + 97.6	2
CG Delhi	2010	595 + 103.0	2
		1193 Team	1
Glasgow	2014	622,2 + 205,3	1

Asian Games/Championships

Venue	Year	Score	Rank
ASC Langkawi	2000	592 +102.9	3
AG Busan	2002	593 + 101.3	7
Asian air gun Bangkok	2005	1775 Team	1
		593 + 102.3	4
ASC Kuwait	2007	1784 Team	1
		592	9
Asian air gun Nanjing	2008	1772 Team	2
		592 + 102.2	7
AG Guangzhou	2010	593	10
		1783 Team	2
Asian Games	2014	625,4 + 187,1	3
Asian air gun Delhi	2015	627,9 + 208,3	1

Grand Prix

Venue	Year	Score	Rank
Luxembourg Open	2001	598 + 104.2	1 – WR* score
Intershoot Den Haag	2001	593 + 101.3	2
Intershoot Den Haag	2002	597 + 101.3	3
NRW Cup Dortmund	2003	599 + 105	1 – WR* score
IWK Munich	2003	598 + 103.7	1
		597 + 103.2	2
3 × Air Colorado Springs	2003	600 + 103.9	1 – WR* score
IWK Munich	2004	597 + 104	1
3 × Air Colorado Springs	2004	600 + 103.2	1 – WR* score
Intershoot Denhaag	2005	597 + 104.5	1
RIAC Luxembourg	2010	598 + 101.4	2
IWK Munich	2015	630,2 + 208	1

* World record

INDEX